Sunrises and Songs

Reading and Writing Poetry in an Elementary Classroom

Amy A. McClure
Ohio Wesleyan University

with

Peggy Harrison and Sheryl Reed
Upper Arlington City Schools
Columbus, Ohio

With a Foreword by
Charlotte S. Huck

Heinemann
Portsmouth, New Hampshire

HEINEMANN EDUCATIONAL BOOKS, INC.
70 Court Street   Portsmouth, NH 03801
Offices and agents throughout the world

Acknowledgments for previously published material begin on page xv.

Every effort has been made to contact the copyright holders and the children and their parents for permission to reprint borrowed material. We regret any oversights that may have occurred and would be happy to rectify them in future printings of this work.

Library of Congress Cataloging-in-Publication Data

McClure, Amy A.
   Sunrises and songs : reading and writing poetry in an elementary classroom / by Amy A. McClure : with Peggy Harrison and Sheryl Reed.
     p. cm.
   Includes bibliographical references.
   ISBN 0-435-08507-7
   1. Poetry—Study and teaching (Elementary)—United States.
I. Harrison, Peggy. II. Reed, Sheryl. III. Title.
LB1576.M3974   1990
372.6'4—dc20   89-19919
                                                        CIP

Designed by Jenny Greenleaf.
Front-cover art by Eddie Perkins.
Printed in the United States of America.
10   9   8   7   6   5   4   3   2   1

For
Charlotte,
who helped us
rediscover our love
of poetry

Contents

Foreword

When I was teaching a graduate class in poetry for children at Ohio State University I used to recommend that my students go out to Mt. Victory, a small rural town of some 650 persons in central Ohio, and visit the combined fifth- and sixth-grade classrooms of Sheryl Reed and Peggy Harrison. I regularly maintained that I knew of no mount and no victory in that small town *except* in the classrooms of these two remarkable teachers.

Both teachers were advocates of the whole language approach to teaching before the name was invented. Persuading their administrator and school board to take down the partition between their classrooms was their first step in initiating their integrated curriculum. Then they deliberately fostered cross-grade interaction by mixing children of the fifth and sixth grades for various subjects and projects. They surrounded children with many books—trade books, not textbooks, and books of various genres including fantasy, realism, historical fiction and biography, poetry, and many informational books. They bought books themselves. They wrote and received a federal grant for $5000. With this money, they set up a program mixing grade levels and bought the books for a literature-based reading program. And they took courses that supported and extended what they were doing at Ohio State University, some fifty miles away.

Both of these teachers enrolled in my graduate course on poetry for children. My major goal in this class was to help teachers become excited about poetry and then in turn to excite their own students. We read poetry aloud to each other in small groups and responded to it. We chanted poetry, sang it, and did choral readings.

We tried writing poetry ourselves as a way of helping us become better observers of our world and the poet's world. Everyone in the class agreed to try poetry with their students and then share their successes, frustrations, and failures. We were all captivated by the descriptions of what was happening with children and poetry in Mt. Victory. Sheryl and Peggy brought in the poems children had written and their illustrations. They described their children's delight with poetry, their developing preference for poems with deep meaning, and the various ways children found to do process writing with each other.

I was invited to visit this classroom. It was one of the most rewarding days of my teaching career. Children were reading poetry, discussing it, writing and revising their poems together, and, most importantly, thoroughly enjoying it. I came away determined that we had to capture how these teachers inspired their students in order that other teachers could read about it and do the same.

Then Amy McClure, an instructor at Ohio Wesleyan University, a former classroom teacher and a Ph.D. student, enrolled in my poetry class. She followed my advice and went to visit Sheryl and Peggy's classroom and was fascinated by what she observed. She too wanted to record and capture the way these two gifted teachers taught. She realized she had found her dissertation topic.

Amy spent one school year visiting this classroom regularly as a participant-observer. She tape-recorded all sessions and took detailed field notes. She also interviewed the two teachers regularly. Gradually, she became more of a participant than an observer, working alongside the teachers, encouraging the children, and recording their conversations and responses. Her research adviser told me that this was one of the most carefully prepared ethnographic studies that he had ever read, and he used it in his class as a model of insightful observations and analysis. The NCTE Research Committee must have agreed, for they gave Amy one of only two Promising Research Awards that year for dissertations. Kappa Delta Pi, an honor society for educators, also named this dissertation the outstanding one done in 1985.

Using the framework from her study, Amy, in collaboration with Sheryl and Peggy, rewrote it—dropping her research voice for an almost poetic description of her year in this lively classroom in which poetry was the heart of the curriculum. She has captured the language of the children (frequently ungrammatical) as they discuss and revise their poems. You meet Jimmy P., who was once labeled a behavior problem, yet who could observe and record the flight of an owl or the orbit of a basketball around a basket's rim. You see how Angela's poem on the sunrise evolved through many revisions over several months of off-and-on attention until she was finally satisfied with her metaphor of the night being eaten by the sun for "Breakfast." You hear the teachers asking questions, guiding but not telling, encouraging children to play with an idea, to consider alternatives to be true to their subject and offer honest, unclichéd visions of their world. They gave the children not false praise but focused praise that made them want to stretch themselves to reach new heights of achievement.

I wish that all teachers who have ever wanted to try poetry in their classrooms would read this book. I hope that teachers interested in process writing will read this account of children voluntarily revising their work. *Sunrises and Songs* is a book that will help teachers learn how to introduce poetry to children and provide ways to encourage children to write and refine their poems. It also provides a superb model for anyone interested in doing ethnographic research. Above all, it is a book that reveals a love of children and fine literature, and the way creative teachers may bring the two together. It is as much a book about the poetry of teaching as it is about the teaching of poetry.

Charlotte S. Huck
Professor Emeritus
The Ohio State University

Preface

This book is intended for teachers, librarians, and others who want to make poetry an important part of children's lives. We believe all children can become poetry lovers. However, we offer no prescriptions, no lists of do's and don'ts for teaching poetry. Nor do we promise children that writing or understanding a poem is easy if only one follows the rules. Rather, we see poetry as an art, the product of much thinking and feeling, with roots in personal observation and experience.

What we have done in this book is tell our story. It is a story of normal, ordinary children in a real classroom, with all the triumphs, frustrations, progress, and false starts that are inevitably part of any classroom. It is our hope that after reading this story you will be stimulated to take our ideas and techniques, focus them through your personal teaching lens, and create your own community of poetry lovers.

Acknowledgments

We wish to thank the children of Ridgemont Elementary School, who have delighted and inspired us as well as affirmed our conviction that once children get into poetry, they really like it. Thanks also to them and their parents for permission to quote from the children's work.

We are grateful to the following for permission to reprint previously published material:

"Beginning" is from *The Malibu and Other Poems* by Myra Cohn Livingston. Copyright © 1972 by Myra Cohn Livingston. Reprinted by permission of Marian Reiner for the author.

Excerpts from "Where Is a Poem?" in JAMBOREE *Rhymes for All Times* by Eve Merriam. Copyright © 1962, 1964, 1966, 1973, 1984 by Eve Merriam. Reprinted by permission of Marian Reiner for the author.

"To Look at Anything" in *Living Seed*, Copyright © 1958 and renewed 1986 by John Moffitt, reprinted by permission of Harcourt Brace Jovanovich, Inc.

Excerpts from " 'I,' Says the Poem" in A *Sky Full of Poems* by Eve Merriam. Copyright © 1964, 1970, 1973 by Eve Merriam. All rights reserved. Reprinted by permission of Marian Reiner for the author.

"Unfolding Bud" by Naoshi Koriyama, *The Christian Science Monitor*, July 13, 1957. Reprinted by permission from *The Christian Science Monitor*, © 1957 The Christian Science Publishing Society. All rights reserved.

"The Fish" by Stanley Cook, from *The Fourth Poetry Book* compiled by John Foster (Oxford: Oxford University Press, 1982). Reprinted by permission of Stanley Cook.

"Posting Letters" from the book *Posting Letters* by Gregory Harrison (Oxford: Oxford University Press, 1968). Reprinted by permission of the author.

"Poem" from William Carlos Williams: *Collected Poems Vol. I, 1909–1939*. Copyright 1938 by New Directions Publishing Corporation. Reprinted by permission of New Directions Publishing Corporation.

"Catalogue" by Rosalie Moore. From *The New Yorker*, May 25, 1940. Reprinted by permission; © 1940, 1968 The New Yorker Magazine, Inc.

"Street Song" is from *The Way Things Are and Other Poems* by Myra Cohn Livingston. Copyright © 1974 by Myra Cohn Livingston. Reprinted by permission of Marian Reiner for the author.

"Crystal Moment" by Robert P. Tristram Coffin. Reprinted with permission of Macmillan Publishing Company from *Collected Poems* by Robert P. Tristram Coffin. Copyright 1932 by Macmillan Publishing Company, renewed 1960 by Margaret Coffin Halvosa.

"Phizzog" in *Good Morning, America*, copyright 1928 and renewed 1956 by Carl Sandburg, reprinted by permission of Harcourt Brace Jovanovich, Inc.

"The Drum" from *Sing a Soft Black Song* by Nikki Giovanni. Copyright © 1971, 1985 by Nikki Giovanni. Reprinted by permission of Hill and Wang, a division of Farrar, Straus and Giroux, Inc.

"April" by Marcia Lee Masters. From *Intent on Earth* (1957) and *Wind Around the Moon* (1986). Reprinted by permission of the author.

Excerpts from "It Doesn't Always Have to Rhyme" in *It Doesn't Always Have to Rhyme* by Eve Merriam. Copyright © 1964 by Eve Merriam. Reprinted by permission of Marian Reiner for the author.

"From the Japanese" from *Rainbow Writing* by Eve Merriam. Copyright © 1976 by Eve Merriam. Reprinted by permission of Marian Reiner for the author.

Excerpt from "The Road Not Taken" by Robert Frost. Copyright 1916 by Holt, Rinehart and Winston, Inc. and renewed 1944 by Robert Frost. Reprinted from *The Poetry of Robert Frost* edited by Edward Connery Lathem, by permission of Henry Holt and Company, Inc.

Finally, we thank our families, who have always supported our dedication to teaching.

PART I

Beginnings

CHAPTER 1

A Beginning

Spring
    happens

out of the cold.

Winter lives inside your skin

old
and
tight

then

buds burst bright

and you
begin.

"Beginning"
MYRA COHN LIVINGSTON

Voices rose and fell...boys' voices. The voices spoke of a kitten and a poem. The janitor whispered to the teacher who had just arrived at her classroom door, "I've been letting 'em into your room early for awhile now. They usually get here around 7:30. They come in to write and talk and share poetry. I kinda enjoy listenin' to 'em."

It was 8:00, thirty minutes before the start of the school day. Johnny, Ronnie, Jimmy, and Matt, four sixth-grade boys, welcomed their teacher, Sheryl Reed, with enthusiasm. All of the boys were talking to her at once. "Put down your book bag." "Sit here." "Johnny has a new kitten and he wrote an entry about it." "It's pretty good but it needs some revision."

After she joined the group, Jimmy told Johnny to first read what he had written the previous night before sharing all the revisions they had worked on that morning.

Johnny said proudly, "My Mom and I watched my new black kitten play with a string I hung over the couch, and I wrote this poetry entry about it."

Kitten

The Kitten creeps
Toward the circling
String
As I jerk it
He attacks
He fights the string
With all his might
Suddenly
He runs away
The string lays still.

"We told him that 'with all his might' sounds like something people say all the time, and it doesn't really make you see a picture of anything," Jimmy said as Sheryl was about to comment on Johnny's entry.

"Yeah," Ronnie interjected, "We asked what kittens fight strings with and Johnny said 'paws' so we said put that down."

"It didn't sound right—the rhythm you know. So we finally decided the paws were the kitten's, and I put down 'kitten paws'," added Johnny.

"And we said he didn't need 'suddenly.' Everybody always says that. It didn't add nothing to his poem either," Matt put in.

Ronnie said, " 'He runs away' just wasn't descriptive enough. It needed to be more specific. We all kept sayin' ideas until Jimmy said we had to think how a kitten really goes away from fightin' a string."

"Yeah," Johnny agreed, "and 'leaps' was just the way a kitten does and we decided 'he leaps away' sounded good so I put that down, then Jimmy says I ought to have a catchier start, and Matt says that 'circling' doesn't sound just right so we thought some more and talked some more and read a whole bunch of cat poems, and then we decided a string dangles if someone holds it so I put 'dangling string.'"

Jimmy interrupted, "And his beginning still didn't catch your attention so I asked how kittens creep."

"And I said," added Ronnie, "'pretty cautious so's as the mice won't hear them.'"

Everybody laughed at Ronnie's usual joke and Jimmy continued, "so Johnny put down 'cautious creeps the kitten.' That's a k-k-k sound and that's neat but it doesn't sound exactly right yet, does it? What do you think's the matter with it, Mrs. Reed?"

She replied, "I like the k–k–k alliteration but I agree that it doesn't have quite the right sound yet. Think about what suffixes might be added to the word 'cautious' to give it more rhythm or make it sound better."

After asking her to remind them whether a suffix went at the beginning or the end of a word, they began playing with different endings. When someone suggested "ly," and the word cautiously was repeated around the table, Johnny squealed, "That's it. That's it!"

Three girls had entered the room during this retelling of how the revision process evolved. When Johnny squealed, they hurried to the table and joined the group. After they heard a shortened version of the poem's evolution, they wanted to hear it too.

Johnny, stumbling over words in his excitement, said, "I'm gonna read my revision." He took a long deep breath. " 'Kitten.' This is just how it really was!"

Cautiously creeps
The kitten
Toward the dangling
String.
As I jerk it
He attacks.
He fights the string
With kitten paws.
He leaps away.
The string lays still.

Everyone applauded. The group broke up with children still commenting to Johnny and to each other about the neat poem. The bus children were arriving and the word passed among them concerning Johnny's piece. Everybody wanted to read it.

Johnny worked on the poem several different times throughout the day and during the week. He then brought it to Sheryl for help with spelling and punctuation. He had also done some revising on his own, changing "the string lays still" to "the string hangs still," explaining that the string was still hanging so "lays" didn't sound right. Sheryl agreed that this change further strengthened the commitment of staying true to a subject that he, Jimmy, Ronnie and Matt had been working to achieve.

5

A Beginning

"It's just the way I want it," Johnny commented after they had finished.

This incident is typical of many that occurred in this classroom. These children loved poetry. Furthermore, they viewed it as an essential part of their lives—as natural as reading, doing math, even eating and sleeping.

These positive attitudes are not typical of most children. Research suggests that most children dislike poetry, viewing it as the literary equivalent of liver. In preference surveys, poetry invariably is ranked near the bottom, along with literary criticism, speeches, and letters (Norvell, 1958; Schulte, 1967; Matanzo and Madison, 1979; NAEP, 1981). Such acute dislike is not inevitable. When children are presented with motivating activities and poetry that appeal to their interests, they have quite positive attitudes (Matanzo and Madison, 1979; Shapiro and Shapiro, 1971; McCall, 1979). However, studies that show these positive responses seem to be more the exception than the rule.

When children do demonstrate a liking for poetry, their preferences for specific elements and forms are strikingly similar across age, sex, demographic data, and time. Generally, it seems that children prefer poems that include elements of humor, nonsense, familiar experiences, imaginative story lines, animals, holidays, and people. In contrast, they dislike poems like Longfellow's "The Children's Hour" or Hughes's "April Rain Song," which they perceive as didactic, meditative, serious, or "difficult to understand." Narrative and limerick forms are enjoyed while more abstract forms such as haiku and free verse are generally disliked. Preferred poetic elements include rhyme, rhythm, sound and repetition. Figurative language is not usually enjoyed (Mackintosh, 1924, 1932; Avegno, 1956; Norvell, 1958; Bridge, 1966; Terry, 1972; Ingham, 1980; Simmons, 1980; Fisher and Natarella, 1982).

Despite the research that suggests children have definite preferences for particular kinds of poetry, teachers often present poems children don't enjoy. Research surveys reveal that teachers often share traditional, meditative pieces rather than contemporary humorous poetry with children and use basal readers and curriculum guides for their choices (many of which fail to include children's favorites). The only exception to these selections is the widespread use of Silverstein's *Where the Sidewalk Ends*. Common teaching practices include line-by-line analysis, memorization, and the relating of the poem to other literary works. Student-directed discussions or activities are rare (Norvell, 1968; Thom, 1969; Purves and Beach, 1972; Terry, 1972; Hecht, 1978; Craven, 1980).

This research on poetry preferences and teaching practices led me to some speculation. Maybe there was more to children's poetry preferences than previously thought. What could explain the discrepancy between the excitement and affinity for poetry observed in Jimmy, Johnny, Ronnie, and Matt and the general apathy displayed by children in other studies? Were their positive attitudes merely flukes? Or were they the result of a particular classroom environment that nurtured and supported them? Maybe previous research had touched only the tip of the iceberg in describing children's responses to poetry. I was intrigued. I wanted to find out what motivated these boys to come to school at 7:30 A.M. to read and write poetry. I contacted Sheryl Reed and her colleague, Peggy Harrison, and they agreed to participate in a study.

A Meeting of Like Minds

As I drove to our first pre-project meeting, I thought back to the real start of the study—before I knew Johnny, Jimmy, Ronnie, and their teachers. The story began almost a year earlier when several Ohio State University professors and graduate students became interested in studying the discrepancies between the theory taught in teacher education methods classes and actual teaching practice. The objective of this study was to interview teachers in all types of teaching situations—rural, suburban, inner city, racially mixed, racially homogeneous—to gain a sense of why some teachers implemented a whole language teaching approach (highly endorsed by the local university), while others felt unable to do so. Sheryl Reed and Peggy Harrison were selected as participants for this study because they were known as strong proponents of the whole language approach.

They also worked in a true team-teaching situation. We'd been told that although each teacher was assigned to a separate grade level, either fifth or sixth, and ostensibly had her own class, such distinctions quickly blurred as children moved freely about the large room that housed both groups. The school administrators okayed the removal of a central wall that originally separated the rooms so children could collaborate with whomever they wished. Sheryl and Peggy then deliberately fostered cross-grade interaction by dividing some of their teaching responsibilities by subject rather than grade level. Although both taught math and reading to their own classes, Sheryl worked extensively with all the children in writing while Peggy helped everyone with art. Frequent whole-group meetings with all the children reinforced the idea that the classes were linked.

On a cold, snowy morning in mid-January, my research partner, Judy Yocum, and I traveled to their school in Mt. Victory, Ohio, for an all-day visit. "Is this really going to be as great as everyone says?" we wondered skeptically. After weeks of interviewing teachers who felt constrained by their environments to teach according to the theory they had learned in teacher education courses, we wondered if we would encounter yet one more instance of people who want to do interesting things but are unable to teach in line with their beliefs.

After twenty minutes in Sheryl and Peggy's classroom our skepticism vanished, replaced by a growing admiration for these women who were implementing their whole language philosophy in a small rural school, with children who had no previous experience with this kind of teaching. We saw children busily working in small groups—discussing novels, writing in poetry journals, constructing art and science projects and helping each other revise stories. Everyone willingly stopped to explain what they were doing and were amazingly articulate about the purposes of each project. I was particularly intrigued by their work in poetry. As I leafed through poetry journals from previous classes and listened while children eagerly shared their current pieces, I was struck by the creativity and thought so evident in poems like the following:

A Bat

A bat
Feeds lavishly
On moths
And beetles,
Flies loops
And twirls,
Catches bugs
From behind.
When the sun
Rises faintly,
The bat
Retires to rest.

CHARLES
PHIPPS, JR.

Combine

Scissoring the weedy ground,
Shaving it
And spitting it out,
Taking it
For a day's harvest.

EDDIE PERKINS

Later, after school, Judy, Sheryl, Peggy, and I met at the Plaza, the local truck stop and only restaurant in town. We had planned a forty-five minute interview session. Two hours later we were still talking. It was as if a dam had burst. Sheryl and Peggy talked on and on about children and literature—particularly poetry. The frustrations of helping children become excited about learning by reading and writing real literature in an atmosphere that did not value these activities quickly became evident. As we explored our common beliefs, understandings and frustrations over coffee, a friendship based on shared purposes and experiences evolved. It was evident to Judy and me that these teachers were deeply committed to their practices, yet welcomed—indeed thirsted—for interaction with like-minded colleagues. When we finally left, the two of us couldn't stop talking and thinking about what we had seen in Mt. Victory. We wanted to know more about these two teachers and their students—how they got children to love fine poetry as well as write pieces that used unusual language, complex imagery, and uncommon structures. As I carefully drove home along the icy country roads, I grew determined to discover what made the difference. I knew this was the environment in which I could test out my tentative hypotheses about children and poetry.

Formulating the Research Design

Traditional approaches to studying poetry have often focused on the text or the writer but rarely on the reader's past experiences and understandings. It has been assumed that readers must possess tacit knowledge of literary conventions and forms before they can uncover the inherent or so-called true meaning of a literary work. As a result research on response to poetry has long been defined as measuring student ability or inability to discern the correct meaning of text (Richards, 1929; reviewed in Purves and Beach, 1972).

These findings, however, were at odds with what I saw in Mt. Victory, and thus I decided a different research technique was needed for this study. Young children's responses are often elusive and spontaneous, frequently articulated in a half-formed, disorganized fashion. Such responses are difficult to document in experimental settings. If I had used traditional experimental methods, I may have derived the same limited results as other studies, even in a classroom like this one where so many exciting things were happening.

I was also greatly influenced by the work of Louise Rosenblatt (1965, 1978) who has defined response not as a one-way transmission from writer to reader but rather as a complex transaction, requiring reciprocal interaction between reader and text. This transaction, according to Rosenblatt, is tempered by the reader's experiences and perceptions that direct him or her to distill the multiple meanings implicit in a particular text. Response, then, is individual in nature, reflecting one's unique view of the world. The function of text in this process is to both guide and constrain the reader's construction of meaning.

But the reader's perspective cannot be considered apart from the context in which it exists. Various elements of social context—the interactions between peers, the relationships between teachers and children—are critical in helping readers construct responses as well as enlarge, deepen, and practice them (Rosen and Rosen, 1973; Barnes, 1976; Hickman, 1979; Hepler, 1982). It is through interaction with both peers and teachers, negotiating meanings through language, that children develop the abilities to reflect upon their unique personal constructs or responses to literature.

These reconceptualized understandings about the experiential and social nature of response and the complexity involved in measuring it made me realize a different research methodology was needed. The chosen method had to allow for continuous observation of a wide range of behaviors that change over time as well as provide the opportunity to document the influence of context on these behaviors. My intention was to move beyond quantifying the occurrence of response to constructing an understanding of the particular conditions that nurture more complex understandings of poetry.

An ethnographic, participant-observer methodology seemed the reasonable choice. Using this approach would allow me to explore the complex relationship between the patterns of children's responses as well as how the social context of the classroom influenced and shaped those responses. I hoped to arrive at insights and understandings that more quantitative, short-term assessments might miss. Further, I hypothesized that the ethnographic method would allow me to interpret classroom events more from the children's and teachers' perspectives. By becoming part of their world I hoped to gain a clearer understanding of their perceptions about the processes of reading and writing poetry. This book documents what we—teachers, children, and researcher—discovered.

CHAPTER 2

A Community of Poetry Lovers

Where is a poem?
As far away
As a rainbow span,
Ancient Cathay,
Or Afghanistan,

Or it can be near
As where you stand
This very day
On Main Street here
With a poem
In your hand.

"Where Is a Poem?"
EVE MERRIAM

The drive from Columbus to Mt. Victory takes forty minutes, but it always made me feel like I was going back forty years. From Columbus, a white-collar community of modern glass office buildings, crowded expressways, and high-tech businesses, I would head out Route 33 to the open rural spaces of Marysville and beyond. As the traffic eased, so did my frame of mind as I settled in for the tranquil drive through the countryside.

From Route 33, I would make a right turn onto Route 31. Along the straight two-lane road, the open fields of rural Ohio stretch for miles on both sides. Along the road I passed meandering creeks, irrigation ditches marked by cattails, small clumps of hardwood timber, and acres of soybeans. The flat landscape is dotted with small family farms with names like Spring Valley, Happy Acres, and Buckeye Valley Farm. Each has the standard weatherbeaten clapboard farmhouse, large barn, silo, and garden. Often, in the early morning, horse trainers would be out exercising their animals. Occasionally, isolated clapboard country churches like God's Country Church and Byhalia Friends Church reminded me that religion is a central part of life for many people in this area. Although sometimes a satellite dish can be seen poking out from behind a farmyard complex and high tension, electric wires cross the narrow road, the impression is one of returning to simpler ways and times.

Occasionally, I would pass an old-fashioned, black horse and buggy as this is Amish country in Ohio. The women and children, dressed in dark, somber clothes, would peer cautiously out as I passed. The men were usually bolder and would often lift their hand in greeting. I was always initially jarred by these encounters. Even in this setting, the sight seemed a bit incongruous. But these feelings were quickly replaced by the sense that somehow these people are a natural part of the landscape.

I was particularly intrigued by the sky. Unencumbered by buildings or hills, it seemed to go on forever. I never grew tired of watching the bright turquoise against the brilliant fall foliage fade to the silver gray and soft blue of winter, then brighten to the crisp hues of spring.

I loved this part of my visits. All the tensions and hassles of life in the city seemed to disappear as I was lulled by the serenity of farmland and sky. Even within the seemingly tranquil, unchanging landscape, there was always something new to see. This feeling was reinforced by the children whose poetry was filled with the rural images that surrounded them. They too found beauty in what others might term ordinary or boring.

Eventually, I would come to Mt. Victory, a small community of about 650 people that reflects the rural character of its surroundings. There are no shopping malls, movie theatres, or fast food restaurants (except for one locally run dairy bar) in Mt. Victory. The downtown is composed of several small businesses (hardware, grocery store, farm implements, etc.), a grain elevator, one gas station, a bar, seventeen antique shops, and the post office. Since most people have a post office box, everyone makes a daily trip there. Elsie, the postmistress, keeps people informed about the latest town news and even sets up chairs so they can stay and talk to one another.

The town has one K–6 elementary school, Ridgemont, which houses approximately 276 students. They come from Mt. Victory, Ridgeway (a nearby town of 400 people), and the surrounding rural areas. About 150 local, Amish children do not attend the school. School enrollment is declining, mainly because young families are inclined to leave town for bigger cities.

Most parents have graduated from high school and are employed by factories in surrounding towns and cities. Some still make a living from family farms, although this is no longer a viable occupation for many. The community is too small to support many professionals; if they choose to live in Mt. Victory, they often work elsewhere. There is also a significant group of transient people who come and go in low-rent housing.

Mt. Victory may seem like an unusual place for poetry to flourish and indeed it has not been easy for these teachers to fan the spark. The response of parents to the inclusion of poetry in the curriculum has run the gamut from hostility to curiosity to enthusiastic involvement. Even though the use of poetry is mandated in the Language Arts Curriculum Guide, it has been difficult to assure some parents of its value.

Some parents, after observing their children's enthusiasm, become zealous advocates. For example, some children reported their mom or dad began reading poetry with them in the evenings. One mother even shyly shared her own journal that was filled with poems about her children and life as a woman in this rural community. Most parents, however, remain suspicious and are not always positive when describing this classroom to their friends and neighbors. This is a tough situation for the two dedicated, hardworking teachers.

The Teachers

Sheryl ("Peg") Reed is the sixth-grade teacher. She has taught for nineteen years, all of them at Ridgemont School in Mt. Victory. She obtained a degree from Ohio State University, then completed a master's degree there in reading and children's literature. Peggy Harrison, the fifth-grade teacher, has taught for twelve years, all of them at Ridgemont. She also received a B.A. from Ohio State, and completed the same master's program.

Sheryl and Peggy had positive experiences with poetry as young children. Both were read poetry aloud by family members who obviously loved the lilt and flow that characterize poetic language. Peggy recollects hearing nursery rhymes and Robert Louis Stevenson's A Child's Garden of Verses. "Even now I can close my eyes and see the counterpane he mentions," she recalls. "What an interesting word to be stored in a child's mind to be savored even now." Sheryl's mother and grandfather frequently read aloud to her from the Bible and many poetry books.

Both teachers characterize their own school years as generally devoid of poetry. All Peggy remembers is a sixth-grade teacher who read "The Village Blacksmith" aloud to the class. What is most vivid about this experience is not the poem (of which she remembers nothing) but rather the way her teacher's diamond sparkled and glittered as she read. In Peggy's junior high, teacher-selected poems were memorized, then recited by each student as the teacher stood sternly in front of the class, gradebook in hand. High school English classes focused on dissecting poems to see what they were made of. Peggy occasionally attempted to write poetry—but always quickly hid it away like Emily Dickinson.

Sheryl cites similar experiences. She enjoyed hearing poetry so much that she began creating her own poems in her mind. Later, as she learned to write, she would record these verses on paper. Her mother read this work but neither praised nor critiqued it. Teachers showed little interest in her writing or in that done by other students.

Sheryl's poems were a great source of personal enjoyment until she entered the fifth grade. As she often finished workbook assignments quickly, she kept a tablet hidden in her desk on which were scribbled poems. One day her fifth-grade teacher spied Sheryl writing furiously on the tablet. She jerked the pad from beneath the workbook and quickly skimmed its contents. Sheryl remembers that the teacher's quavering voice echoed from every corner of the room as she announced that Sheryl was wasting her time writing poetry again and that her fate would be that of those who choose to lead a "less than productive life." Although she didn't use the word "bum," Sheryl was sure she would become one. The teacher then dramatically tore up the writing and threw it in the wastebasket.

For years after that incident, Sheryl wrote poetry only occasionally and only late at night, always tearing it up and throwing it away the next morning. As she says now, "I longed to write but I was ashamed to do so and was always afraid of the fate that awaited me if I did."

Despite these negative experiences, both teachers have always enjoyed poetry with their students. They frequently read it aloud and occasionally provide time for poetry writing. Initially, those experiences were not particularly rewarding. "I tried poetry several times," commented Peggy, "yet felt very frustrated because the children wiggled and squirmed when I read a poem a day. But all I ever did was read it. I never asked them what they thought, tied it in with anything else, or had them get right in the middle of a poem."

Both agreed it was Charlotte Huck's course in children's poetry that expanded their perceptions as to how teachers can get children excited about good poetry. Sheryl enthusiastically describes the rekindling of her love for poetry and how that excitement could be communicated to children in the following way:

> Charlotte carefully steeped us in a brew of fine poets and poetry. She had us make poetry collections which would help children make the connection between their own lives and the broader realm of poetry. The feeling of success children experience from reading and writing poetry, the expectation that poetry set-ups or books made by children be beautifully done, the effect sharing has on the reading and writing processes and the significant influence a teacher has who loves poetry were but a few of the mix of "fine teas" offered in Charlotte's Poetry for Children class.

It was Myra Cohn Livingston's book *When You're Alone, It Keeps You Capone*, also discovered in the poetry course, that particularly influenced how these teachers organized the classroom for poetry as well as how they responded to children's oral comments and writing. Livingston believes that children should hear fine poetry as well as attempt to write it. The teachers decided to include both elements in their own teaching. They further agreed with Livingston's perspective that children respond readily and benefit more from honest comments than hasty, insincere praise. Livingston contends that premature or false praise is neither honest nor helpful. Rather, it becomes an excuse to do only enough to elicit more such praise. Conversely, negative or premature corrections can rob children of their willingness to experiment, take risks, or maybe even write again. Livingston, and Sheryl and Peggy, see this as a tragedy. They realize that few, if any, of their students will ever become poets or professional writers. But if they stop writing and reading poetry, they will have lost a source of personal joy and introspection, a vehicle for expressing their thoughts and as Sheryl says, "a means of touching the quietness of life."

Both teachers are now once again avid writers and readers of poetry. They keep their own poetry journals in which they record observations, snatches of phrases that pop into their heads and sometimes whole poems. These journals are freely shared with the children who are invited to suggest changes. Sheryl, in particular, finds this writing exhilarating:

> I experience a powerful satisfaction every time I write. I struggle as a writer...I agonize...I am sometimes crippled. I sometimes fly. I am exhausted yet jubilant after each writing session....I write in my mind, when I'm in the car alone, in the shower, in bed and when a rhythm or the music of words play without ceasing in my head.

They also read poetry alone, to each other, and to the children. These readings are usually accompanied by discussions in which children and adults alike savor the poem together.

All this study and experimentation has led to the belief that enjoying poetry with children not only helps them succeed in academic subjects but also contributes to their social, emotional, and aesthetic development. The following statement reveals Sheryl and Peggy's thinking:

> We feel that involvement with poetry increases children's sensitivity and awareness, helps them become more observant, causes them to look deeply within themselves, and to reach far beyond themselves to universal truths, provides them a vehicle to get in touch with the feelings of others as well as their own feelings, brings to the surface that spark of truth within each of them, gives them the opportunity to be in communication with the aesthetic side of life, and initiates a habit which can bring joy to them for the rest of their lives.
>
> Reading, hearing and especially writing poetry helps children become better overall writers and readers. Their prose becomes more poetic, more truthful, more fluent, and more to the point. They learn to say what they mean in a few words—to be concise. We develop a sense of the uncommon and endeavor to make the common come alive.

Both teachers also held certain philosophical convictions about teaching and learning that were consistent with their ideas about poetry. They viewed their teaching role as that of facilitator of a developmental process, which meant they believed it was essential to guide, suggest, respond, and question. They supported the children's emerging understandings rather than arbitrarily designating what these understandings should be.

Both teachers advocated learning that was compatible with their view of the teacher's role. They believed children learn best when encouraged to develop naturally and can interact with peers and adults as they mutually negotiate meanings through language. They organized the classroom so children could interact with peers as they explored ideas through individual and small group projects. Topics were frequently integrated, blurring the common distinctions between math, language, social studies, and science. The emphasis was on self-selection and self-direction rather than passive acceptance of adult direction.

Most importantly, both teachers were strongly committed to their beliefs. As Sheryl confided that first winter's day at the Plaza, "I could never go back to teaching the way I started out. . . . I would give up my career before doing that." This strong commitment to

Beginnings

their approach required a heavy investment of personal time and effort. Both often spoke of "planning twenty-four hours a day," of "planning even as we're sitting here talking." Peggy even often joked about keeping scraps of paper in the pocket of her bathrobe to jot down ideas.

The picture that emerges of these teachers is that of committed professionals, concerned about supporting children's learning. Further, they were early lovers of poetry—having been denied it, they had rediscovered it and possessed a keen desire to share their own joy in it with their students.

The Children

The children who attend Ridgemont Elementary are a curious blend of old-fashioned and modern. They often build tree forts, go frogging in the creeks, and aren't averse to getting mud between their toes to collect a choice piece of skunk cabbage or moss to write about. Yet they also know all the latest break-dancing steps, MTV lyrics, and sweatshirt styles. It seems that while television has exposed them to the outside world, they are still capable of enjoying the simple joys of life in a small town.

Most of the classrooms in the school have children with a range of abilities. However, the group in Sheryl and Peggy's room this year seemed to have more than its share of problems. When the children first arrived, they seemed defeated. They felt "like they couldn't do anything well," according to Peggy. She describes them as frightened about math, writing, reading "hard" books—just about anything that presented a challenge. They were unwilling to reach out, to take risks or to try something new.

Standardized test scores confirmed the expectation that these children would struggle academically. Several of the children could be classified as learning disabled or developmentally handicapped. Over a third had test scores that were low enough to qualify them for special reading help through Chapter I. No one in the class had scored in the unusually bright or gifted range.

So it would seem that this group of children would struggle with academic work. They were destined not to succeed in school and certainly would not respond to the abstractions and unique language of poetry. They were certainly not the upper-middle class suburban children one normally associates with complex literary response. Yet somehow when we—teachers and researchers—began focusing on them as individuals, ceasing to worry about what they couldn't do, we began to discover the desire for self-expression and the unique voice of each child.

Several individuals stood out in the group, particularly those of the sixth-grade male "gang." There was Johnny, the boy with the new kitten. Dark-haired, stocky Johnny had a speech impairment that made him difficult to understand unless you listened carefully and made him slow down. Yet, through extreme determination, Johnny had greatly improved his speech. This intense self-motivation carried over to his academic work. Although good in math, he qualified for the Chapter I reading program. However, he constantly announced his intentions to challenge himself with hard books and poems. Johnny enjoyed helping other children with their work and sometimes came across as bossy. If you looked beyond the brash exterior, it was evident that this was Johnny's way of making friends and covering up a lack of self-confidence.

Johnny's best friend was Jimmy, a tall, thin, sensitive boy who reminded me of the stereotypical romantic, English poet. Jimmy had also been in the Chapter I reading program, until third grade. His parents had divorced the previous year, causing him much anguish: at one point during this time he even stopped eating. This upheaval seemed to make Jimmy sensitive to the nuances of events around him, and he frequently seemed distant and pensive. His poetry was melancholy. It had a sense of standing outside and looking at something from an observer's perspective. While most of the children wrote about hopscotching, their pets, and nature, Jimmy often wrote about things like death, war, and freedom. This sensitivity, rather than putting off the other children, seemed to draw them to him. They would frequently seek his advice, particularly on how to make their poems have "deep meaning."

Ronnie, in contrast, was the class clown. From an Appalachian background, he spoke with the rhythm and lilt of hill people and always had a joke or funny observation to share. He was also a messy person. Everything he used was wadded up, disorganized, and strewn from one end of the classroom to the other. The girls constantly tried to organize him, but it never seemed to do much good. Ronnie was another child who qualified for Chapter I reading assistance, but in this classroom, he chose books to read like *Adam of the Road*, *Otto and the Silver Hand*, and *Johnny Tremain*. His comments in class discussions usually got to the heart of a book or poem.

Both teachers remember the children in this group as unusual in one respect: the amount of interaction that occurred between boys and girls. The children sat next to someone from the opposite sex without squealing and helped each other with projects, personal problems, and poetry.

Jennifer was particularly close to the gang. Dark-haired, tall, and stocky, Jennifer was a child with a great deal of depth and intelligence. She had read Little Women in first grade and had enjoyed challenging herself with complex books from then on. Jennifer was also one of the few children who would write on her own, then join the boys or her friends Jenny and Becky to give advice or get reactions to what she'd written. She reminded me of the stereotypical writer holed up in a garret like Jo from her favorite book, Little Women.

Angela, in contrast, sought lots of social contact and feedback in her writing. I could usually find her reading her poems to a few close friends, like Becky and Angie, asking them to give her another word or suggest a different way to write a line. She too was bright but somehow never fully succeeded in school due to an inability to maintain consistently strong effort. But she possessed a creative flair that showed up in both her reading and writing.

Several other sixth-grade girls responded in various ways to poetry. Stacie and Carrie, the cool cheerleaders, would make sensitive, insightful comments in small group discussions and often gathered groups of children together to read poems. Stacie was also known as a good "critiquer" or analyzer of other people's poems, although she wrote little poetry herself. Angie, who loved to experiment with words and ideas, occasionally displayed astonishing insights in her poetry, yet she was shy about talking in a discussion group. Becky, a Chapter I candidate, would often surprise everyone by coming up with perceptive comments.

The fifth graders were identified through test scores as being more able than the sixth-grade group although again few were considered gifted. As with the sixth graders, there were separate groups of boys and girls who worked together, then intermingled when they felt the need for fresh ideas or different insights.

The central fifth-grade male group included Aaron, Jeremy, Tommy, and Mike J. These were the cool boys, interested in basketball, MTV, and girls. Aaron was considered the class leader and was often asked for advice on writing poems. Tall, quiet Jeremy was the creative one. He would join his friends for a poetry discussion, then suddenly disappear to be found later in the windowsill or under a bench writing furiously on a piece he would later bring back to the group. Tommy and Mike J. seemingly followed the dictates of the others, yet often would create their own poetic observations about the thrill of hunting with their dogs, basketball, or the delightful taste of a favorite candy on the tongue.

Jimmy P. often worked with this group, although he was never an insider. Labeled as having behavior problems, he often crashed around the room, bumping into furniture, knocking over jars of paint and stepping on work in progress. Yet, he also could observe and record with astonishing insight the flight of an owl or the orbit of a basketball around a basket's rim.

Mandy, Robin and Dolly made up the most cohesive group of fifth-grade girls. Feminine, blond-haired Robin was the leader. She always had good ideas and could get everyone else organized to do a project. Happy-go-lucky Mandy with her bright smile and brown hair caught up in a ponytail would often go along with Robin but also had her own unique observations about "hopscotching" fall leaves and the way milkweed floated through the air. Shy Dolly would offer tentative comments to her friends, then find her own quiet spot to write observations about friends or nature.

The Poetry "Curriculum"

What these teachers did with poetry is an interesting mixture of writing and reading, sharing and listening, establishing structure and allowing freedom. To acquire a general sense of this subtle tapestry of interactive forces, I asked the teachers to meet with me in late August, prior to the beginning of school. It was not my purpose to question their practices or to somehow change what they did to fit any image I may have subconsciously created of the perfect poetry teacher. Rather, I wanted to subtly ferret out their ideas, perceptions, and realizations as to how they created the community of poetry lovers that seemed to inevitably evolve year after year.

"How do you get them to begin writing?" I asked first. I wondered about this in particular as I'd often observed children in other classes (including my own) staring at blank pages, then wailing, "I can't think of anything to write about."

"They write in their poetry journal every day," responded Peggy. She pointed to a stack of lined tablets with Ridgemont Gophers printed boldly on the front. "A daily entry can be a new poem, a revision of a poem written previously, or a brainstormed list of topics. They don't have to write a new poem every day. They can just go back to anyplace in the book and revise. Often, they pull out a poem they wrote weeks ago and discover they feel differently about the topic. Then they change the poem."

"We have to be observant of this, however," added Sheryl. "Some children just change one word and call that their journal entry for the day. Or they'll write a few lines one day, change the lining the next and call that their entry. We really hope they'll make substantive changes and we try to support and encourage them when they move in this direction. Our goal is to help them become more and more able to express themselves in a few words."

"But you know," said Peggy, "It's something a lot of kids complain about in the beginning because they think it's so much easier to sit down and dash off a story. We have to show them a lot about lining and polishing—and that's not always easy."

I began to wonder about how they differentiated the excellent pieces from the more superficial. "How do you indicate to a child that a particular poem is good?" I asked.

"Well," said Sheryl, "that's something we've been struggling with. In the past we put checkmarks on poems we thought were ready to be typed up. This didn't mean a poem was perfect or finished, just at a stage where some meaning was being expressed in a unique way. The problem was they'd write a poem and bring it up right away, expecting a checkmark. Then it would be a blow to their ego if we said it needed more work."

Peggy added, "Sometimes I'd check something that I didn't feel was the child's best efforts because I could just see what was happening to him."

"So we thought about it and decided it's not a good idea to make checkmarks when they've just completed a first draft of a poem," continued Sheryl, "because they feel very strongly about it at the time. Later on, after they've written new things and they've rethought what they said before, it's easier to take a second look."

"Are you not going to checkmark poems at all this year?" I asked.

"Yes we still will do this," she responded tentatively, "but I think I'll look at a group of poems from one child and comment on the parts that have some potential or checkmark those the child has really worked on and thought about. We want them to view all their poems as in progress, never finished. We're not making poets here, just appreciators of the way poets can capture the essence of experience in a few words."

I was curious about the kinds of things the teachers wrote in these journals. Were there the usual red marks for misspellings and punctuation errors? Were the children given specific ideas of what words to change or how to make the meter come out properly according to the formal rules of poetic form? Or was anything the children wrote considered okay as long as they were expressing themselves?

When asked about this, Sheryl commented, "We used to write many comments in their journals, but now we don't do much of that. The children were not responding to our comments, and we realized our suggestions were affecting ownership and were sometimes overwhelming in number. We decided there needed to be more dialogue, and that we should be less directive so more of their ideas would be generated as they continued to work on their poems. This year we are going to try saying general things like 'What more can you do with your topic' or 'You have a strong beginning, but your ending isn't quite as strong. How can you help that?' or 'This poem has potential—play with it some more.' Then the changes will come directly from the child."

One other thing was still bothering me. "How do you handle punctuation, spelling, and all those other issues?" I asked. In a conservative district like Mt. Victory, I thought surely this would quickly become an issue if children were permitted to use non-standard forms.

Peggy was quick to respond. "Before anything is typed for display or checkmarked to be recopied, all proofing must be completed. We try to encourage them to have their friends do this but often it ends up that we provide this help. But they don't have to worry about these things when they're writing and revising. Sometimes we show them where punctuation might go by reading the poem aloud. They can get it that way. But it really depends on the poem. Sometimes they don't use any punctuation in a poem—and that's okay, if the meaning is clear. Many of them don't really know what a poem looks like. They know in the book, but there is a lot of difference when they try to get their own ideas down. That's a part of revision—where they put the words. Some of the kids will write their ideas down in a paragraph first, then work from there."

"Do you expose them to much poetry written by professionals?" I asked. It seemed that something must serve as a catalyst to inspire the children's own work.

"We read a lot of poetry aloud together, rereading each poem several times," responded Peggy. "Each time we might change it, saying it in a high or a low voice, encouraging the children to join in on certain lines, talking about their favorite parts."

"We also try to tie in things that happen around us," added Sheryl. "For instance, on a foggy morning last year we shared Carl Sandburg's poem about fog. It's a way to help them link the ideas they have with established poets' ideas about things. We encourage them to notice how many times one poet writes about the same thing over and over and how his perspective changes with time. We also try to call attention to how poets say things in special ways ... how they use a unique group of words to say something. But we caution them to be careful that they're not copying what the poet wrote."

I wondered, "Do you lead them to particular poets? How do they know where to look to find a poem on fog or cats or any other topic that interests them?" Frankly, I was thinking privately that I might have difficulty knowing where to look.

"No," responded Sheryl. "We share poetry aloud several times a day from which they gain experience, then they look for poems on their own. We used to show them where to find almost everything or suggest they read about given subjects. That took ownership and independence away from them. Sometimes Peggy and I give them a specific task, but now we usually just send them to the poetry area to see what others have written about or to examine a poet's style they might like to try."

I would soon learn that this kind of encouragement was an integral component of the classroom. But both Peggy and Sheryl constantly struggled with defining the fine line between total freedom and supportive intervention. As Peggy told me that day and both reiterated many times through the year, "they grow and learn from each other more than they do from the teacher and that's hard for a teacher to let go of. But if you have a guiding hand and not a manipulative hand, you and the children are going to be a lot better off." It sounded easy when she said it, but it wasn't such an easy principle to put into practice. Both teachers continually wrestled with maintaining the balance.

This philosophy of guiding rather than directly teaching also influenced how they introduced the children to poetic devices and form. They stated that they rarely did specific lessons highlighting these ideas. Rather, as Sheryl described it, "When these things come up in our group reading sessions, we just talk about them. I might use the words 'comparison,' 'metaphor' or 'simile' and show examples in the poetry we are sharing, so eventually they see a connection. But I never say 'today we are going to learn about metaphors.' And I never test the children on these things. I just notice that they start using the terms in conversation with each other. That's how I gauge the change."

"It's going to be hard to find time to do all this with poetry this year," Peggy was quick to add. "We used to do our whole group poetry sharing right after lunch. Sharing the children's own poetry and poetry they'd found in books, we really established our poetry then because we did it every day. The children knew this was part of our daily routine so they seemed more focused when they worked on their own or in small groups. With our new lunch schedule we won't be able to do this. It's going to be hard to find time, but we will."

Making time—the perennial problem of teachers. With so much competition for class time and attention, it's no wonder that poetry often gets pushed aside. These teachers thought it was important, so they made time for poetry. I was beginning to see that this commitment was a critical element of their program.

If one looks superficially at Sheryl and Peggy's responses, they might seem to belie the image of supportive teachers who encourage their children to follow their own inclinations. I really felt this was not the case. Rather, they seemed to be examples of what often makes whole language teaching successful: a sense of order, structure, and expectation that lays the foundation for freedom and spontaneity. Children know their limits and are thus somewhat freed from figuring out what the teacher wants. This allows them to concentrate on more personally interesting things.

It was time to go. I felt I'd gained a glimmer of what these teachers did with poetry. Yet I felt there was much more—things the teachers were not even aware they did, things this year's children would do that would alter the very practices being described to me. I sensed this would be fine. Life in this classroom was meant to be fluid, dynamic, and changing. Everyone—teachers and children—saw themselves as learners, willing to explore together the exciting possibilities of poetry.

A Community of Poetry Lovers

Literary responses do not occur in a vacuum; they are inextricably connected to the context in which they occur. As Geertz (1974) asserts, "Man is an animal suspended in webs of significance... spun through interaction. These webs are entangled with the webs of others' understandings, knotted, and superimposed one upon the other." We can never perceive ourselves and our understandings as detached from the world, but rather must view them as integral parts of a larger social matrix.

Thus, although the children were individuals with unique perceptions, backgrounds, and abilities, their responses were tempered by their rural environment, families, and classroom experiences. They, in turn, modified this context by the responses they made to it. The teachers similarly shaped and were shaped by their own perceptions and actions and those of the children. I was looking forward to watching the interplay of all these factors, of documenting how a group of individuals evolved through communication and collaboration into a community of poetry lovers.

CHAPTER 3

First Impressions

To look at anything,
If you would know that thing,
You must look at it long:
To look at this green and say
I have seen spring in these
Woods, will not do—you must
Be the thing you see:
You must be the dark snakes of
Stems and ferny plumes of leaves,
You must enter in
To the small silences between
The leaves,
You must take your time
And touch the very peace
They issue from

"To Look at Anything"
JOHN MOFFITT

It was one of those perfect, hot, early September days when I drove to Mt. Victory for my first day of actual research. I was filled with a mixture of anticipation and nervousness. It was already the third day of school, and I expected that enough of a routine had been established so that I would avoid the usual first-day-of-school chaos and be able to see some interesting things. However, I was as concerned as Sheryl and Peggy were by the fact that this year's children were different from those of previous years: more tentative, less self-confident, and less experienced with poetry. Their responses might never approach the complexity achieved by children in previous classes. It wasn't going to be an auspicious start.

As I entered Ridgemont Elementary School, a square, old-fashioned brick building one block from the main street, I was struck by the contrasts. The usual stark, plastered walls were covered with large murals of book characters: Sendak's Wild Things, Brink's Caddie Woodlawn, Charlotte from *Charlotte's Web*, Clifford from *Clifford the Big Red Dog* and the like. I was assailed by the profusion of color, movement, and personality in these drawings. (I later learned that Peggy's daughter had done this in an attempt to liven up the halls.) Once past these, however, the stark grayish-white walls and concrete stairs closed in. As I walked through the halls I caught glimpses of neat teacher-designed bulletin boards, orderly rows of quiet children and brisk teachers going efficiently about their jobs. I got a sense of tradition, that this was how school should look, had looked and functioned for decades.

Entering Peggy and Sheryl's classroom felt like coming up for air after nearly drowning in a sea of gray, formless matter. The room was alive with motion, color, and creative energy. Children were scattered everywhere, working on writing, art projects, math papers, or quietly reading. No one had an assigned seat. Personal materials were kept in bins and children moved freely between tables placed strategically about the room. All this movement and energy might seem chaotic to some observers. But if one looked closely, an air of purpose was vividly evident. Everyone seemed to have a task to do—and was doing it.

The teachers didn't have desks either. These had been made into display areas in which drawers were filled with cow horns, brass bells, shells, and other interesting items to stimulate creative writing or artwork. Instead the teachers moved freely about the room, providing assistance where needed. Each had an area where she most often conducted the many small and large group sessions that comprised much of her teaching. I was to learn that these places were implicitly defined as "where one first looks if in need of teacher assistance."

Materials were everywhere, carefully organized by subject matter. For example, the science area housed microscopes, books on science topics, live animals, shell collections, and similar materials. The math area contained such things as graphing supplies, counters, measuring equipment, task cards, and puzzle books. In the art area, children had access to chalk, paint, markers, inks, crayons, simple printing equipment, and a wide variety of collage materials to illustrate their poems, stories, and reports. Hundreds of books, arranged by genre, then by author within genre, lined one wall. Other shelves around the room contained extra texts, reference materials (dictionaries, thesauruses, encyclopedias, nonfiction books related to content areas), and other items of a similarly general nature.

Even at this early date, wall and bulletin board space was

already filling up with children's work. The displays were mainly stories or poems accompanied by complementary illustrations. I was to learn that this was a favorite way to validate the worth of one's work, and the children willingly took great pride in carefully editing their pieces so they were suitable for public viewing.

I settled myself in what I hoped was an inconspicuous spot and began taking notes—frantically. How was I ever going to capture everything before it stopped happening and eluded me? I felt compelled to adequately describe the room, the students, teachers, what they said, where everyone moved. I was sure I would miss some vital activity or conversation and thus lose forever a critical insight.

I was also already feeling the pull between my new role of researcher and the comfortable familiarity of my usual teaching role. I was beginning to suffer from withdrawal: rather than sitting quietly, notebook in hand, I wanted to plunge in and teach. I had to continually fight this feeling throughout the year. Although I had my university students, it had been a while since I'd had my own classroom with real children. I was beginning to realize how much I missed it all.

Gradually, things began to sort themselves out, and I was able to make some tentative sense from the events I was observing. I moved over to one of the large group meeting areas where Peggy was reading a novel, *Summer of the Monkeys*, aloud to the fifth graders. They were listening but seemed bored. Some of the girls were braiding each other's hair while boys were snapping the velcro strips on their shoes open and closed. Sensing their lack of interest, she decided to change the pace a bit by discussing the process of writing a story through sharing her own struggles in writing a story about a boa constrictor found in her daughter's apartment. The children are enthralled. "Wasn't she scared? I'd be," they shivered. Stimulated by Peggy's choice of topic and carefully probing questions, they began offering suggestions about ways to start her story, the perspective from which it should be told (the snake's? the person's?), the events that should be included and so on.

I noticed that Sheryl seemed to be doing some activities related to poetry with her sixth graders so I moved over to that side of the room. Johnny was sharing two poems, "Questions" and "Comparison," from Mary Ann Hoberman's collection, *Yellow Butter, Purple Jelly, Red Jam, Black Bread*. When asked why he chose those particular poems to share, he responded, "because they describe how I've grown this year."

"That's an interesting observation," answered Sheryl. "Anyone else want to say anything about these poems?" No one responded.

"Well, how do they relate to our unit on time?" she persisted.

Again, no one answered. After some additional prodding, a few offered tentative comments like "they're about growing" and "they show change." No one seemed willing to risk a more adventurous response. Sheryl flashed me a discouraged look and changed the focus by opening Mollie Hunter's *The Kelpie's Pearls* and reading aloud to the group.

Eventually the afternoon work session began. During this time, children were allowed to do a variety of activities including math, science investigations, art, reading, story writing, and poetry. Children selected informally from these options; that is they could organize their time as desired as long as certain things were done every day or by the end of the week.

I decided to sit in the poetry area to get a sense of what children were choosing to read at this point in the year. This area consisted of a bookcase filled with poetry books written by a wide variety of poets ranging from Robert Louis Stevenson and Langston Hughes to those like Myra Cohn Livingston and Jack Prelutsky, who wrote more exclusively for children. There was also a small rug, a table, and some chairs.

I felt a bit conspicuous, sitting there, notebook in hand, obviously writing down every comment and movement. I didn't want to miss anything, yet I also didn't want to squelch any natural interactions that might occur. After enduring curious looks and a considerable amount of avoidance behavior I decided it might be better to appear disinterested in their activities. I began pulling books from the shelves, leafing through them, then writing down titles. As I physically and mentally melted into the background the children's activities began moving to the forefront of my mind and eyes.

I realized that already there were instances where children orally shared poetry with each other. This happened mostly with partners although in a few instances a small group gathered together for a shared reading. One girl (I later learned her name was Shelly) read riddles aloud to another, pausing to let her friend guess the answer, then reading it from the book. They both giggled then continued on to the next. I noticed another girl reading Lobel's *Pigericks* aloud to herself, although she was so quiet I could barely make out the words. Her body moved to the rhythm of the words. She had a look of intense pleasure. I watched still another girl (Angela) leaf through Nancy Larrick's *Piping Down the Valleys Wild* collection, suggesting possible writing topics to a friend—things like "wind," "shadows," and "grizzly bears." Suddenly Angela came upon Kay Starbird's hilarious account of summer camp, "Eat-It-All-Elaine." "My favorite!" she exclaimed, and began reading aloud. Three other girls joined in and a spontaneous choral reading evolved as they took turns reading different lines aloud, then joined together on others. I wondered if this was something they'd created entirely on their own or if a previous teacher had organized something similar. But I dared not ask as I didn't want to intrude on the spontaneous interactions happening around me. I wasn't invisible yet, but I had certainly not been the focus of much attention or curiosity after the first hour. I wanted to maintain that anonymity as long as possible.

Several children were writing poetry at the small table. Although it was difficult to discern the topics without craning my neck, they seemed to be about seasons, animals, the weather, and similar topics. The writers didn't seem involved with their pieces. Rather, they appeared to be going through the motions, as if it was something they had to do rather than feeling compelled to get thoughts and images recorded on paper.

Occasionally friends were asked to comment on a poem's content or to suggest a new topic. The responses to such requests were limited to "that's nice" or "I don't know." Not much assistance. The only poem I could see clearly without being too obvious was one about pigs:

                    Pigs
                        Pigs
                            Pigs
                    Pigs are quite
                    Big and small
                    They oink, oink, oink
                        Pigs
                            Pigs
                                Pigs
                    Oink
                        Oink
                            Oink

                                LESA

It was a beginning. Lesa had some sense of the difference between poetic and prose forms. Yet it was a far cry from the pieces I'd seen produced by former class members.

Suddenly, Johnny, the boy who had shared the Hoberman time poems in the large group session, plopped down beside me and began a conversation about poetry. "I like to read it out loud and talk about it," he told me proudly. "Arnold Adoff, Mary Ann Hoberman, and Arnold Lobel are my favorites. Adoff has good descriptions and the poems go all over the page. I think that's neat. He [Adoff] also loves food like I do!" Adoff had visited the class the previous year as a poet in residence, thus the children knew a great deal about him and his poetry.

Johnny then offered to read aloud his favorite pieces from Hoberman's *Yellow Butter, Purple Jelly; Red Jam, Black Bread;* Lobel's *Pigericks;* and Adoff's *Eats.* After reading Hoberman's "Comparisons" he mused, "That's a good one, she switches things around in a neat way."

Generally, however, few children seemed to have any real affinity for poetry or a strong sense of its unique characteristics. Selections of what to share were made randomly, perhaps based on what was familiar from previous years or what could generate laughter from friends rather than a fondness for particular poems. Johnny's insights, limited as they were at this point, were the exception rather than the rule.

Reflection and Regrouping

That evening we met at the Plaza truckstop for a debriefing session on our perceptions of the day. Both teachers were discouraged that nothing much was happening in poetry. They had noticed the absence of responses in small group sharing sessions, the superficial selections for independent reading, and the lack of freshness and originality in the children's writing. They knew this class would have a slow beginning. Although the fifth graders had been exposed to some reading of poetry in fourth grade, they had written little but prose. The sixth graders had been exposed to poetry as Sheryl and Peggy's fifth graders and had profited from observing the older sixth-grade students that year. However, they seemed to have absorbed little from this influence. Even these normally optimistic teachers were daunted by the group's seeming lack of focus and perception.

When we got to know each other better, Peggy and Sheryl confided some of the worries they had had that day. "We wanted you to have a good experience, but we were pretty worried that we wouldn't be able to get this group to gel," they told me. "We were also worried that our apprehension might rub off on the children and make them feel anxious about performing."

I sensed this anxiety. I was anxious too. After all, I too wanted the project to go well. When I forced myself to look beyond my immediate personal needs, I wondered, were we looking for the right things? Were we expecting too much from children who had little exposure to poetry and even less opportunity to reflect on what they learn in school? Most importantly, were we so concerned about ourselves, that we were failing to observe what the children were doing? Were we learning from what we saw? Maybe we needed to do what Moffitt suggests and "enter in to the small silences" and "take time," allowing ourselves to become immersed in observing from the children's perspective. Only then might we truly see what was happening around us.

I began to view what the children were doing as they began to explore new territory. Surely they could be expected to hang onto the familiar and take only tentative steps into this new uncharted ground. Yet the potential for rich discoveries was there. What we were seeing now was typical of responses cited in previous research. I was optimistic that richer understandings were to come.

To help them we mapped out a plan that evening. The teachers decided not to wait passively for a community of poetry readers and writers to develop on its own. Instead, they would meet regularly with small groups for sharing, writing, and critiquing poetry. Children would not be formally placed into these groups but could participate when they wished or when they were encouraged to do so. The teachers would make it fun and challenging so children would come of their own accord. We hoped small successes would become bigger successes, and we would be on our way.

PART II

Building a
Community
of Poetry Readers

"I," says the poem matter-of-factly,
"I am a cloud,
I am a tree.

I am a city,
I am the sea,

I am a golden
Mystery."

But, adds the poem silently,
I cannot speak until you come.
Reader, come, come with me.

" 'I,' *Says the Poem*"
EVE MERRIAM

A poem is a living thing, given first breath by its creator, the poet. Although it owes its creation to the poet, it owes continued life to its readers and listeners: those who hear its song and are touched by the ideas and messages it presents. It not only tells about experience but also invites participation in that experience. From this perspective, then, the task of bringing children and poetry together must be viewed as an artistic endeavor, one in which an emotional connection is forged between literature and listeners.

Unfortunately, many teachers do not view the teaching of poetry in this way. Rather than stressing enjoyment and love of poetic language, they tend to equate their task to the teaching of biology: just as one dissects a frog, they dissect poems to see what makes them jump for the listener. Or they require memorization for later class recitation and testing. Unfortunately, when such activities are the focus, something vital and alive is lost: the poem no longer jumps for the listener.

This section will chronicle how Peggy and Sheryl helped children come to poetry, giving them the resources and understandings to unravel its golden mysteries. The changes did not occur overnight. Nevertheless, they did occur—gradually, imperceptibly—until a community of poetry readers, bonded by a common love of the genre, had formed.

CHAPTER 4

Early Responses
to Published Poetry

One is amazed
By a water-lily bud
Unfolding
With each passing day,
Taking on a richer color
And new dimensions.

One is not amazed,
At a first glance,
By a poem,
Which is as tight-closed
As a tiny bud.

Yet one is surprised
To see the poem
Gradually unfolding,
Revealing its rich inner self,
As one reads it
Again
And over again.

"Unfolding Bud"
NAOSHI KORIYAMA

The golden days of September drifted into multicolored October. As the weeks progressed, the class settled into a rhythm of activity. From my original perch in the poetry center, I discovered I needed to expand my horizons both physically and intellectually. First, I realized I needed to broaden my definition of what constituted a child's "encounter" with poetry. Reading with a friend or teacher, curling up in a corner with a stack of poetry books or chanting rhymes on the playground were all examples of poetry encounters. These didn't happen at a set time but occurred throughout the day. When I understood this, I knew I would need to roam throughout the room and become a more active participant in the class. Yet I had to make these changes in a way that was natural and unobtrusive. My role up to this point had mainly been that of an observer—sitting quietly in areas where small groups were working or placing running tape recorders on tables. I would smile and talk to children like Johnny and Angela, who sought me out. Otherwise, I sat quietly.

I began initiating tentative conversations with all the children and they soon began doing the same. These talks weren't always about poetry. Sometimes we'd discuss break-dancing, parents, and sibling problems. By the end of October a few were still wary of me and all my notebooks, microphones, and tape recorders. Most, however, were coming to view me as just another member of the class community—not teacher or child but someone in between.

As I grew more comfortable with the children and they with me, it became easier to sort out the different kinds of interactions that occurred with published poetry. From the ebb and flow of activity, I identified the following typical incidents:

- Large group sharing with a teacher.
- Choral reading.
- Oral sharing of published poetry with peers or reading aloud to self.

I initially observed a fourth category: small group sharing with a teacher. However, after the first few days of school, it rarely occurred so I dropped it from the list. Later in the year I added another category, sharing outside the classroom context, when I observed the children talking about poetry on the playground, at lunch, and after school.

Large Group Sharing with a Teacher

The most common incidents occurring in relation to published poetry at the beginning of the year were teacher-led large group sharing sessions. Generally each teacher held these sessions with her own class, although mixed-grade sessions were occasionally organized for variety and to expose the fifth graders to the complex, diverse responses sometimes offered by the more experienced sixth graders.

The sessions were usually held after lunch. Children would enter the room and immediately find a seat on the floor or in a chair. Each grade met in an open area at opposite ends of the room to minimize distractions from the other's activities. Those who had been asked to share some favorite poems would peruse the poetry collection, find the appropriate book, then settle down into a comfortable spot with the others.

On this particular day, as usual, the fifth graders had gathered after lunch. Peggy settled several playground disputes, then began to talk. "I thought you might like to think about this poem. It relates to our social studies topic of time." She began reading.

The Fish

Like an angler in the river bank
With his back bent over his line
The colliery headgear with its steel rope
Fishes the ground for coal.

It fishes through millions of years
And half a mile of earth
With a cage to bring up its catch
From the forests of the past.

The silvery fossil of a lost species
On a lump of coal that was buried ages
Goes by on the conveyor too fast
To be saved from the crusher.

STANLEY COOK

"What do you think about this poem?" she asked. No one responded. Most looked down at the floor, hoping, perhaps, they wouldn't be called on. Peggy focused her attention on Aaron and Jeremy. "You guys are studying archaeology. What do you think this is about?"

Aaron ventured a tentative guess. "Bones...fossils?"

"Okay," responded Peggy. "Here, I'll read part of it again. That might help you." She reread the first verse aloud. "What could that be, 'his back bent over his line...Fishes the ground for coal'?" She then reread the rest of the poem.

"Now what happened? Anyone want to take a guess?" she asked.

Again only one child ventured a response. "Someone's gonna get in and get the fossil like coal?" she asked tentatively.

"Okay, what's coal?" continued Peggy.

"Rock...like that which you can burn," answered the same girl.

Peggy continued probing for a more refined definition, "What do we make it from?" she asked. "Millions and millions of years of pressure—then what? You archaeologists, what's coal? Something that turned dark but what was it really?"

"Oh yeah, I know. It was plant life," answered Aaron. "Plant life that was probably dead and got pressed in the rock."

"Okay," said Peggy, "Does it take very long to do something like that? Do you have any idea how long?"

The discussion continued with the children speculating about the number of years the process would take. Although the topic was not a central part of the poem, Peggy seemed to sense that it was a part they could respond to. She soon realized, however, they weren't really into the poem and decided to move on to another. She leafed through the book.

"Oh, here's one. We're going to have to get ready for this time of year."

"You mean Halloween?" asked one child.

"Well—sort of," responded Peggy. "See if you can figure out the time of year the poet is talking about." She began to read aloud, deliberately omitting the title so as not to narrow their thinking. As she read, her voice became more rapid and breathless, to reflect the poet's description of being scared.

> There are no lamps in our village,
> And when the owl-and-bat black night
> Creeps up low fields
> And sidles along the manor walls
> I walk quickly.
>
> It is winter,
> The letters patter from my hand
> Into the tin box in the cottage wall;
> The gate taps behind me,
> And the road in the sliver of moonlight
> Gleams greasily
> Where the tractors have stood.
>
> I have to go under the spread fingers of the trees
> Under the dark windows of the old man's house,
> Where the panes in peeling frames
> Flash like spectacles
> As I tip-toe.
> But there is no sound of him in his one room
> In the Queen-Anne shell,
> Behind the shutters.

I run past the gates,
Their iron feet gaitered with grass,
Into the church porch,
Standing, hand on the cold door ring,
While above
The tongue-tip of the clock
Clops
Against the hard palate of the tower.
The door groans as I push
And
Dare myself to dash
Along the flagstones to the great brass bird,
To put one shrinking hand
Upon the gritty lid.
Of Black Tom's tomb.

Don't tempt whatever spirits stir
In this damp corner,
But
Race down the aisle,
Blunder past font,
Fumble the door,
Leap steps,
Clang iron gate,
And patter through the short-cut muddy lane.

Oh, what a pumping of breath
And choking throat
For three letters.
And now there are the cattle
Stirring in the straw
So close

I can hear their soft muzzling and coughs;
And there are the bungalows,
And the steel-blue miming of the little screen;
And the familiar rattle of the latch,
And our own knocker
Clicking like an old friend;
And
I am home.

"Posting Letters"
GREGORY HARRISON

Early Responses to Published Poetry

A silence followed her reading. The children seemed intrigued but puzzled by some of the references in the poem. They sat quietly, waiting for Peggy's comments.

"Well—what's this person doing in the dark? Where was he going? What was he going to do...just an ordinary thing?" asked Peggy.

"Going home?" asked Missy tentatively.

"Well, in the end he was going home," responded Peggy. "But first he was going to do something. What was it he was going to do? Listen again." She read aloud several lines:

> It is winter;
> The letters patter from my hand
> Into the tin box in the cottage wall;

"Yours may not be on a cottage wall. Yours might be on a pole in front of your house. This is an ordinary thing, something done every day."

"You mean mail letters?" asked Mandy.

"Okay, this is talking about mailing letters," responded Peggy. "The person walks out to mail letters and all this is happening in his mind before he gets back."

The discussion continued in this same tentative manner. Peggy, sensing that the group had had enough, closed the poetry book and began reading a chapter book aloud.

It seemed that the fifth graders hadn't yet formed any strategies for responding to a poem. They seemed to view poetry as mysterious, senseless gobbledygook that was comprehensible only to the teacher. Ideas were offered only tentatively—and only after considerable questioning and prodding from an adult.

I moved over to the sixth grade side of the room to see if there were any differences in the children's responses. Sheryl had asked the children to find poems about cats to share with the group. Few had been able to do this. So she decided to search for some together in hopes of showing them how to find poems on a special topic or theme. "Let's look for the one by William Carlos Williams," she told them. "It's called 'Poem,' it's not called 'Cat.'" She leafed through *Reflections on a Gift of Watermelon Pickle* until she found it. "This is talking about writing a poem that appeals to one of your five senses—taste, smell, touch, sight, or hearing," she continued. "Williams' poem can be your model. I'm going to ask you when I read it what sense it uses." She began to read aloud.

Poem

As the cat
climbed over
the top of

the jamcloset
first the right
forefoot

carefully
then the hind
stepped down

into the pit of
the empty
flowerpot.

WILLIAM CARLOS
WILLIAMS

"Well, what sense?" Sheryl asked the group. She turned to one child who seemed somewhat interested. "Ronnie?"

"Seeing?" he ventured a tentative guess.

"It was a sense of sight, wasn't it? Williams used his sense of sight and this is what he saw. Listen and see if you can see the picture too."

She read the poem again but this time I noticed the children were listening much more avidly. Somehow, Sheryl had piqued their interest with those few sentences. After reading, she continued the discussion:

> Now, I want you to take a look at what he did with the lining of that poem. If I read it line by line, and I'm going to do that, how does that change what has been said? See how there are no more than three words per line and sometimes two and sometimes one? I'm going to read it line by line because right now we are lining our own poems so that we get meaning line by line. But this isn't always the best way to read a poem. If I read this line by line, it would be . . .

She read the poem again, this time stopping at the end of each line. The effect was jerky with the poem's meaning almost indecipherable due to the strange division of thought. Several children wrinkled their noses. Sheryl continued her questioning: "Do you see what I mean? I didn't look for what this time? It didn't make sense this time, did it? You had to look for what to make sense?"

Several children shrugged their shoulders, but no one responded. Finally, with additional encouragement from Sheryl, a few tentatively ventured a guess. "Meaning?" they asked. "Yes," responded Sheryl, "I didn't look for the meaning. I just read it line by line. So that's one of the things to keep in mind.

"Here's another poem called 'Catalogue.' Now, what would you think of if you saw a poem with a title like 'Catalogue'?"

"A cat who was sleeping on a log?" guessed Jenny.

"Okay, what else?" asked Sheryl, laughing at the literal interpretation. "What else would you think of if I were going to read a poem called 'Catalogue'?"

"A cat shaped like a log?" guessed Stacie.

"Okay, shaped like a log," answered Sheryl. "What else? If I just said 'Catalogue,' what would be the first thing everybody would say?"

Johnny had obviously read the poem and could hardly contain himself. He knew it had nothing to do with lists or logs. "I won't tell them," he grinned. "Let them wait." With that, the children chorused, "Okay, Mrs. Reed, come on, read it to us!"

"Okay," said Sheryl. "This is Rosalie Moore's 'Catalogue.' " (As she read, she frequently stopped to allow children to interject some of the rhyming words at the end of lines.)

Catalogue
Rosalie Moore

Cats sleep fat and walk thin.
Cats, when they sleep, slump;
When they wake, stretch and begin
Over, pulling their ribs in.
Cats walk thin.

Cats wait in a lump,
Jump in a streak.
Cats, when they jump, are sleek
As a grape slipping its skin—
They have technique.
Oh, cats don't creak.
They sneak.

Cats sleep fat.
They spread out comfort underneath them
Like a good mat,
As if they picked the place
And then sat;
You walk around one

As if he were the City Hall
After that.

If male,
A cat is apt to sing on a major scale;
This concert is for everybody, this
is wholesale.
For a baton, he wields a tail.

(He is also found,
When happy, to resound
With an enclosed and private sound.)

A cat condenses.
He pulls in his tail to go under bridges,
And himself to go under fences.
Cats fit
In any size box or kit,
And if a large pumpkin grew under one,
He could arch over it.

When everyone else is just ready to go out,
The cat is just ready to come in.
He's not where he's been
Cats sleep fat and walk thin.

"Did you ever think about cats in those terms?" Sheryl asked the group. "It might be interesting if you are writing a poem on a certain subject to look at what other poets have said about the same subject. Of course you won't be able to find them all because we don't have all the poetry books in the world here. But we can find out something with what we have—how many times or what kinds of poems poets have written about cats or whatever else is of interest to us. Jeremy just wrote a poem called 'Midnight Express.' It's about a train. And he might want to read what other poets have said about trains. You might look at what other poets say about the same subject after you have had an idea or even after you have written something. Look at what one poet said about cats—like, here, Valerie Worth had two poems and she described cats in two very different ways. What are some subjects you have noticed that poets write about over and over again?"

"Cats," suggested Johnny.

"Dogs," answered Bryan.

"Yes, a lot about dogs," agreed Sheryl. "Snakes... nature... What else?"

"Spring." "People." "Summer." "Fall." "Leaves." "Rainbows."
Many voices called out suggestions.

Because the sixth graders had more previous experience with poetry, they were able to respond in more complex ways than the fifth graders. However, these responses were nevertheless tentative and cautious. No one was yet willing to experiment with different ideas or go beyond the parameters of discussion offered by Sheryl.

As I observed these discussions over several months, I began to make my own tentative generalizations about their format as well as the kinds of interactions that generally occurred. There began to be a rhythm and predictability to the talks. Far from causing boredom, I thought this structure helped free the children from having to figure out the teacher's agenda. It enabled them to concentrate on enjoying the experience, then exploring what it was about a poem that contributed to this enjoyment.

The format was essentially the same: both teachers began with some sort of introduction that heightened anticipation and suggested purposes for reading the poem. Next the children were encouraged to offer a variety of responses. Finally, the teachers tried to deepen the children's appreciation of more complex aspects of the poem; they discussed, for instance, its particular literary techniques, its unusual imagery, or how it compared with others they'd heard. Most sessions included sequences of all three types, although this was not true for every discussion recorded, particularly in this early part of the year.

A typical session might begin with the teacher reading a poem's title, then asking children to predict its content. The teacher also often suggested that students identify the poet by listening for his or her unique voice. Sometimes children were asked to discern how a particular poetic device was used or to listen for something special like an interesting image, unusual rhyme pattern, or different meaning. The following is an example of how this was done:

SHERYL: This is called "A Narrow Fellow in the Grass" by Emily Dickinson. From the title, can we make any predictions?
CHILD: An ant in the grass?
SHERYL: All right. It could be narrow. What else could be narrow . . . a narrow fellow in the grass?
CHILD: A caterpillar?
SHERYL: Okay. Any other possibilities?
CHILD: A snake?
SHERYL: Maybe. Now let's listen to the poem.

Peggy's reference to "We're going to have to get ready for this time of year" before reading the "Posting Letters" poem and Sheryl's suggestion that the children pay attention to the different ways poets describe cats are other instances of these introductory sequences.

After reading a poem through once, each teacher requested initial responses from the children. The emphasis at this point seemed to be on encouraging students to offer hypotheses about a poem's meaning and purpose. The children were also often encouraged to link their own experiences with the poem so as to make sense of it. Neither teacher created a lesson plan of questions to ask. Rather, they just felt their way along, preferring to guide the discussions in response to the children's ideas, impressions, and questions. I noticed a few questions like the following were repeatedly asked to facilitate reflection:

- What do you think?
- What did you like about this poem?
- Does this remind you of anything you know about?
- What is the poet saying here?
- Any comments about that?
- Let's discuss what is going on here.
- What is this about?

The poem was then usually reread several times so as to elicit more complex responses. Again, the focus was on constructing meaning, using one's knowledge of reality in conjunction with the images conveyed in the poem to more fully delight in and appreciate the image.

That poetry must make sense, that a logical, rational connection between the real world and the world created in the poem, differentiated these sessions from the usual poetry interpretation activities I'd seen other teachers do. To Sheryl and Peggy, a poem was not a mysterious puzzle that alluded to obscure images discernible only to the knowledgeable reader. Rather, a viable response to a poem was thought to be available to anyone interested in exploring it. In fact they believed a poem might have several meanings depending on one's personal perspective or expectations.

A poem, however, was never divided into discrete parts that were analyzed separately to determine this meaning. Rather, the emphasis was on enjoying the poem as a whole, developing an appreciation for how the parts—rhyme, rhythm, imagery, and figurative language—contributed to that whole. The distinction is subtle, yet critical and is important, considering the research on children's attitudes toward common teaching practices for poetry. The findings from this research suggest that children generally dislike talking about poetry, often citing the necessity to construct a "right" interpretation as one of the most salient factors contributing to their dislike. Evidence for this assertion comes from many surveys. For example, Painter (1970) interviewed preservice college students to discover their attitudes towards poetry. Of all explanations for negative feelings, the one most frequently cited was an insistence on "correct" interpretation. As one student commented:

> My interpretations were never the same or even close to what the teacher or some of my classmates found. Even after reading the poems over to myself several more times, I still missed the point. I used to dread poetry and cringed at the mention of the word. (Painter, 1970)

Verble (1973), in a survey of elementary students, found similar attitudes. When he asked the children why they didn't like poetry, the majority responded "because I can't understand it" and "because my interpretation is never right." Their dislike seemed to be directed less at the poetry itself than what they were expected to do with it in class. Matanzo and Madison (1979) also documented strong negative feelings toward poetry, with respondents citing frustration with critical analysis as a major cause of their alienation. Surveys by Craven (1980), Baskin, Harris, and Salley (1984), and others support these conclusions.

Perhaps we have been too concerned about teaching children that there's a "right" way to interpret poetry and that interpretation is the only thing one does with poetry. In effect, we've taken poetry out of the hands of children and put it into the hands of adults. In contrast, Peggy and Sheryl were trying to create a community where everyone could share in the delight poetry can bring. Interpretation was a part of this. But the emphasis was on building enjoyment by looking carefully at what the poet was trying to say and how he or she said it. They were not always successful at maintaining the balance; sometimes they too found themselves asking questions that were too narrowly focused and too concerned with finding a prescribed meaning. Yet, they constantly endeavored to go beyond these limitations.

The children were not yet fully aware that the teachers were open to diverse responses. At this early point in the year they were unwilling and unable to make more than very tentative comments and connections. Although I observed discernible patterns in the sessions, the children still seemed unsure of what was expected and were more concerned about offering "correct" answers than exploring alternative possibilities. It wasn't easy to overcome years of conditioning. Later, after they knew me better, many confided they were initially scared they'd be wrong and would experience the ultimate preadolescent nightmare of being laughed at. I couldn't blame them. We were patient. A child's initial reluctance to respond was accepted. We knew it would take time for the children to become comfortable with poetry and with venturing a response to something so unstructured. Both teachers continued to encourage experimentation, playfulness, and risk-taking.

Because of this reluctance to take risks, the interactions in the early sessions were primarily teacher to student. One of the teachers would ask a question and children would respond directly to her. The teachers would then usually try to extend or clarify these often ambiguous responses until the children became more used to the process. Students rarely offered ideas on their own nor did they discuss things freely with each other.

The teachers hoped these poetry reading sessions would meet several objectives. They wanted the children to become familiar with the look and sound of poetry. Poetry is a genre with unique characteristics that clearly differentiate it from prose. The teachers wanted their students to intuitively recognize and appreciate these differences. A related common objective was to help children become familiar with much excellent poetry written for both children and adults. Concurrently, they hoped the children would expand their appreciation of the more unusual, complex pieces. As Sheryl commented, "I want to lift them beyond what they might ordinarily read or experience." To this end she constantly strove to make the children think more deeply about poetry, to go beyond obvious superficial responses to more complex understandings. Both teachers also wanted the children to become aware of how poets use poetic devices (rhyme, rhythm, metaphor, alliteration, etc.), transferring this awareness to their own writing.

The poetry selected for the discussions reflected these avowed purposes. Both teachers shared a wide variety of poems, representing many poets, subjects, themes, and forms. Poems using a wide range of literary devices were also presented. Thus, discussions could range from a focus on topics ("cats" or "fall," for example) to consideration of how a poet used certain words to convey an image or how two poets described the same phenomenon in totally different ways.

It seems that the children were being exposed to much fine poetry as well as strategies for talking about it in the large group sessions. They were also building a foundation for appreciating increasingly abstract images and complex ideas in these works. Certainly these understandings were half-formed, fuzzy, and often unarticulated, but they existed, even at this early stage.

Choral Reading

Choral reading is widely advocated as an appropriate classroom activity for fostering interest in poetry. Many teachers contend that children derive enjoyment from physically responding to the rhythm and rhyme of poetry. Further, they learn much about interpretation as they plan ways to present a poem (Huck, 1987). Choral reading deepens appreciation while simultaneously providing an enjoyable group activity. Knowing this I was interested in how choral reading might affect the children's responses.

The first choral reading I observed was a class performance of Livingston's "Street Song." Sheryl began by giving the children an initial idea of how to do choral reading. "We'll try to read it without much sing-song, but we want a bit of rhythm in it too," she told them. She began reading:

> Oh, I have been walking
> with a bag of potato chips,
> me and potato chips
> munching along,
>
> walking alone
> eating potato chips,
> big old potato chips
> crunching along,
>
> walking along
> munching potato chips,
> me and potato chips
> lunching along.
>
> "Street Song"
> MYRA COHN LIVINGSTON

Although initially most children had refrained from joining in, by the end no one could resist the infectious rhythm. Many began spontaneously clapping and moving their bodies in time to the rhythm. Several called out, "Read it again," after she had finished.

"Okay. This time let's try something a little bit different," Sheryl suggested. "What could we do for 'munching,' 'crunching,' and 'lunching'?"

"We could clap our hands," said Jennifer.

"Do you want to do that on all the words?" responded Sheryl. "Does this remind you, this munching and crunching, of Mike J's poem about the lunchroom? He used words like munching and crunching." She read the poem aloud:

> "CRUNCH"
> I hear as the people
> Crush their chips
> In the munch room.
>
> MIKE J.

"Okay," she continued. "Let's try it with clapping the rhythm."

They read the poem together again, clapping enthusiastically, if not always exactly in rhythm. "Now what else can we do?" asked Peggy. "What's another sound or rhythm thing we can do? How about snapping your fingers on the first stanza?"

The children loved this idea. "Then let's click our tongues on the next part," suggested Bryan. A new reading was organized using several different sound effects.

The group reread the poem several more times, changing actions, voicing patterns, and pitch. Ronnie and Bryan even performed their own version, complete with exaggerated gobbling movements and backwards walking.

After everyone enjoyed a laugh, Sheryl began to probe deeper. "What did Myra Cohn Livingston do to get rhythm in her poem? What kinds of words did she put in to carry her rhythm?"

"Lots of 'ing' words that go together like 'crunching,' 'munching' . . . stuff like that," said Stacie.

"And a lot of 'ch' and 'sh' words," added Jennifer.

"Yes, those words are fun to say," responded Peggy. "Potato chips . . . those are words that roll over your tongue. They have a rhythm with each other. So just putting those two words together has a rhythmic sound to begin with. This is a thing to remember in your own poetry. You can make rhythm by just putting certain words together."

The group broke up. As they moved on to other activities, I noticed that several children were still chanting the poem to themselves. An hour later, I noticed Jim P. walking rhythmically across the room, chanting the poem and clicking his fingers. It seemed as if he couldn't get the poem out of his head. Poetry can definitely be addictive, I thought.

Despite the success of this activity, I rarely saw any other instances of formal choral reading. I was initially puzzled by this. Certainly, there was time for a vast array of other activities related to poetry. Why not choral reading? As I thought about it, however, I surmised that actually it may have been the format of this activity that was the critical factor. Organizing choral reading is a rather formal teacher-directed process. These teachers may have believed that the children's spontaneous responses were much more interesting and valuable.

My intuitions were strengthened as I observed subsequent discussion sessions. Often, when the teachers read a familiar selection or one that rhymed, the children would spontaneously join in, essentially creating a choral reading of the poem. They would frequently do the same thing when sharing poetry with each other. Thus, for example, I observed several boys dividing "This Is My Rock" into segments, taking turns reading individual lines, then joining together on the last two. It seems that the teachers provided a model for responding to poetry through choral reading, and the children shaped the activity to fit their own needs. Choral reading did not have to be a formal, organized activity. It certainly wasn't in this classroom. Rather, it occurred spontaneously in response to particularly rhythmical lines or repetitive passages in familiar poems.

Listen to This: Sharing Poetry with Peers

Since I had extended my vision beyond the poetry corner I was able to observe more and more instances of poetry sharing among the children. Boys and girls alike would come together, select a stack of books and settle down to read aloud. Although the most frequent combination was partners, often a small group of friends would gather to share their favorites. Sometimes I observed a child reading alone, but this was not a common occurrence.

In all cases, the teachers both supported and encouraged these efforts. Often they would suggest that children "find a friend and look through some poetry books to see how other poets treat this subject." Or when a new child was enrolled, they would urge the others to hold a read-aloud session as a way to introduce the newcomer to class routines. Even without this encouragement I think the children would have gravitated to this activity. Sharing poetry with a friend was not only fun but also a sanctioned way to do something together.

A session involving two fifth graders, Bryan H. and Earnie, was typical. They leafed idly through William Cole's *Poem Stew* collection, stopping at "Pop Bottles." "Here's a funny one," exclaimed Earnie.

They read the poem aloud in unison, tripping over the alliterative phrases. They were giggling so hard they could barely get the words out. In another instance Bryan and Johnny came over to the poetry area and picked up Lobel's *Pigericks*. As Bryan flipped through the pages, Johnny peered over his shoulder and commented, "That one's a doozy" or "That one's so funny, read it aloud." The boys took turns reading *Pigericks* to each other, then asked me to join in. "You know," said Bryan, "that pig in the first poem looks a lot like Arnold Lobel. I've seen pictures of him." "Why do you think Lobel did this?" I asked in what I hoped was a properly interested yet not too pushy manner. Bryan just shrugged his shoulders, seemingly uninterested in such issues.

Although the procedures followed in these groups varied somewhat due to group composition as well as the particular poems being shared, the children seemed to have created an implicit ritual for conducting these sessions. Participants usually gathered a stack of poetry books and arranged themselves in a circle on the floor. If partners were involved, they often sat across from each other. Sometimes a group wanted more privacy. In that case they would move into the taping shed (a large built-in area in the corner at one end of the classroom), the hall, or behind the bookshelves.

The selected poems were always read aloud with an attempt to use good expression. Often one child would play teacher, first reading aloud, then showing illustrations to the group. I was surprised, however, to observe that groups routinely paid only cursory attention to the person reading. Instead I observed them flipping through pages to find new selections. Occasionally they'd make an appreciative comment like, "That's a good one—it's funny" or "This one's my favorite." I rarely heard analytic or evaluative comments this early in the year. It seemed the purpose of these peer read-aloud sessions was primarily shared enjoyment. It was not a time to think deeply, to question, or to probe for a poet's intended meaning.

This interest in enjoyment was confirmed when I considered the kinds of poems selected for these early sessions. Choices seemed to be made quite randomly. Usually children would idly flip through the pages, stop (especially, they told me, when they saw a title or an illustration they liked), then read a selection aloud. When selections were made purposefully, the criteria seemed to be whether the poem was humorous, rhythmical, or easily read (i.e., didn't include many hard words). Thus, I noticed that books like Lobel's *Pigericks*, Adoff's *Eats* and Hoberman's *Yellow Butter, Purple Jelly, Red Jam, Black Bread* were frequently selected. When the children selected anthologies like the *Random House Book of Poetry*, they inevitably turned to the thematic sections on animals or humor. Those who ventured into more complex kinds of poetry rarely did much with it. For example, I observed Angela select a copy of Hornsby's *Poems for Children and Other People* (a thick book with few pictures) from the bookcase. She idly leafed through it for a few minutes, then quickly exchanged it for a more cheerful looking volume by Adoff. In other instances, I noticed children sorting through the bookcase, invariably pulling out the books with eye-catching covers or appealing titles.

When the children did choose more complex pieces, it was often because they wanted to reread something the teachers had shared in a large group session. Thus, after Peggy had read aloud some poems from the *Fourth Poetry Book*, I observed Aaron alone in a corner, lips moving silently, as he read the same poems to himself. In another instance, I was initially surprised that Mandy and Robin were moving away from the tried and true by sharing selections from *Reflections on a Gift of Watermelon Pickle*. I then remembered that Peggy had read aloud selections from this book the previous day.

I was still curious as to why particular poems were selected for these informal sharing sessions. Were they chosen deliberately? Maybe my hunch that this was entirely a random activity was correct. Or maybe the children were selecting poems on the basis of accessibility or capacity to entertain a friend. I wanted to explore these questions in more varied ways although I was also concerned that the normal classroom routine remain as unchanged as possible due to my presence. This precluded giving a standardized test or even using structured informal assessments like the tapes and response guides created by Ann Terry (1974) for her study.

The teachers helped solve this dilemma. They routinely asked their classes to complete a simple poetry survey at the beginning of the year. Since they had not taken the survey yet, we modified some of the questions and created an instrument we thought might provide interesting information to supplement my observations. This helped me construct a more comprehensive view of the children's evolving preferences for particular poems, their awareness of poets, appreciation of various poetic elements, and the like.

I gave the survey in late September, asking the children to respond to the following items:

- What are your favorite poems?
- Who are your favorite poets?
- List the names of poets you know.
- List your favorite kinds of poetry.
- What are your favorite things to do with poetry?

The results supported my initial hypotheses: these children knew little about poetry at the beginning of the year. When asked to list their favorite poem, many claimed to not have one or stated they couldn't think of one to list. Only a few specific poems were listed. Nor could many of them list specific poets or particular kinds of poetry they liked. Evidently the limited choices, random page turning, and reluctance to move beyond the tried and true stemmed from a lack of familiarity with poetry. The children had little idea of its varied dimensions and even less about how to expand their horizons.

As I thought about this I began to see that, rather than being purposeless, the children were actually being quite purposeful in these groups. By examining poetry books on their own, stopping to read what appealed to them, the children were building a foundation for understanding and enjoyment. Maybe, I thought, this seemingly aimless exploration was necessary for effecting the transition to more purposeful sharing. Time to explore, on the basis of one's own interests and perspectives, might well be a necessary precursor to more focused, thoughtful responses.

Unfolding Buds

These children had little experience with poetry at the beginning of the year. Further, they were afraid of taking risks, of experimenting, of reaching out to find the "richer inner self" of a poem. To them, poetry was "as tightly closed as a tiny bud."

As they gained more experience with poetry, savoring it in many ways, they began to see the new dimensions and rich possibilities lying beneath the external black and white marks on a page. Most importantly, they began to trust the teachers, each other, and themselves. We hoped repeated encounters with poetry in this supportive community would lead to new growth and appreciation.

CHAPTER 5

Crystal Moments:
A Growing Appreciation
of Fine Poetry

Once or twice this side of death
Things can make one hold his breath

From my boyhood I remember
A crystal moment in September.

A wooded island rang with sounds
of church bells in the throat of hounds.

A buck leaped out and took the tide
with jewels flowing past each side.

With his high head like a tree
He swam within a yard of me.

I saw the golden drop of light
In his eyes turned dark with fright.

Fear made him lovely past belief
My heart was trembling like a leaf.

He leaned towards the land and life
With need upon him like a knife.

In his wake the hot hounds churned
They stretched their muzzles out and yearned.

They bayed no more but swam and throbbed
Hunger drove them till they sobbed.

Pursued, pursuers reached the shore
And vanished. I saw nothing more.

So they passed, a pageant such
As only gods could witness much,

Life and death upon one tether
And running beautifully together.

"Crystal Moment"
ROBERT P. TRISTRAM COFFIN

It was a cold, gray day in early February. The leaden skies seemed to promise snow but as yet had not fulfilled that promise. After recess the children gathered as they usually did in the corner of the classroom. Fifth and sixth graders were now regularly meeting together for large group poetry reading sessions as the few original class and grade distinctions had for the most part melted. Many of the children carried around books of poetry that looked well used— slips of paper were stuck between pages to mark favorite parts, pages were turned down at the corners and covers were rather ragged around the edges. The group looked up expectantly as Sheryl began to talk.

"I was thinking last night about what might lift you beyond some of the things you ordinarily read," she said. "I chose some because I thought they might give us some things to think about. The first one is called 'Phizzog' by Carl Sandburg. Listen and think about what he's saying here."

This face you got,
This here phizzog you carry around,
You never picked it out for yourself,
    at all, at all—did you?
This here phizzog—somebody handed it
    to you—am I right?
Somebody said, "Here's yours, now go see
    what you can do with it."
Somebody slipped it to you and it was like
    a package marked:
"No goods exchanged after being taken away"
This face you got.

"Well . . . what do you think about this poem?"

There was a short silence. The silences I was now observing, however, were different from those at the beginning of the year. Rather than nervously looking around and fixing their eyes on the floor in hopes of remaining inconspicuous, the children seemed to be quietly considering the implications of the poem. Jimmy P. was the first to offer his opinion.

"In the beginning when you started it, I didn't understand it," he said. "But I thought it was like...um...he was giving away something. When he was at the end [of the poem], um, it was like he was saying something about your face, um...how you would keep it. Now I think I understand...at the beginning it was strange."

Although Jim did not clearly articulate his insights, he was nevertheless groping toward an understanding of Sandburg's poem. Sheryl continued to encourage him. "So what do you think?...The poet is talking about what?" she asked him. "Go ahead, you said it."

"Like a face," responded Jim.

"Okay," answered Sheryl. She turned her attention again to the whole group. "Any other comments about that?"

Several children offered their opinions. Some expanded on Jimmy's ideas while others offered new insights of their own. Occasionally there was disagreement or a request for clarification of an idea. Eventually, the group concluded that Sandburg was saying, as Stacy put it, that "you're an original and you can't return [your face] even though you might like to exchange it." Through the interchange I was particularly struck by the fact that children readily disagreed with each other. Conversely, they often helped each other rephrase a comment so it was understandable to the group. The reticence I'd noticed earlier had largely disappeared.

They then began discussing why Sandburg used the word "Phizzog," speculating that this caught the reader's attention and made one really pay attention to the poem. Jennifer compared it to the use of nonsense in Carroll's "Jabberwocky." Several children also commented on the unusual topic. As Jim P. stated, "It's not a poem like about rain or something like that. It's very different. When they [other poets] do write about it [faces], they are usually telling about what you've got on your face—or how you use your face." Others speculated about why people are always trying to cover up their true selves.

Finally, Sheryl asked them to consider some of the techniques Sandburg used to make his poem unique, notably the use of repetition and questions. In typical fashion, however, she didn't just tell the children about these things. Rather, she read selected lines, such as the first and last, then told the children, "Let's talk about the beginning and the end of this poem. Notice anything interesting about the beginning and the end of it?"

Many children responded, "He repeated."

"Yes," answered Sheryl, "it begins and ends the same way and the rest of the time he is talking about this face you've got. Anything else you noticed about it?" She reread four lines:

> You never picked it out for yourself,
> at all, at all—did you?
> This here phizzog—somebody handed it
> to you—am I right?

"He asked you a question," Jennifer broke in eagerly.

"Sometimes two questions," added Jim P.

"He acted like a detective or something. He asked you questions," added Aaron.

"Is he drawing your attention?" Sheryl asked the group.

Many voices rose in a chorus of "Yeah!" Then Stacie added, "It makes you think, gee, what's he gonna do next?"

This discussion led naturally into the reading of a second poem, Nikki Giovanni's "The Drum." "Now you are really going to have to think about this one," Sheryl told the group, "It's very short, and there is a lot of meaning packed into it so think about how this poem affects you."

> Daddy says the world
> Is a drum
> Tight and hard
> And I told him,
> I'm gonna beat out my own rhythm

As usual, a brief silence followed as the children thoughtfully considered the poem.

"Sounds like a poem about how you're gonna live," stated Carrie.

"He's gonna find his own way," added Robin.

As usual, Jim P. speculated aloud as to the various possibilities he was considering. Although initially stumbling, he soon arrived at a definitive opinion.

"It sounds like the father is telling her what to do . . . or whatever . . . do what she . . . her father sounds like . . . but she is going to do what she wants to do."

Stacie cut in, "I don't agree with what Jim said," she stated, "Because Jim said it sounds like she's doing what her father said and then he switched to a completely different thing."

"No, I didn't say that," countered Jim P. "What I said was her father was telling her what to do and how to do in the world and the girl said that she didn't want to do that."

"Do you agree with that . . . that the father is telling her how to live?" asked Sheryl. "Let's listen." She read the poem aloud again.

"Like the world out there. It's hard when you don't have enough money or anything. It's just better to like make your own way," said Deon. She seemed well aware of some of the harsh realities of everyday life.

"How do you feel about that?" Sheryl asked the rest of the group.

"I agree," said Jennifer.

"Do you think the Dad is telling her how she has to live?" Sheryl asked again.

"No. Telling her what it's like. Like it's hard and everything," answered Jennifer.

"What do the rest of you think?" Sheryl asked the group. Many agreed with Jennifer's comments.

"I think her father is trying to tell her what the world is going to be like—and she can't have her own way every time," said Mike H.

"And then what?" asked Sheryl. She had noticed some children, particularly Jennifer, shaking their heads. "Well, disagree with him. Go ahead and talk back."

Jennifer and Mike H. then began a lively debate about each other's ideas, eventually coming to the realization that they essentially concurred on their understandings. The group listened quietly; such disagreements were not only allowed but encouraged because they frequently led to new insights.

When she felt things had been resolved between the two, Sheryl turned to the group and asked, "Do [the rest of] you agree that the father is saying she can't have her own way all the time?"

"I think Mike's right about that because she goes, 'But I'm gonna beat my own rhythm'," said Stacie.

"Is that always possible?" asked Sheryl. A chorus of "No" greeted her question.

She continued, "Sometimes and sometimes not, maybe? Why isn't it? Why can't you always beat out your own rhythm?"

"Because if you do your work or something—the boss will tell you what to do, or the president or someone," answered Jim P.

"Other people have higher rhythms, they have bigger jobs," added Robin.

"They have bigger drums," said Mandy.

"And harder rhythms," said Jimmy R.

Sheryl and I exchanged glances. We were both surprised and stimulated by the turn the discussion had taken. What interesting ideas evolve when children are given the opportunity.

"What do you think about this poem," Sheryl asked again, hoping to stimulate more insights.

"It has a lot of meaning to it," answered Angela.

"Like what?" Sheryl wanted to know. Aaron seemed eager to offer an opinion.

"Well, when Mike said about when the father was telling what the world was going to be like—he said the world is a tight drum. He said it is, not it will be," Aaron answered, seemingly intent on examining each word carefully so he understood the poet's message.

"Yes," agreed Sheryl. "Why did the father say the world is a drum, tight and hard. Why did he say it *is* instead of it *will be*?"

"Because it is right now," answered many voices.

"Because he is the one that has to pay all the taxes and make a living," said Stacie.

"Why does the father know that and the girl doesn't," Sheryl asked again, intent on helping them delve as far into the poem as they could.

Many voices again responded: "Because he's out in the world." "He knows about life." "He's lived longer." And similar comments were offered.

"Going back to that old [concept of] experience that we find in books so many times," added Sheryl.

Carrie had an interesting observation. "This reminds me of that poem by...I forget...the one you read yesterday to us about the crystal stairs." She was referring to Langston Hughes' moving poem, "Mother to Son," in which a black mother gives advice to her child about not giving up in the face of adversity. "The part... when he said the part about the drum, is tight," she continued, "that's the part that reminded me of the [Hughes] poem because it talks about nails and spots without any boards and no carpet. That sounded the same."

"That is an interesting connection because Langston Hughes and Nikki Giovanni could well have had similar experiences growing up," answered Sheryl. "Do people who heard 'Mother to Son' see any relationship between these poems?"

Jennifer had an idea. "They're both talking about how life is or was. Like the mother was talking about how hard hers was and the dad—he is talking about how hard his life was."

"It also seems like they're alive and it could happen," added Aaron.

"Like my dad," said Deon. "My mom and dad...he always says things like you can't get your own way—just like that poem."

"All right," responded Sheryl.

"I think that in both poems—that this one and the one we're

comparing it to—that they're warning their children of what life will be and they should be ready for it," said Jennifer.

"And in 'The Drum,' how is the child responding to that?" Sheryl asked the group.

"She's gonna beat her own rhythm," answered Stacie and Deon together.

"Is it okay to do that?" Sheryl wanted to know. Many children shook their heads no. "If you didn't, what would you be like?"

"Boring," said Stacie, wrinkling up her nose in distaste.

"You would be the same as everybody else," added Mike.

"Or at least the same as what?" asked Sheryl. "Do you think the father was telling her she *had* to live her life a certain way?"

Her question was greeted by a strong chorus of "No."

"She chose to live that way," added Angela.

"But he is trying to warn her what life is going to be like. Nevertheless she is going to try—just like the mother in Langston Hughes' poem, she is going to climb her stairs," said Sheryl.

The group then began discussing the similarities and differences between the ideas expressed in "Phizzogg" and "The Drum." Eventually Sheryl leafed through the books on her lap until she found a new poem, "Small Discovery" by Harry Behn, adding a different dimension to the discussion by reading it.

Changes had occurred in these groups. They had happened slowly, like a cat uncurling from a warm nap, stretching first one paw then another; eyelids blinking away shadowy visions; legs stretching then materializing underneath. The children too were on their feet; we could see the glint of discovery flickering in their eyes.

The interaction was no longer only teacher to student, with the teachers asking a question and the children barely responding to it. Although the sessions were still teacher controlled in that teachers devised the purposes, selected the poetry to be discussed, and controlled the focus, the proportion of student to teacher talk was more equal. I would characterize the interactions as more like a process of mutual collaboration to discover meaning than the transmission of information from a skilled to a naive reader. Increasingly, it was the children who initiated new directions in discussions, argued among themselves as to a poet's intentions, and spontaneously made connections between similar poets and poems. Their comments were more analytic and reflective; they were starting to be capable of going beyond "I like it" to describing what Rosenblatt (1978) terms "the lived-through experience"; the particular thoughts and emotions evoked as the work was read. Meaning was less likely to be perceived as a right answer. Rather, several answers often evolved out of the interaction between content, theme, poetic elements, and participants.

These changes did not progress in a consistent, linear fashion. A child might offer insightful responses one day and then be unable to move beyond superficial comments on another. Additionally, some children still rarely commented during these large group sessions, making it difficult to ascertain the development of their responses. But these less publicly verbal children frequently made comments to their friends and to me that indicated they, too, were becoming capable of more complex responses. Angie, who soon became my friend, would often initiate a private discussion with me and one or two friends following a large group session. "I just don't like to talk in front of those other kids," she would say, "but I think...." Then she would share her insights, seemingly more comfortable in the smaller group.

When I asked the children why they talked more now, few could articulate any specific reasons. All they could tell me were things like "I really loved that poem" or "I just felt like no one would laugh if I started talking." No one knew exactly why, but it was evident that many were becoming more adept at building on one another's understandings, refining their own responses in light of other's insights Few ever reached a point where they could construct a viable meaning on their own without the scaffolding that the group had built. In this classroom, making sense of poetry was essentially a collaborative activity as children "talked their way towards each other's understandings and outwards along the paths of their own experience" (Rosen and Rosen, 1976).

As the year progressed, my conclusions were increasingly confirmed. More children participated, expressing unique insights and keen observations. Rather than only listening to selections chosen by the teacher, many began bringing their own favorites to share. There were disagreements, but generally the children had respect for different viewpoints. It seemed that what was being created here was a partnership between teachers and children in which everyone was encouraged to experiment and go beyond the obvious. Most importantly, they seemed to have become poetry lovers.

Making the Difference

Determining why the changes had occurred was not easy. Sometimes it seemed that a particular poem captured their imagination and insights developed spontaneously from something that deeply touched the children or that related to their personal experiences.

This seemed to be the case with pieces like Coffin's "The Crystal Moment," Hughes' "Mother to Son," and Frost's "Invitation." These rural children easily found a kinship with the subject matters of hunting, farm life, and parental advice.

It may also have been the combining of fifth and sixth graders that made a difference in stimulating new responses. The fifth graders were exposed to the responses offered by the more experienced sixth graders. The sixth graders, in turn, were stimulated by the perspective of their younger classmates.

Further, the teachers continually helped the children make connections between poets and between poems with similar themes or styles, thus communicating the idea that poetry is a body of literature with common ties to content and technique. To this end they helped children build their knowledge of poets' names as well as an ability to discern the unique voices of different poets like Carl Sandburg, Robert Frost, David McCord, and Myra Cohn Livingston. Gradually, as the children became acquainted with a wide variety of poetry, the teachers would challenge them to make their own connections through questions like the following:

- Does anybody know anything else by this poet?
- What kinds of poems does this person write?
- What did we think about when we read other poems by this person?

Eventually, the children became so skilled at this that the teachers would often introduce a poem without stating the poet's name, then challenge the children to guess who wrote the poem by listening to its voice.

The teachers made similar connections between poems with analogous topics, themes, moods, and the like. Thus, in the large group sharing sessions, they would select several poems about spring, or those which expressed a common intense emotion. The subsequent discussion would then focus on similarities, with teachers asking the children, for example, to compare how each poet describes spring or tell how the poets showed fear in their poems. Sometimes a poem was read that spontaneously reminded the children or teachers of a previously read poem. Generally, when this occurred, the group would find the original poem and reread it. The ensuing talk then often revolved around how the poems were similar yet different in their description of the event or phenomenon.

The teachers also alluded to similarities between the themes used by professional poets and these same ideas in poems written by the children. Angie, for example, wrote the following poem about a seashell:

A Sea Shell

As I walked along the sea
I stumbled over something,
A shiny orange seashell.

I picked it up and took it home,
and laid it on my dresser
By the picture of an orange cat.

ANGIE
Grade 6

When her teacher read it she commented, "Have you read 'The Red Wheelbarrow' by William Carlos Williams? Your poem reminds me so much of that one." Together, they found Williams' poem and began comparing how both had created a "poem picture." Or when Jimmy R. wrote a poem about friends, his teacher found Hughes' "Friends" and helped him see how the two poems dealt similarly with the topic of friendship. Often, these connections were made with the whole class. Thus, when various children shared their own poetry in whole group critiquing sessions, others would be asked to comment on how professional poets described the same subject.

As a result of the connections built between poets and among similar poems, the children began developing strong preferences for their favorite poets and types of poetry. It seems that these linking activities afforded them the opportunity to develop a sense of poetic literature and to make judgments about what they did and didn't like.

The opportunity to try one's hand at writing poetry also undoubtedly affected their responses. As children began discovering how poets made their pieces unique, they experimented with this tentative understanding by trying the techniques out in their own writing. As a result, they began using elements like repetition, figurative language or nonsense words in attempts to make their own pieces "sound more poetic," as they termed it. In turn, they came to the discussion sessions with fresh insights and a heightened appreciation of what's involved in writing poetry.

Most importantly, however, I sensed that the children felt secure. They knew they could express their ideas and feelings freely, sure that they would not be laughed at by peers or corrected by

65

the teacher. This secure feeling, I think, stimulated more experimentation and divergent thinking. Both teachers encouraged this by continually telling the children to "play with" ideas, and "to think of possibilities." As Peggy commented in an after-school interview session:

> You have to always ask [the children]...what are the possibilities here? Are there other ways to look at that? I think we should constantly challenge them to look at all sides of a thing and maybe somebody else could see something from quite another viewpoint and open everyone else's minds where they had been closed before.

This flexibility had its limits, however. Although Peggy and Sheryl encouraged children to explore various potential meanings, they did not encourage interpretations that were clearly unsupported by the text. The following discussion occurred after a reading of Dickinson's "A Narrow Fellow in the Grass." It illustrates how a misunderstanding or misinterpretation was redirected. Several children erroneously concluded that Dickinson was referring to a garden hose, rather than a snake, in her poem.

SHERYL: We can hardly tell what [the object] is but here she wants you to use your imagination and guess what it is and think about it.
CHILD: She could also think of some other stuff that might be in the grass...like a hose.
SHERYL: All right. Let's talk about that possibility.
CHILD: A hose don't move.
CHILD: When you move it, it does.
CHILD: Would she be scared of a hose? Would she be "zeroed to the bone" by a hose moving through the grass?
CHILD: If it sprayed her. If she got wet by it.
CHILD: That wouldn't scare her. It might startle her.
CHILD: She would be frozen if it was cold out.
CHILD: What if it was warm water? It might be warm water.

At this point Sheryl decided to intervene.

SHERYL: Listen to this. "The grass divides as with a comb. A spotted shaft is seen. And then it closes at your feet and opens further on."
CHILD: That's why it's a hose because water comes out of one side of it and not out the other.
SHERYL: Do you know what she is saying? It's impossible for her to

say this if it were a hose. She says, "the grass divides as if with a comb. A spotted shaft is seen and then it closes at your feet and opens further on." Now, listen to this: "He likes a boggy acre. A floor too cool for corn." Does a hose have any likes or dislikes?

CHILDREN: No.

CHILD: It doesn't have any feelings.

SHERYL: So, as we play with the poem and read it and think about it we keep coming back to the conclusion that it must be a snake.

It is evident that flexibility was valued and encouraged in this classroom. Children were directed to think of possibilities and to play with various shadings of meaning to derive increasingly complex understandings of poetry. But it was equally clear that flexibility has its limits, bound by the conventions and meanings intrinsic to a specific text.

Selecting Poetry to Read Aloud

Choosing poems to read aloud is an art. It's tempting to select the pieces that get the quick laugh and instant positive response. Children love reading such poetry. But does it challenge them? Does it sharpen their perception of the English language or make them look at the world in a way that has a lasting effect on their lives? Probably not. Everyone enjoys the immediately satisfying experiences. Having only these sorts of experiences, however, makes for an unbalanced diet. We'd all eventually get sick of eating only chocolate and ice cream.

Thus, we believe teachers should select poetry that balances the literary diet of children and develops their taste for the more complex and interesting types. Children need help in reaching beyond their initial preferences to discover new challenges and delights. This is what will help make them life-long readers—and lovers—of poetry. Eve Merriam once commented:

> I find it difficult to sit still when I hear poetry or read it aloud. I feel a tingling all over, particularly in the tips of my fingers and toes, and it just seems to go right from my mouth, all the way through my body.

This is the kind of response we want to build in children.

Passive Listening Isn't Enough

When we explain these techniques at in-service workshops, teachers sometimes question the necessity of doing anything with poetry. "Shouldn't we just read it aloud and let them enjoy it without asking them to do anything with it?" they ask. We agree that it is important to let children "just enjoy" poetry. Enjoyment is a fundamental premise of the program, but it doesn't just happen. We've all had poetry just read to us, and although we may have enjoyed the lilt and flow of words, we probably rarely experienced the joy of discovering the reason for our delight. Understanding can deepen enjoyment. Thus, we think that teachers are depriving children if they don't show them how to uncover the subtle nuances of meaning and what poets do to forge an emotional connection with the reader. Such activities are infinitely rewarding because they open up new possibilities for enjoyment that go far beyond a passive or superficial acceptance. Also, what better way to develop those higher-level thinking skills mandated by many schools than by using something real that is worth thinking about? Now this does not mean that teachers should use activity sheets asking children to fill in the blank or make a choice on a multiple choice test. Such exercises are constraining and always focus on a meaning being imposed on the child rather than allowing children to create a meaning for themselves.

There is a subtle difference between imposing meaning on someone and helping them discover this meaning on their own. It is also not an easy thing to do. These teachers weren't perfect. They sometimes jumped in and tried to explain or steer the conversation in a certain direction. However, their general tone was to support the children's ideas by suggesting possibilities rather than stating probabilities.

Crystal Moments

One incident epitomizes the community of poetry lovers that had developed. Sheryl had chosen to begin a sharing session (with both fifth and sixth graders) by reading aloud Coffin's "The Crystal Moment," a poem in which the poet describes a perfect suspended moment of time when he observed life and death "running beautifully together." (The complete text is at the beginning of this chapter.) It is a powerful poem with vivid images and a compelling rhythm, and it causes the reader to share the speaker's intense emotional response to the incident described. After Sheryl read the poem, there was total silence for several minutes. The children seemed deeply moved. Several broke the silence by requesting, "Read it again." After the second reading, they began a lengthy discussion about hunting (a common pastime in this community) and how they felt about killing animals. This led into a discussion of death. The session lasted over an hour, not because the teacher had planned it but because the children were involved and interested for that long.

After the session was over, Stacie and Carrie remained. They asked Sheryl for the book she'd read from that day. Turning to "The Crystal Moment," Stacie commented, "Oh, I just love this poem. Read it to me again." She closed her eyes and rocked quietly in the rocker as Carrie read the poem to her. Watching them, Sheryl commented quietly, "If we can give these kids one crystal moment in poetry, I'll feel we've accomplished our goal." She and Peggy seem to have succeeded.

CHAPTER 6

Reading Poetry
with Friends

Once I saved a fairy.
Three wishes she gave me.
Knowledge one was,
The second a great big climbing tree,
As the third came to mind,
I told her—
I want all the poetry books
In the World.
They all appeared
And I was happy
As could be.

"Three-Wish Fairy"
BRIAN
Grade 6

As the tenor and quality of discussion changed in the large-group sessions, I began noticing similar changes in the small group and partner-reading sessions. To document this I knew I would have to become a more integral part of the group. I continued to exchange views on pets, hairstyles, and basketball with the children, but now I began participating more actively in poetry discussions.

As a result, most children no longer hesitated asking me to join their peer poetry reading sessions. After weeks of being interviewed (termed "having a talk with Amy"), they now often voluntarily told me about discussions they'd had with their friends when I wasn't present, vividly describing what was read and what everyone had said. I still sought out and interviewed children who were shyer about initiating conversations so my data would not be skewed toward the more verbal and outgoing children.

Small peer poetry reading communities formed, disbanded, then reformed. Depending on particular purposes and needs, children read poetry with other children at different times throughout the day. Thus, when they wanted to read humorous poetry, they might seek out Carrie or Robin who were not only good readers but also knew the funny poems and often provided a running commentary on the group's activities. Similarly, when children wanted to share more serious poems, they would seek out Aaron, Jennifer, or Jimmy who were known to be skillful at refining a poem's meaning and liked poetry with what they called a "deep meaning."

By the middle of the year, however, several stable communities were composed of members who seemed consistently to seek each other out for sharing sessions. Generally group members were either all boys or all girls although the sixth grade "gang" included both. The groups also tended to include children from only one grade level, although occasionally a child from another level would become a temporary member.

All the peer-reading groups continued following the turn-taking procedures I had observed earlier in the year, taking turns selecting poems and reading them aloud with one child serving as teacher while the others listened. But now, subtle changes were occurring in what was being said about the poetry. Rather than just making comments as to whether a poem was "good" or "bad," "funny" or "sad," they were beginning to comment on specific aspects of content. The kind of talk that had evolved in the teacher-led sessions was occurring in their own conversations about poetry. We felt this was a significant change. It was one thing to engage in such conversations in the presence of adults who initiated them. It was quite another thing to realize the children were becoming interested in these ideas on their own. Sometimes they would ask a teacher for confirmation of their opinions or to answer a question, but the initiative was coming from them.

One of the most common type of comments compared one poem with another. Often this evolved directly from the large group teacher-led sharing sessions. Thus, for example, after Sheryl had read aloud Coffin's "Forgive My Guilt," I noticed that several sixth graders had borrowed the books and were busily comparing the poem on their own with Coffin's "The Crystal Moment."

I walked over and sat down with them. "It's interesting to me that you're connecting those poems," I said. "How come? What's alike?"

"Well, they're both about killing animals and the person feels real guilty," answered Jimmy R.

"And they're both real sad and about nature," added Johnny.

"The words are a lot the same [in both poems] . . . I don't know . . . like that part where the birds swam out to sea and cry? That sounds like he [Coffin] described the deer that was dying [in 'Crystal Moment']," added Jennifer.

Later, I saw that Jimmy R. and Johnny had borrowed the Langston Hughes collection that had also been read that day and were rereading "War" and "Peace." They puzzled over the lines "Death is the broom / I take in my hands / to sweep the world clean," before asking Sheryl what they meant.

"What do you think?" she countered.

"Well . . . maybe it's talking about sweeping up the bad guys so there won't be any more," answered Johnny.

"Who are the bad guys?" asked Sheryl.

Jimmy looked thoughtful. "Maybe it's everyone if they fight in a war," he said slowly. The boys walked away, still arguing about what the poet was saying about war and the concept of enemy. Later, I saw a powerful poem Jimmy had written in response to his thinking about Hughes' poem. It had evolved from the ideas discussed in the large group session, then the more intense, focused conversation he'd shared with Johnny.

War

War is me,
War is you,
It's your fault,
No yours,
I kill you
You kill me,
It doesn't matter,
We're both as good as dead
War is a waste of time,
War is a waste of my time, enemy.

JIMMY R.

Often the children made these connections between poems completely on their own. For example, I watched Ronnie and Johnny read Edwin Hoey's "Foul Shot" in *Reflections on a Gift of Watermelon Pickle*. "Where's that other basketball poem?" asked Ronnie. They leafed through several books, eventually finding Adoff's *Eats* and looked up "The Coach Said," to compare the two poems.

" 'Foul Shot' is really like it is to play basketball," Johnny commented appreciatively. "It's like the poem Jim P. wrote." They scurried over to the bookcase and found Jim P.'s anthology. Turning to his basketball poem, they read it aloud:

One Point Behind

Motionless,
A boy stares at the net,
Sweating in anticipation.
He bounces the ball,
Concentrates,
Shoots,
And follows through.
The ball orbits the rim,
Hesitates,
Falls,
The game is lost.

JIMMY P.

They then began comparing how each poem described the game.

Generally, however, the most common comments were "This poem says it [the meaning] in an unusual way" or "This one has deep meaning." No one could fully explain what they meant. As in the beginning of the year, the purpose of these groups was still primarily to enjoy poetry with each other.

More telling changes were evident when I documented which poems were chosen to read with friends. Although I still observed random page-turning, choices increasingly seemed more planned and deliberate, suggesting repeated experiences with the poetry books. Because the children had become familiar with a wide variety of specific poems and poets, they could be more discerning in their choices. I noticed Jimmy R. moving back and forth between pages in Ted Hughes' Under the North Star. He told me later that he was rereading and comparing the poems about the snowshoe hare and the rabbit—"the words he [the poet] used to describe nature." Jennifer would frequently report that she and Johnny read poetry together, particularly enjoying books by Robert Frost (her favorite), and Karla Kuskin (Johnny's perennial first choice). " 'The Road Not Taken' is my favorite," she declared. "It's serious and has a different meaning."

I must admit I was initially a bit discouraged by the sessions I was observing in April and May. I had originally hypothesized that based on their comments in large group sessions and obvious enjoyment of the poems read at these times, they would abandon some of their earlier favorites for a new kind of enjoyment with the more complex poetry. This simply did not happen. While I did see many instances of children spontaneously sharing imaginative, complex poems with each other, I also saw them still reading things I thought they'd outgrown—very simple poems that offered them few challenges. For example, I observed Jimmy R. and Jeremy with their friend Bryan sharing Livingston's A *Circle of Seasons* (a thematic collection using complex imagery) and Frost's *You Come Too* along with a book of silly riddles. When Carrie, Kellie, and Teava were asked to teach a new child how sharing sessions worked, they selected "Jabberwocky," "Stopping by Woods on a Snowy Evening," and "The Crystal Moment" as the basis of their instruction. Yet they also used Ciardi's "Mommy Slept Late and Daddy Fixed Breakfast" and "Purple Cow." I began to wonder. Were they really not growing in their appreciation of fine poetry? Did they select the more challenging pieces only because they thought this was expected and would please their teachers, all the while really preferring light, humorous pieces? I thought I needed to keep pursuing this question, using other ways beyond observation to interpret what was happening.

I began by carefully documenting the kinds of poems children selected for inclusion in their personal anthologies. These were collections of their favorites that were made into books, then illustrated. Many of these were organized thematically around topics like "Christmas," "animals," "nature," and the like. But often sometimes a favorite poem could not be placed under a discernible theme. These were collected into a general anthology with a generic title.

Many of the children put both complex and light, humorous pieces in their collections, providing evidence that they were beginning to enjoy challenging poetry while still appreciating their earlier favorites. For example, among simply rhymed poems about animals and nature, Jeremy and Earnie added Ted Hughes' "The Osprey."

"Why that one?" I asked.

"We like the part where it says 'God hides below in the shadow,'" answered Jeremy. "It sounds mysterious, and it's got deep meaning."

I noticed they had also included Ted Hughes' "The Heron."

"What about that one?" I asked again.

"I liked the part where it says 'the sun is an iceberg in the sky' because it was a neat way to describe the sun," commented Earnie. Then, almost as an afterthought, he said, "You know his [Hughes'] poems give me good ideas for writing on my own."

Similarly, Dawn included "Valentine" in her collection because, she told me, "it was funny" and "Garden" solely because she wanted a poem on seasons. Yet she also included "The Toaster" (a poem comparing a toaster to a dragon) because of the comparison. "It's really different," she said. Mike J. and Aaron added "The Toaster" to Fresh Poetry, their collection of personal favorites, for the same reason. "It's neat to look at a toaster and think it's a dragon. We never thought of it that way before," they commented. They also included Tippett's "Sunning," not because it was about a dog but due to their sense that it presented a vivid description of that dog, a description that they told me kept running through their heads.

In another instance Robin, Mandy, and Dolly chose poems like Ciardi's "Pop Bottles" (for its entertaining alliterative sounds) and Hoberman's "Yellow Butter, Purple Jelly, Red Jam, Black Bread" (because it was "fun to say"). They also included Langston Hughes' "Hold Fast to Dreams" among their favorites. This poem was quite different from the others they had selected because of its more complex imagery.

"Why that one?" I asked again.

"We love the way the words flow from each other," answered Robin. "And, well, the meaning is just like I really feel about dreams." The other girls nodded in agreement.

I gathered more responses in informal conversations after school, during work sessions and other opportune times. As I listened to their ideas, I formed new conclusions about their choices. Rather than preferring one kind of poetry over the other, they liked both. They seemed unwilling to give up the fun and camaraderie of reading the light pieces together. Yet they were excited about the new possibilities to which they'd been introduced and wanted to explore these with friends who were engaged in the same process of discovery. Maybe they needed the assurance of the familiar as they began exploring the unknown.

The May poetry survey results confirmed even more clearly that when asked to make a choice, quality usually won out. In contrast to September, poems listed as "favorites" by fifth graders were quite diverse, seemingly representing familiarity with a wide variety of forms and topics. McCord's "This Is My Rock" was the most favored. But many other poems were mentioned, ranging from Tippett's "Sunning" and Thurman's "Flashlight" (an unusual poem comparing a flashlight's beam to a sniffing hunting dog) and Langston Hughes' "Hold Fast to Dreams," to David Amey's "My Uncle Jack" and Fyleman's "Mice." The fact that every child listed a favorite and some listed several was further evidence that the fifth graders were developing a repertoire of poems they knew and enjoyed. Although they still often preferred poetry that was funny, rhythmical, and rhymed, many were beginning to appreciate more depth and complexity.

The sixth grade surveys revealed even more striking changes. Many children felt compelled to list several choices as they found it impossible to select one favorite. In contrast to the fifth graders', their choices reflected more consensus in that several poems received a high number of votes. Langston Hughes' "Mother to Son" was the most popular followed by two of Frost's poems: "Stopping by Woods on a Snowy Evening" and "The Pasture" and Sandburg's "Buffalo Dusk." Poems receiving one vote each ranged from Marcia Masters' "April" (a poem uniquely describing the sounds and smells of April) to "Sun Tiger" (a metaphorical piece comparing the sun's pattern on a sidewalk to a tiger's stripes) to Sandburg's "A Dust of Snow."

The sixth graders' reasons for selecting particular poems further revealed their growing preferences for poetry that related to their lives, made them think, or struck them as particularly good examples of poetic technique. Because these comments were written and offered spontaneously by the children, the adults were reluctant to question and probe for clarity or extension of a short comment. On their own, the children had perceptive reasons for selecting a particular poem as their favorite. Stacie wrote she selected "Dust of Snow" because "it brightens my day whenever I read it." Jennifer stated she chose Masters' "April" because "it's a poem that makes you really think of what the poet meant to say." And Jimmy wrote he liked Frost's "The Pasture" because of the last line which he stated "is like an invitation. I like how it says 'I shan't be gone long—you come too.' "

Just as the children were developing an appreciation for more complex poetry, their knowledge and appreciation of poets who wrote this kind of poetry grew. Although Adoff was the top favorite of the fifth graders, many others were listed, including David McCord, Arnold Lobel, Robert Frost, Valerie Worth, Myra Cohn Livingston, and Aileen Fisher. Several children named more than one favorite as they couldn't decide which was the best. When asked why they preferred a particular poet, the fifth graders' responses revealed a growing appreciation for how poets craft their pieces. For example, Bryan and Earnie wrote they liked Adoff's poems because "he puts things together in a neat way" and "he draws you into his poems and the words just slide out of your mouth." Lesa stated she liked Aileen Fisher because of "how her poetry is all about the outside. She describes it well." Certainly, these children were not yet expressing a complex awareness of poets and poetic technique, but they had made a start.

Even more interesting was the increase in the number of poets each fifth grader could spontaneously list without adult prompting. Although Adoff was still the most familiar poet (every child listed his name), many other poets were listed. These included familiar ones like David McCord, Shel Silverstein, and Arnold Lobel. Nevertheless, a wide variety of poets usually less familiar to children, including Myra Cohn Livingston, Eve Merriam, Harry Behn, and even e. e. cummings (named by seven children), were listed.

Survey results from the sixth graders showed that they also were beginning to recognize and appreciate fine poetry. When asked to name their favorite poet, Robert Frost was the overwhelming favorite (receiving 14 votes) followed by Langston Hughes, David McCord, Emily Dickinson, Carl Sandburg, and a host of others. It's probably no accident that Robert Frost is Sheryl's favorite poet while Carl Sandburg is one of Peggy's. It is likely teacher enthusiasm contributed to the children's enthusiasm for particular poets.

When asked to write why a particular poet's work was enjoyed, their responses demonstrated a growing awareness of many poets' particular styles as well as an appreciation for their skill with various poetic techniques. For example, although many stated they liked Frost because of his focus on nature (a predictable result considering their rural background), several commented further on his ability to "make you think." Jennifer wrote she preferred him because "his poetry makes you really use your brain to get the message he's trying to tell you." Stacie stated she enjoyed Frost because "his poems are different than anyone else's in how he sets the mood in them." Similarly perceptive comments were made about other poets. Brandon stated that he liked Langston Hughes "because of the way he writes good metaphors" while Jenny S. wrote that Hughes was her favorite because "when he writes a poem he sounds really different."

When asked to list as many poets as they knew, an astonishing number was generated. Only three children listed fewer than eight names and many listed more than ten. Langston Hughes was the most frequently named, followed by Robert Frost, Carl Sandburg, Eve Merriam, e. e. cummings, Arnold Adoff, David McCord, Emily Dickinson, and Harry Behn. Over thirty additional names were listed. The results are even more astounding when one considers that the children received no help from adults and were not told in advance that they would be asked to do this. Nor were the names checked off on a list. The children had to write every one on their own.

I began to realize that I had been a bit of an elitist in labeling some pieces as inferior. From Silverstein to Merriam to Shakespeare—it was all poetry. Each piece just provided a different kind of experience; a different way of looking at the world. The children seemed to need such diversity. This is equally true for literate adults. We make shifts in our own literary diet, one day reading *People* magazine or a romance novel, then moving to a piece of research in a professional journal or a critically acclaimed novel. Realizing this, my perspective changed. Rather than hoping children would appreciate only good poetry, I hoped they would expand their ability to appreciate the imagery and perspective of many different kinds of poetry. It seems that this was in fact what had occurred.

Teachers Make the Difference

What caused these changes? I kept asking myself what was it about these classrooms that helped the children develop increasingly discerning preferences for many kinds of poetry and an interest in sharing poetry with their friends? As I sifted through the notes from all my observations and interviews it seemed that, just as with the large group sharing sessions, my evidence once again revealed the subtle yet powerful influence of the teachers.

There seemed to be several specific things Peggy and Sheryl did that encouraged the children to explore poetry with each other. First, they would periodically make certain books visible and accessible. Thus, after Peggy had arranged several books by Thurman and Worth on the chalk rail, I observed Lisa and Cathy reading Worth's *More Small Poems* and Thurman's *Flashlights and Other Poems* together. The same thing happened when she displayed Karla Kuskin's books. This practice seemed to help the children become more focused when they made their own selections of what to read. Rather than randomly choosing a book based on interesting cover or title, they began deliberately choosing those by particular poets.

In other instances, poems that were read aloud in the large-group sessions would be made available for rereading. The teachers hoped that once the children got a taste of a poet's work, they would choose to examine it more closely on their own. The teachers rarely handed a book to a child and told him or her to read it. Rather, after a book was shared, it would be left casually on the table so the children could naturally gravitate to it. This was the case with Johnny and Jimmy who reread Hughes' "War" and "Peace" in the incident described previously. In another incident, two fifth-grade girls, Mandy and Robin, selected poems from Livingston's "O Frabjous Day" to share because they told me, "Mrs. Harrison read us poems by Myra Cohn Livingston, and we liked them so we thought we'd read some more." It seems that the intimate, informal nature of these sessions provided the opportunity to reexperience as well as savor the emotions and enjoyment evoked by the original reading. The children would probably never have selected these poems without the influence of teacher direction.

Children also discovered more complex poems and unfamiliar poets through specific assignments. This usually involved finding poems to illustrate a particular topic, theme or subject area. Aaron, Jeremy and Mike were carrying out such an assignment when I observed them looking purposefully through *Crickets, Bullfrogs and Whispers of Thunder, Reflections on a Gift of Watermelon Pickle,* and *A Dog's Life.* Peggy had suggested they look for dog poems to go with *Sounder,* their current group novel.

"I think I found one," Aaron said excitedly. "Listen to this." He read Tippett's "Sunning" aloud. "Yeah, that's a good one!" responded Mike. They found a scrap of paper to mark the spot, then continued searching.

In another instance, Jim P. coordinated a class collection of poems that were designed to reflect the themes of Leo Lionni. The children found poems like Worth's "The Turtle" and "Caterpillar" and Oliver Wendell Holmes' "Chambered Nautilus." The children probably would not have encountered the diversity of theme, genre, poet, or complex use of poetic elements without this teacher guidance.

Most importantly, the atmosphere of support and trust, developed in the large-group sessions, carried over to the small-group sessions. Children were trusted to conduct their sessions independently, secure in the knowledge that teachers would not dictate their choice of poems or control what was said. Rather than abusing this freedom I think they found it quite liberating and were generally purposeful when they gathered to share poetry.

Sharing Poems

It was now early May. The snow had melted and the smell of spring was definitely in the air. Instead of huddling against the school building to keep out of the cold, the children were organizing kickball games and practicing for cheerleading tryouts. Trooping in after lunch, they grabbed well-worn copies of *The Arrow Book of Poetry* and gathered as usual for a sharing session.

I'd been talking to the teachers during lunch. Both had noticed an interesting phenomenon. Rather than accepting whatever the teachers decided to read aloud, the children were now frequently bringing their own favorites to share with the group. This was sometimes prompted by a teacher request, but more often the children initiated the selection as a result of their own peer sharing sessions.

Today, the teachers tell me, the children have asked to share their favorite poems from *The Arrow Book of Poetry*. Although they have encouraged the children to read this book (even providing multiple copies), it is the children who have organized the session and selected the poems by first trying them out with each other.

Matt, one of the class strugglers, began by reading Kuskin's "I Woke Up This Morning." Sheryl laughed as he finished, commenting, "I know why you read that! You felt the same way this morning [as the person in the poem]. I know because you told me."

"Yeah, I felt really sore after baseball practice yesterday, and this poem really talks about how I felt," responded Matt.

Jennifer was next, reading aloud Livingston's "Whispers." After finishing, she commented, "I like this poem because it sounds neat the way it says 'Whispers tickle through your ear, telling things you like to hear.' I love how the words roll around together and rhyme." Many of the children nodded in agreement and several asked her to read it again. A few followed along quietly to themselves when she got to the favored lines.

Deon next read Langston Hughes' "April Rain Song," chosen because she particularly liked the line, "Let the rain kiss you, let the rain beat upon your head." "That's an unusual way to say it," she commented, "I've never heard rain described that way—but it's true."

"Would anyone have guessed it was by Langston Hughes?" asked Sheryl. A few children nodded "yes" but most shook their heads "no." "Most of the poems we've read by him are about people and their problems," ventured Stacie, "This one is different."

"It's a lot different from [Merriam's] 'Summer Rain,'" added Angela. I knew this poem was one of her favorites, and she knew it by heart. "That poem has more, you know, rhythm to it because of the words."

"What words?" asked Sheryl, pushing Angela to extend her comment.

"You know, like 'tickle,' 'sprinkle,' 'tangle,' and stuff like that. It's a different way to describe rain—and it's different from the one Deon read." Since the poem was also in *The Arrow Book of Poetry*, the group urged Angela to read it aloud. Again, I noticed several children following along on some of the more familiar lines.

Bryan, one of the quieter students in the group, offered to read McLeod's "Lone Dog." "I like the way the poet talks in this poem. She makes the dog sound real sad."

"How does she do this?" asked Sheryl, again trying to get Bryan to extend his ideas.

"She uses real sad words, and she puts words together so

80

they rhyme good and sound good together." Appreciative nods from many of the other children confirmed that they agreed with Bryan.

Stacie went next, reading aloud Aileen Fisher's "Weather Is Full of the Nicest Sounds." "This poem has good rhythm. I like the way it makes me feel. It's also lined kind of different." She held the book up and showed the group what she meant. Several commented that it looked like the kind of lining Adoff uses.

The group eventually broke up and afternoon activities began. Although a few put their copies of the book back on the shelf, many kept them for later sharing with friends or a quiet read on their own. I notice slips of paper were marking new poems in several cases. A community of people, bound by a common love of poetry, had evolved.

A Community of Poetry Lovers

That this was a community of poetry lovers was increasingly evident as I caught snatches of the children's conversations. I overheard Jimmy P. and Brandon talking about how they memorized their favorite poems, then took turns reciting them to each other on the boring bus ride home. Ronnie confided that he often "pulled poems out of his head" when something he saw while walking along the road prompted an association. His favorite walks were with Jimmy and Johnny during which they took turns reciting their favorite pieces.

Many commented that their families had begun reading poetry together at home or they used it like a glass of warm milk at night to fall asleep. As Stacie told me: "If it's the afternoon or morning, I like to read books because you don't have to concentrate so much on them. But at night I read poetry . . . I read a lot at night before I go to bed."

James Britton (1982) states that you must read and reread poetry before it becomes understandable and you "own" it. It seems to me that this was exactly what the children were doing. They read and reread the same selections, sharing their favorites again and again with a friend or their inner self. This was possible because they had acquired a repertoire of "poems in their pockets" (to use the title of a poem by Beatrice Schenk de Regniers) that they could pull out anywhere they went or as often as they wished—skipping along a creek bed, walking on a dusty road, or at night in bed.

PART III

Building a Community of Poetry Writers

Some footprints in the sand
Are of a sandpiper
Working tiny feet
Over a long stretch of beach.
Following quietly, I retrace his footsteps.
What a long way to go for such a small thing.
The footsteps swerve and curve.
Hopping this way and that,
He looks back to see his footsteps,
His own.
Triumphantly he turns,
Strutting and jumping effortlessly.
Proud of himself,
He puffs out his chest.
His footsteps are tiny,
But still footsteps.
He turns around
And with pleasure,
Looks at the final draft
He had been revising
Over and over again.

"The Poet"
ANNE
Grade 3*

W riting poetry is not a linear process in which one's initial thoughts, captured on paper, are inviolate. Rather, a poet works circuitously, becoming involved in the experience, then drawing away to gauge the effect, then continuing to experiment with different ideas until something pleasing has been achieved.

Just as with the reading of poetry, these children did not begin writing poetry with an understanding of this process. Nor did their

*Poems written by third and fourth graders were all done by Upper Arlington students of Peggy and Sheryl in years following the study described in this book.

understanding develop immediately. Rather, as with the reading, awareness developed gradually in response to much experimentation with others engaged in the same process.

This section documents how the children learned to take footsteps that "swerve and curve / Hopping this way and that" in their journey to becoming a community of poetry writers.

CHAPTER 7

Initial Attempts at Writing Poetry

A poem, a poem
I can't write a poem
Cause my brain, won't work,
My pencil won't write
And I think I've lost my appetite
With all this untouched white
Staring up at me.

> "Stupefied"
> KATY
> Grade 3

When I first began observing the children writing poetry, I was disappointed. For a long time, things didn't change much. Just as the children didn't quite seem to know how to go about discussing poetry, they were similarly unsure about how to write it. I noticed quite a bit of aimless paper shuffling and little sincere commitment to the task. They seemed to be writing with words and rules borrowed from what they'd been told about poetry rather than with ideas and images from their own experience.

Poetry journals would be passed from one child to another, the day's entry read (aloud or silently), then the book would be passed back to the writer. Occasionally a child might offer a comment like "that's nice" or "I like that" after reading a friend's piece. But direct, focused assistance was rarely given and even these general comments were rare.

A group of fifth-grade girls was typical. While writing, their conversations seemed to revolve exclusively around topic selection with little attention given to creating a piece that was personally satisfying. Rather, the attention seemed to be on finding a topic so they could "get something down."

"What should I write? You guys got any ideas? Maybe I could write about cats. I got a cat at home," said Mandy to her friends as I sat observing one day in late September.

"You could write about dolls. There are some doll books you could look in to get some ideas," answered Robin, who immediately got up, collected several doll books from the class library and deposited them on the table.

The girls began aimlessly leafing through the books but no one seemed particularly inclined to put something down on paper. Soon Peggy stopped by to check on their progress. Realizing that the girls seemed stuck, she offered a few suggestions.

"Did you look at some of these doll books here?" she asked. "You could talk about some of these dolls. Or do you have a special doll? What could you say about that? Missy, you said you never liked to play with dolls. What can you say about that?"

Peggy moved on, leaving the girls to consider these possibilities. They began discussing their friends and the various kinds and numbers of dolls each had. Yet, none could really muster enthusiasm for writing a doll poem.

"We could write about horses. Like, Missy, you could write about your horse and how you got it," someone finally suggested. "Or we could write about rainbows," said another.

Everyone agreed these ideas might work and began to write furiously, eventually producing poems like the following:

Horses

They are fun and
They are very nice
They are brown, white and black and spotted

Rainbows

Rainbows, Rainbows, Rainbows
Colorful rainbows high in
the sky, that shows us
that God still cares.

This kind of poetry was typical. I commonly observed many pieces in which the topic would be repeated several times at the beginning or end of the poem. In other instances the writer would create lists in which an object would be described by repeating some element, like a color or an action, over and over. Shelly's

"Rainbow" poem and Johnny's "Dream" piece are examples of this pattern:

Dreams	Red rainbows
Dreams are nice	Pink rainbows
Dreams in the night	Blue rainbows
And at day.	Rainbows
JOHNNY	SHELLY
Grade 6	*Grade 6*

I termed this "grocery list" poetry because that was exactly what it reminded me of. It appears the children had some sense that poets used repetition but had little idea of its real purpose in creating rhythm or mood. Tiffany articulated the perceptions of most of her peers. When asked why she wrote as she did, she responded, "I'm just thinking about words and getting them down." She was genuinely unaware that expressing a personally significant meaning was part of the process.

When a topic was finally selected it was usually something abstract or esoteric like "rainbows," "stars," "unicorns," and the like. The children seemed to share the views of many their age that poetry can only be about "Truth," "Beauty," and other sentimental ideas. When they did write on a topic closer to their own experience, like horses or going to the county fair, they seemed detached from it. Most were content to write descriptions rather than investing any emotion in what they were saying.

Some at least seemed to have a sense of what poetry looked like and how it differed from prose. These children would write one line under another and realized a sentence didn't always end on one line but could continue on to the next. Nevertheless, quite a few were writing what I came to term "paragraph poetry." These were paragraphs similar in form to prose. Yet they possessed a slight poetic quality due to the use of some description or a slight rhythmic feel that led me to classify them as part of the initial stages of poetry. Although some of the sixth graders initially used the form, paragraph poetry was more typical of fifth graders who had less experience generally with poetry. Thus, for example, Earnie wrote his poem about walking in the woods in the following fashion:

Walking through a dry creekbed
Into the dense woods smells of a
dead animal is in the air
crickets chirping squirrels

chattering I start walking
to the meadow. Tall grass
swallows me up as I walk
through it milkweed puffs come
out of the meadow weeds are all
over the meadow as I walk home.

EARNIE
Grade 5

Another day he wrote a paragraph poem about walking outside on a scary night.

The Scary Night

The dark clutched at my
throat, as I walked past
the cemetery, the wind blew
through the trees, I heard a raven
squawking, I heard moans and
groans in the darkness
of the night.

Certainly, the use of the paragraph form and stereotypical images like ravens (rarely, if ever, observed in Mt. Victory) are not particularly poetic. Yet the teachers and I began to think there was poetic possibility in phrasings like "dark clutched at my throat," "in the darkness of the night," and Earnie's reference to tall grass that "swallows me up."

Revision, when attempted at this point, tended also to be superficial with little understanding of *why* revisions might be made to one's piece. The children seemed to know revisions were part of poetry writing: the teachers had emphasized it from the first day of school, but they didn't really seem to understand its purpose. Often they would add or delete a word and announce they had "revised." Usually the change seemed arbitrary. This was true for Lesa, a fifth grader, when she revised her "County Fair" poem. The following is her first draft:

The soft teddy bear just lay there
Till the grizzly bear said,
 Let's go to
The Hardin County Fair and
they walked off
 hand in hand.

Her revised version was exactly the same with the words "Hardin County" left out.

"Why did you make that change?" I asked her.

"Well, Mrs. Harrison told us poems have fewer words than stories do," she replied.

Similarly, Jennifer completed the following first draft and a revision that substituted one word for one she perceived as a "big" word:

Dreams (first draft)	Dreams (second draft)
Floating in heads, Getting smaller and smaller Until . . . Poof! Your dreams are TRUE!	Floating in *noggins* Getting smaller and smaller Until . . . Poof! Your dreams are TRUE!

Both Lesa and Jennifer seemed to be following a formula with no understanding of why the formula had been devised or why they should or shouldn't make changes.

Another popular way to revise was to reline. Again, this was done with little understanding of why. Children would just write the words in a new pattern on the page—putting different words on subsequent lines or indenting another way. Lesa's second revision of her "County Fair" poem looked like this:

The
 soft
  teddy bear
  just
   laid
    there
     till
      the
       Grizzly Bear
        said
       Let's
      go
     to
      the
     Fair
     and
     they

        walked
         off
        hand
       in hand.

    We were concerned. Would the class ever move beyond writing lists and paragraphs to creating poems that would reflect their personal perceptions of the world? As we initially perused the daily entries, this didn't seem possible.

    As we began watching and listening, then carefully examining the entries, then listening some more, however, we began to discern glimmers of insight that suggested there were possibilities for new understandings. For instance, Ronnie had an early poem called "Farm Songs" that incorporated the element of repetition in a somewhat more purposeful way than I'd observed previously:

Farm Song

birds cherp, roosters
crow, cows moo
dogs bark, pigs oink
  cherp
    crow
      moo
    bark
     oink

RONNIE
Grade 6

Jeremy tried to use some unusual language to evoke a scary feeling in his piece, "Night Wind":

Night Wind

The wind howls
The trees blow
The night creeps up on you
You slither down in covers
And you swiftly go to sleep
Then morning comes again.

JEREMY
Grade 5

Jennifer attempted a metaphor when she tried to describe the wind:

Cool, wild, whistling wind
Going through my hair
Like a comb.

JENNIFER
Grade 6

She did a similar thing with her "Milkweed" poem.

Milkweed

Waiting and waiting and waiting
in a pod.
Seeds keep waiting for a wind
to come until suddenly...

Whish
There they go
Gliding in the wind like silk butterflies
to their new home.

JENNIFER
Grade 6

Johnny tried to move beyond description to express some strong personal feelings in the following first draft of his "Puppet" poem:

I am on strings
Just like a puppet
Moving when I have to
Standing stiff
Until used again.

JOHNNY
Grade 6

Some might consider these images unimaginative and somewhat clichéd. Indeed, we knew they were not poetry. Yet pieces like these written by Ronnie, Jeremy, Jennifer, and Johnny showed us some potential was there if only we could guide the children toward expressing it.

Just as they had needed guidance with the reading of poetry, we realized they similarly needed guidance in writing it. We recognized they were explorers in new, uncharted territory. Maybe, we reasoned, they needed a map; some guidelines as to how one goes about creating a poem as well as some emotional support to help them over the rough spots along the way. We thought we could nudge them into new challenges while acknowledging the risks and tentative testing of the waters they were already attempting.

CHAPTER 8

Helping Children Learn to Help Themselves: Poetry and the Revision Process

Writing poetry is like baking bread. You have to shape it, knead it, punch it down, leave it alone for a while in a warm spot...then start again. Good poetry, like good bread, requires hard work.

SHERYL REED

Because the children seemed to have little understanding of how to write poetry, the teachers knew they had to first communicate some basic tenets about the process, particularly the idea that revision was an integral part. Children learn best, the teachers believed, when situations are created that challenge them, dislodging their current perceptions so that new ones can be created. If the children were ever to move from their current limited perceptions about writing poetry, they would need to become familiar with alternatives.

Revision was never required but the teachers strongly encouraged children to do it and frequently complimented those who had done much revising to create a poem. The process was often compared to using a scalpel. With a pencil, unnecessary verbiage was cut away to create a piece that was succinct and used the most appropriate words to describe the essence of something. One child (from another year's class) dubbed this "getting rid of the excess baggage" and was inspired to write the following poem to describe it:

Writing a poem
Is like piloting a plane
If it's not flying smoothly,
Throw out the excess baggage.

RAFE
Grade 3

Children were encouraged to view the writing process as analogous to baking bread, kneading, punching it down, leaving it alone, then kneading some more until satisfied that a unique statement had been made. They were told to cross out, brainstorm a list of words down the side of the page, add new ideas in tentatively with a caret, and so on. Messy pages were encouraged but erasures were not. Since the teachers realized first drafts revealed as much or more about a child's thinking as a final version, they told everyone to cross out rather than erase so the path followed to the last version was clear. Poems were never viewed as finished. Even when a poem had been checkmarked, children were encouraged to revisit it, maybe to consider a new perspective, change a word or play with the line pattern. In short, emphasis was on both process and product. Product was important but process, in which the true experimentation and thinking took place, was critical.

The teachers also tried to communicate several principles about writing poetry that they thought might make the process easier. One of the most basic was topic selection. Topics were never assigned—even at the beginning of the year. Peggy and Sheryl wanted the children to find their own voices and discover topics that had personal meaning. Initially, the children selected topics indiscriminately, reflecting a perception of poetry as something that had to be beautiful—what Livingston (1971) termed "Poetry with a capital P." But, as the students struggled to revise initial drafts, many quickly realized that creating something meaningful out of a vacuum was quite difficult. As Bryan stated, "If you don't know much about something, it's hard to revise."

In response to this, the teachers encouraged the children to write about things they knew—pets, holidays, seasons, and everyday experiences. When children wrote poems on these topics, the teachers would write comments in the margins like "this one has potential—play with it" or "This one really describes how ——— is." Children who continued to write about unicorns were asked questions they couldn't answer like "How do unicorns look?" or "How can you describe the unicorn more carefully?" They were encouraged to research and read more about something they had little knowledge of before attempting to write a poem about it.

The teachers also tried to help the children appreciate how poets go beyond the obvious and trite to make their poetry unique. Good poets, agreed Sheryl and Peggy, notice what others usually miss, seeing more comprehensively as well as perceiving unexpected relationships. Sheryl remarked to Shelly at one point: "What we're trying to get you to see here is that many poems are about ordinary things. Some of the most famous poets have written about very ordinary things. But by the way they've put their words together, or by using very few words, or doing something to make it uncommon or extraordinary, they've caught our attention." To get this point across, they would frequently point out interesting comparisons or particularly unique images in the work of professional poets. When reading Masters' "April," Sheryl commented, "Who would ever think of April as a roller-skating, scissor-grinding day, or ginghamwaisted." As she continued reading the poem, she pointed out other images. "'And the sidewalks overlaid with a glaze of yellow yellow like a jar of marmalade.' What is she talking about here?" she asked the group.

"The sun," responded Johnny.

"The sun," agreed Sheryl. "What a way to say it! She didn't say the sun shone on the sidewalk like marmalade, but listen, 'the sidewalk overlaid with a glaze of yellow yellow like a jar of marmalade'."

"I like how she said the mower. Read that [part] over," Jenny begged Sheryl.

Once again Sheryl read the requested lines aloud: "It's the mower gently mowing / and the stars like startled glass. / While the mower keeps on going / through a waterfall of grass."

"I like that," said Jenny. "Because that's what we have in springtime."

"Do you have a different picture of April? Is it somewhat different than any of the other poems you have read about spring or certain months of spring?" Sheryl asked the group. Her question was greeted with an enthusiastic chorus of "yes."

The teachers then tried to develop sensitivity to this concept in the children's writing by constantly suggesting they ask themselves whether or not their poem conveyed a thought, description or meaning in a unique way. To this end they continually asked, "Have you said something new or something old in a new way?" This line of questioning, they hoped, would lead the children to an appreciation of how poetry brings a new perspective to common and ordinary things.

Additionally, the teachers showed the children how professional poets subtly evoke a mood through indirect description, refined shadings of meaning, and judicious word selection without directly telling an intended meaning. Termed "showing, not telling," this idea was often discussed when poetry by professional poets was shared. For example, when Sheryl read aloud Moore's "Autumn Leaves", she told the children: "Listen to what she does with the leaves . . . She starts out in a very ordinary way, then she catches us up in it. Does she tell us about it? No, she shows us."

Similarly, when reading aloud Dickinson's "A Narrow Fellow in the Grass," Sheryl's response to Jennifer deepened the children's awareness of the poet's unusual description of how she felt about the snake.

"I like how she said she is scared of it," Jennifer commented.

"Yes," agreed Sheryl, "she writes 'zero to the bone' instead of telling us she is scared. She *shows* us how she feels about the snake."

"She didn't have to tell you 'cause you know she is getting scared," added Bryan.

"Right. She showed it. 'Tighter breathing' and 'zero at the bone' and right away we know that she was scared," said Sheryl.

The teachers then tried to extend this awareness to the children's own writing. Frequently, after reading a poem's initial draft, they would ask the writer, "How can you show the same thing without telling it?" Or they might suggest, "Try to say this so it conjures up a picture in someone's mind or makes them feel it."

These attitudes were always communicated informally. Sheryl and Peggy never sat the children down and taught these ideas as formal language arts lessons, complete with ditto sheets, fill-in-the-blank exercises, and punitive red ink marks on "wrong" answers. Rather, they helped the children become aware of what seems to work for many readers and writers.

They also frequently organized large- and small-group critiquing sessions during which they modeled the revision process. These sessions also served a second purpose: through them the teachers could support the children's initial tentative attempts at writing poetry, providing a forum to help them expand upon their original ideas and perceptions. Considering what had happened thus far, we knew this was critically important.

Small-Group Critiquing

The most frequent type of session was termed "small-group critiquing." These were organized in a rather informal manner. A teacher (usually Sheryl) would just announce she was critiquing and invite children who felt they needed help with a poem to participate.

Sometimes specific children were asked to join the group. These tended to be those the teachers had identified as "good critiquers" (and thus could be counted on to keep the session going) or those the teachers thought could benefit from the ideas of others but tended to avoid these groups.

Once the group was settled at the round table, she would usually work on each child's poem in turn, offering suggestions to one, encouraging another to try out an idea on his or her own, challenging a third to think of a different way to express a meaning, then returning to the first child to monitor progress. Peggy and Sheryl never deliberated ahead of time over which questions they would ask. Rather, they responded to the immediate conversation. They asked questions and made suggestions based on their knowledge of children and poetry. The children sometimes offered comments to help each other (particularly those who were good critiquers), but more commonly I observed them working quietly on their own poetry until their turn came.

I was particularly fascinated by the way the teachers moved back and forth from child to child, giving advice as well as checking on how they were doing. A session I observed in early October, which included both fifth and sixth graders, provides a good illustration of how this often occurred. In this example, Sheryl is working with Tommy on his "Wind" poem, Angela on "Sunrise," and Angie on "Halloween." Jennifer was also present, although Sheryl did not work as closely with her as she did with the others.

Sheryl began with Angela.

"Let's think about the sunrise and talk about it. What do you think of when you think of a sunrise? Just tell some of the things that it reminds you of and write them."

Sheryl turned to Jennifer. "Jennifer, do you still need me? Good, you figured it all out by yourself."

Sheryl then moved to Tommy. "Now, Tommy, could you use another form of the word riding?"

Tommy thought for a moment. "As I ride against the cool wind?"

"Let's listen to it." suggested Sheryl. "'As I'm riding against the cool wind' or 'as I ride against the cool wind.' Play with it and see which you like better."

Sheryl moved back to Angela.

"Why don't you list some things you notice about the sunrise?" she asked. "Not all sunrises are the same. Sometimes the look of the sky changes. Think of all these things."

She turned back to Tommy, to read another part of his

poem aloud. "Blowing up my shirt, blowing down my shirt, as I ride against the wind." "That sounds more poetic, Tommy. Now let's talk about the line patterns here and what you could do with that." They began experimenting with different line patterns, trying one thing, then another, to discover the most effective way to convey the exhilarating feeling one gets while riding a bike in the wind.

Leaving Tommy to sift through the possibilities they had generated, Sheryl moved to Angie. As with the others, she began by reading Angie's poem aloud:

> Snip, snip, clip, clip
> See the scissors cutting.
> Soon there will be gorgeous orange pumpkins
> many more will dance and haunt
> them til Halloween comes and passes.

"Hmm," said Sheryl thoughtfully, " 'many more will dance and haunt /them . . .' 'many more will dance and haunt . . .' What do you think, Angie? Does it sound better with 'them' or without 'them'? Why don't you play with that? Now let's talk about this word." She pointed to "passes" at the end of the poem. " 'You have til Halloween comes and passes.' What do you think? How could you cut out some things so that it sounds more poetic?"

Angie began to generate various possible words in the margins of her journal, crossing out some of her original ideas, inserting new ones into the poem only to cross these out and try still another idea. This was exactly what Sheryl had hoped would happen. She sensed the session had been helpful to the children.

Sometimes, instead of moving from child to child, the teacher would work extensively with one child and directly invite other children to comment, hoping this would help them understand the critiquing process better. This occurred when Sheryl began working with Johnny on his "Time" poem.

"Do you have something you want to share?" she asked him.

"I have this time poem I started," he responded. "But the last line kind of breaks it up."

"All right," said Sheryl, "Let's hear what you have so far."

Johnny read his poem aloud.

> People change with time
> In the future, in the past
> In the olden days
> People just get older.

"The last line needs to have some work on it," he again declared.

"Well, what are you thinking of changing?" Sheryl asked him. Johnny seemed stumped. He shrugged his shoulders and said, "I can't think of anything." Sheryl read the poem aloud several times, trying to get a sense of its rhythm and meaning.

"Okay, wait a minute. You're saying people are changing . . . then you're talking about the past. Where are the future, the past, or the olden days taking your poem?"

"Maybe I should take out the stuff about the past because . . . well, people change in the past, but we're talking about now," said Johnny.

"Yes, maybe," answered Sheryl, "But it may be just the word you need to carry you into the rest of the poem." (She read the poem aloud again.) "How could you work the past into the next line?"

Again, Johnny seemed unsure about how to proceed. Sheryl decided he might benefit from come additional ideas.

"Stacie, are you at a point where you can do some critiquing?" she asked. "We need some more people over here, especially sixth graders."

As Stacie moved to the table, Sheryl continued questioning Johnny, trying to help him find the focus of his piece.

"What's the main thing you're trying to get across to people, Johnny, when they read your poem?"

"To tell what happens with time?" he responded.

"What about using some figurative language here . . . a metaphor, or simile. . . . What might you do with something like that? What else changes with time?" Sheryl's voice trailed off as she waited for Johnny to think.

"Days change with time," he tentatively ventured.

"Okay . . . days change to what?" Sheryl asked again.

"Weeks," answered Johnny.

"All right," said Sheryl, "Days do *what* into weeks? People change with time and days do *what* into weeks?" She seemed to be trying to get Johnny to think divergently and consider unusual ways to describe change.

"They *grow* into weeks?" he offered.

"They *form* into weeks?" suggested Stacie.

"That's a good idea, Stacie," said Sheryl. "Listen, though, he had an interesting one."

Johnny read aloud:

People change with time
Like days grow into weeks.

Helping Children Learn to Help Themselves

"What do you think?" Sheryl asked him. "That's a good comparison because humans grow and days grow and change too. I like what you have so far."

Sheryl moved on to other children. Johnny, in contrast to his previous tentativeness, seemed confident and motivated as he vigorously scribbled ideas, experimenting with various words and meanings. He had received some precious gifts from Sheryl. First, his ideas had been praised as worthy, as having the potential to turn into something others would enjoy reading. Second, he had received specific help as to what was good, what could be changed to become better and why. Johnny had his "map" and with it he could continue on his own.

This is precisely what he did. Working independently, he created what I thought was a remarkable third line that expressed a universal truth in a simple, yet unique way: "the past is grandparent to the future." Maybe he would have thought of this without the stimulus provided by his teacher. I tend to think not. Working with Sheryl seemed to help him clarify and focus his ideas, illuminating the direction to go next.

Several days later Johnny once again brought his poem to Sheryl. She was amazed by what he had created but sensed he wasn't done yet.

"What else do you want to talk about?" she prodded. "Where are *you* in all this?"

"I am now," answered Johnny. "Hey, that sounds good, I'm gonna write it." The revised poem read as follows:

Time
(checkmarked version)

People change with time
Like days grow into weeks
The past is grandfather to the future
And I am now.

Sheryl beamed. "I think you've written something very beautiful. It's like generations of time. What do you think, Stacie?"

Stacie smiled and replied, "I love it! It's such an unusual way to say it."

Johnny could have earned no higher praise.

Johnny wasn't the only one to gain from these sessions. The others also benefited from the teachers' careful questioning about their pieces. For one thing, their work was affirmed as valuable. Both Peggy and Sheryl continually expressed appreciation for the new things the children tried or risks they had taken, regardless of the outcome. Additionally, they hoped the children were discovering how to help someone else make a poem better. The teachers were usually direct in pointing out which parts didn't quite work or make sense. Yet they tried to refrain from suggesting specific changes. They encouraged experimentation and offered alternatives rather than suggesting specific solutions. These were perspectives they hoped the children would assimilate and use.

Large-Group Critiquing with Teacher

These small group critiquing sessions were supplemented by similar ones held with the whole class. Both teachers felt these were as important as those held with small groups and individuals. It was in the large groups that the teachers could be assured all children had the opportunity to observe the critiquing process. Some children rarely attended a small group teacher-led critiquing session A few never did. The whole class situation exposed them to critiquing techniques that they could subsequently use in sessions with their friends.

The format was similar to that followed in the small group sessions with the exception that attention was always given to just one poem at a time. Usually someone would volunteer to read his or her current poem-in-progress aloud, then invite peer response. Sometimes a child who was working on something particularly interesting or who hadn't done much critiquing would be asked to present his or her ideas to the group.

A fifteen-minute session I observed in March was typical. Held as usual at the end of the day, the entire group gathered in one corner of the room. Sheryl began by discussing the concept of haiku. She asked the children to tell her some of the characteristics of this genre. One by one they responded, revealing their familiarity with haiku through their many experiences reading and writing it.

"Brandon, why don't you read us your 'Spring' poem," Sheryl suggested. "It's a good example of haiku."

Brandon, who was normally a shy, quiet child, stood up proudly and read his poem to the group:

> A brook moves slowly
> Carrying signs of spring
> Into sweet summer.

"I used alliteration to make it sound more poetic," he told the group.

"Like what?" asked Sheryl.

" 'Signs of spring' and 'sweet summer' and stuff like that," he responded.

"I like how it sounds," said Carrie. "It's real slow-moving like a creek is in the summer."

"Is he true to his subject?" Sheryl asked the group. Her question was greeted by an enthusiastic chorus of "Yes!"

The group was next asked to respond to a haiku by Jimmy tentatively titled "Deer." Jimmy had volunteered to share his poem because he couldn't think of a good word for the second line. Sheryl suggested he read it aloud, leave a blank, then invite suggestions:

In leaf crisp forest
Deer ——— in the fall leaves
Leap away soundless.

When he finished, Sheryl turned to the class. "What does 'leaf crisp forest' tell you?"

"It's fall," answered a chorus of voices.

"Yes, now, what did he do here?" Sheryl asked the group.

"He showed," commented Johnny.

"Yes, he showed us fall without saying fall," answered Sheryl. "Now what word do you actually have here?"

"Dear *roam* in fall leaves," answered Jimmy.

"What about prance?" suggested Ronnie.

"Everybody uses that," said Jimmy.

"Yes, that's about worn out, isn't it?" said Sheryl. "What else could deer do in the forest?"

Various children offered ideas such as "play," "eat," "leap," and "wander."

"What are some other words for 'leap'?" Sheryl asked to get them thinking more divergently.

There was a silence while everyone thought. Johnny ran over to the bookshelf and found the thesaurus, turning to the page with "leap" on it.

" 'Scamper' . . . 'spring' . . . 'bolt' . . . 'bound' . . . 'vault' . . . 'run away,' " he read.

"I don't think 'bound' sounds good," said Brandon. "It makes it sound like the deer are moving up and down rather than forward."

The children began discussing the merits of using various words. Sheryl continually suggested they keep in mind how real deer move so they could make a conscious decision as to which word would best fit Jimmy's poem. Jimmy finally decided "vault" was the best word to describe what he really wanted to say and wrote it in the appropriate spot in his book. He seemed to have a new perspective and revived interest in refining his poem. I watched him work on revisions for several days. He wrote busily, erased, thought, and wrote some more. Finally, he shared the checkmarked version with me.

Haiku

In leaf crisp forests
Deer bed down. When frightened, they
Vault away soundlessly.

JIMMY
Grade 6

Although Jimmy's poem reflected his own original thinking, he certainly had gained much from sharing his poem with the members of the class as did they. Not only did they learn about the importance of selecting the most precise word, but they also learned how one goes about giving and receiving help with poetry. Most importantly, they realized that being critiqued was not a scary experience but rather a time when support and validation of a friend's efforts were offered.

Writing Poetry Is Like Making Bread

Bread baking is an art. One is given a recipe to follow, but good bread requires ingenuity and a creative hand because the recipe is never exact: "Add flour until smooth." "Use a pinch of salt to taste." You then add the various ingredients to create a variation to suit your personal taste. Once the ingredients are measured and sifted you knead it, punch it down, then knead some more—molding it into the shape you want.

This is just what the teachers wanted the children to do with the writing of poetry. Sheryl and Peggy provided the basic ingredients, which would nurture the development of the children's work. But the children were then encouraged to incorporate their own ideas and experiences into the writing. Just as with bread baking, guidance was offered, but the children were encouraged to find their own way in the company of others engaged in the same process.

The evolution of one of Ronnie's poems showed how far the children had come in their understanding of all this. Through the year we saw Ronnie's pieces change from silly and nonsensical to work that reflected his exposure to well-written published poems and to the ideas he gleaned about poetry from his teachers and peers.

He collected every ingredient he could find as he basked in his newfound awareness of poetic form. He became particularly intrigued by the subjects poets chose for their poems and as a result soon began to more carefully examine his own choices.

One spring day when his dog was killed on the road before school, Ronnie was ready to put together everything he had been assimilating about poetry with his own deep feelings about the experience. He came to Sheryl, seeking a word that would precisely describe the way blood and life had slowly left his pet. Together, they talked about words, looking up possible choices in the thesaurus. Simultaneously Sheryl encouraged him to talk about why this had happened to his dog and how he felt about it. After a morning of searching, Ronnie chose the word "seeping" as the best one to describe what he had witnessed.

The cooks were angry with us that day. No one even thought about lunch. We were all gathered in a bunch before the chalkboard for a spontaneous whole-class sharing session. Ronnie had shared his poem, then asked for help on creating a title. Out of the hushed and reverent silence that followed his reading came the first idea, then several others. Soon eight to ten suggestions filled the board. We all voted for "Crossing the Line," which Ronnie himself had originally proposed. " 'It crossed the line' means more than crossing the white line in the road," he told the group. They listened with growing respect as Ronnie explained the dual meaning: "My dog did get hit when it crossed the line into the other lane on the road, but I also meant that it crossed the line from life to death."

"Say it one more time, Ronnie, say it again," the children begged, with awe in their voices. Ronnie said it again:

Crossing the Line

The children prayed
For the dog,
For that day
It crossed the line,
And in an instant
Lay helpless,
Seeping life.

RONNIE
Grade 6

Ronnie had crossed the line in his evolving writing style. He had successfully used the ingredients of poetry and shaped them to fit his own purpose.

CHAPTER 9

Classroom Environment: Supporting Children Writing Poetry

Never say
  you won't do well.
Never say
  you can't do swell.
Never say your poem is dumb,
  and give it thumbs up
  when you're done!

"Facts about Poems"
KELLEY
Grade 3

"I finally finished 'August'!" Jennifer told me triumphantly one day in late April. "Hooray!" I told her. "You've been working on that poem a long time." And so she had. Since early February, Jennifer had played with words, manipulated lines and experimented with different images—all to get just the effect she wanted.

Jennifer had originally titled the poem "April" and had written it in response to hearing Marcia Masters' poem "April" read aloud. Her rough draft consisted of a series of images that she associated with that month:

April
(Revision 1)

April is a child to March.
April is a daisy opening up into the world.
April is a daisy opening.

April is a daisy.
April is a mother to May.
April is a daisy opening up.
April is a lamb, baaing down to sleep.
April is a bird singing in May.
April is a bird chirping to wake up it's child.

For weeks, Jennifer periodically returned to the poem, trying out different images she associated with April and experimenting with various line patterns. Although she was intrigued by the subject, she was not yet satisfied with the ideas she was associating with it. Then one day in early April, she crossed out everything except the lines, "April is a child to March" and "April is a mother to May," deciding to focus on the idea of months as succeeding generations. But April somehow didn't seem to be the best month for sustaining this metaphor.

"I think August is better," she told me. "Because everything gets kind of older and dies after August."

She started over. Using August as the central focus and the idea of successive generations as the theme of her piece, she once again experimented with ideas, images, and patterns. When she finally showed the piece to me, she was elated to have conveyed a unique idea in just a few short lines:

August
(checkmarked version)

August is a
child of July,

Mother
To September

Grandmother
to October,

And a faded memory
to November.

JENNIFER
Grade 6

I was struck by the fact that Jennifer had been given the time, opportunity, and encouragement to pursue this piece until she reached a satisfying conclusion. How unusual to have such freedom in school! Her efforts made it clear there was still another essential ingredient in the poetry-making process: the classroom environ-ment. The supportive, nurturing environment created in this class-room encouraged the children to experiment; to take risks and dream dreams that they felt comfortable expressing in poetry.

As I sat among the children, watching as well as participating in the swirl of activities, I began to identify several interwoven themes in the tapestry of classroom life. These included the sanc-tioning of peer interaction, flexibility in time, communication of adult fallibility, support for experimentation, acknowledgment of the struggle involved in writing, the use of focused praise, and the establishing of clear, well-defined expectations. Each of these fac-tors will be described as to its contribution to supporting the chil-dren as they made tentative, then increasingly more confident attempts at writing poetry.

Sanctioning Peer Interaction

These teachers not only valued peer interaction, they actively en-couraged it by organizing activities that caused the children to work cooperatively with each other. Often they would directly suggest that talk be an integral part of children's interactions with writing poetry. To this end, Sheryl made the following statement early in the year to the class:

> We [the teachers] feel you need to be talking while you're writing. Play with ideas together. Other people can ask you about your poem. You then consider, "Do these suggestions mean anything to me?" "Do these help my poem?"

Another time she gathered a group together, then tried to extricate herself so they would begin working more independently, telling them:

> I have a feeling that if I moved away you could talk a little more about it, right? . . . You get started talking about ideas— things to write about. Write about things you know. Keep in mind that using words that start with the same sound helps rhythm . . . I want you to talk. I want to hear some talking.

At other times, the teachers would directly invite someone to attend a critiquing group or solicit help from a friend. "Anyone interested in giving ideas in a small critiquing group should come over here now," one would announce. Or "We could use a couple more people. Some of you don't involve yourself in these revision groups, and it would really help your writing." Inevitably a small group would gather.

Several children were perceived as catalysts for the critiquing process as they were able to keep things moving in a purposeful way, often imitating the teachers' styles and even specific wording. As a result, the teachers often suggested that someone work with these children to "learn the ropes" as Sheryl told Matt when he asked for help.

"Go over to Jimmy or Carrie and ask them to help you. Johnny knows how to do this and so does Jennifer. They'll show you how to improve your poem."

The teachers monitored these activities in several indirect ways. Often children who had worked together in a particularly effective way would be praised. As Peggy told one group:

> Tommy and Jeremy worked together a long time yesterday and got a lot done. Jeremy has a good poem started and got a lot of ideas from Tommy.

The praise was usually focused, providing clues as to the specific strategies that differentiated productive from unproductive groups. Sometimes unproductive associations were gently alluded to:

> Lesa, you always work with Tammy. How about Angie? Has she helped you some? You're going to have to be more critical to get good advice about poems.

Usually in such cases, alternative strategies were offered so that the children would work more productively in the future.

Rather than constantly trying to keep the children quiet, Sheryl and Peggy viewed peer interaction as a valuable and integral part of learning about poetry. They firmly believed that collaborative learning, in which children explored and negotiated their tentative understandings with one another, was essential. The children quickly realized talking was okay, thus they began regularly forming their own critiquing groups.

Time

Time is an elusive yet critical aspect of a classroom environment. Long stretches of time to think, to make false starts or to explore new, sometimes meandering paths are essential to good writing. Yet we seldom allow for this kind of time in our schools. We segment it; put it in little boxes labeled "reading," "math," or "language," rarely giving enough time for one subject to spill over into another.

This classroom was different. The schedule was quite fluid and flexible, changing in response to specific tasks, evolving interests or

Building a Community of Poetry Writers

individual needs. As Sheryl remarked to me once, "We have an idea where we're going—a flexible idea. But if that's not working right we're open to changes."

Time was particularly flexible across weeks. Although certain assignments had to be completed every day (math, for example), the children were allowed to determine how much and when time could be spent on other projects. This was particularly true for poetry. Often, children would work on the same poem over several months, putting down an initial idea, leaving it, then returning later to make revisions. This led not to discontinuity but rather to the creation of poetry that was complex in both thought and form.

Conversely, if someone wanted to work intensely on one poem for a day or two, even to the point of temporarily neglecting other things, that was fine. The teachers believed everything balanced out in the end. If inspiration struck they wanted the children to feel free to pursue their ideas.

The daily schedule had more definite parameters although flexibility was still permitted and encouraged within these broad guidelines. Children were required to make a daily poetry entry, participate in daily group math lessons, work on projects if a theme was in progress, and read a certain number of pages in their self-selected, and in-depth discussion books. Once these tasks were completed, how one structured the rest of the day was left to individual choice. Sometimes the children arrived early, stayed late or chose to stay in from recess completing required tasks at these times so as to free their work time for more personally interesting activities like poetry.

Because the children knew they were expected to do something with poetry every day they could plan ahead for writing at night in bed, on the playground, or on the way to school. Often, children would enter the classroom in the morning and immediately pull out their poetry journals telling me, "I thought of an idea last night, and I got to write it down before I forget it." When Angela shared the evolution of her "Sunrise" poem with me, she stated she'd gotten the original idea from riding in the car to Columbus one Saturday. She'd taken her poetry journal with her to get some ideas for the next week and was struck by the beauty of the early morning landscape. In another instance I observed Peggy with Angie examining an unusual little weed growing by a rock in the corner of the playground.

"That little weed looks so lonely there," Angie commented. "That would be a good thing to write about for a poem."

Peggy agreed. I later noticed Angie had written a rough draft of "The Little Weed" as her poetry entry for the day.

It seemed the children perceived time in this classroom as flexible yet predictable. It was this option to control time rather than be controlled by it that was a critical factor in nurturing thoughtful, more complex responses to poetry.

Support for Experimentation

Flexibility in time was coupled with a similar flexibility in thinking. Children were encouraged to experiment and consider alternatives to the obvious. As Sheryl commented to me once after school:

> You always have to ask them [the children]...what are the possibilities here? I think we should constantly challenge them to look at all sides of a thing. Maybe one person can see something from quite another viewpoint and open everyone else's minds where they had been closed before.

The children were continually told, "Think of possibilities." "Play with it." "Say something old in a new way." So when Sheryl was helping Jeremy with his "Train" poem in which he described the train as "speeding down the track," she asked him, "What are the possibilities here? How else could you say the train was going fast?"

This experimentation did have limits. Although the children were encouraged to explore various possibilities for expressing their ideas and feelings, nonsense was clearly frowned upon. Purposeful nonsense like that used by Lewis Carroll in "Jabberwocky" was fine. In fact Jennifer experimented with writing nonsense poems in the style of Carroll. But random, unrelated thoughts or ideas put together merely for the sake of creating a rhyme or a description, and which were completely illogical, were not encouraged.

Teachers Are People Too

Both teachers regularly espoused a personal conviction that adults are fallible, subject to the same frustrations in writing and understanding poetry that children experience. To communicate this they would pull out their own poetry journals, showing the children how various poems had evolved as well as how they had struggled through the writing process. As Sheryl remarked to two children during one of these sessions, "This one [poem] I couldn't finish— it's one I could never get to work out. I never even did a revision, but I did a lot of thinking about it....I knew what I was trying to say but I couldn't get the right words in the right order." The children were sympathetic.

"Yeah," responded one. "Like you know what you're gonna

write but then when you write it you just can't think of how to put it." Another time Sheryl told the children how a certain poem evolved from an experience she found intriguing:

> You know the spider webs that are made along fence rows? I tried to write a poem about them....I'm still struggling with it. The whole poem is down but it doesn't say exactly what I felt. You can't see those delicate spider webs unless the dew or rain is on them. Suddenly, they are transformed...I just had to stop my car to write down what I saw. I'm still playing with it, but I don't have it right yet.

How human she sounded. Here was an adult who didn't claim to have all the answers and know everything. This must have been so freeing to these children who were entering adolescence, continually conscious of having to be grown up and perfect.

In addition to sharing their frustrations, the teachers also encouraged the children to comment on their work. As a result critiquing sessions focusing on the teachers' poems were common. Often these sessions were initiated by the children as when Jimmy and Johnny pulled out Sheryl's journal.

"Why don't we have a writing session with your book?" suggested Johnny to Sheryl. "You give me good ideas."

"Do mine? Why don't we?" she answered. "I haven't written anything for a long time. Maybe you can help me."

The children seemed to enjoy the opportunity to turn the tables and critique the work of a familiar adult. They also incidentally learned how to conduct such sessions in a constructive manner.

It was evident to the children that their teachers felt compelled to write poetry even though they perceived it as a challenging undertaking. Further, they were comfortable sharing their frustrations with the children and, in fact, believed it was essential that the children realized even adults struggled and sometimes failed. Their attitude seemed to help the children become more relaxed, more willing to take risks with poetry. Because no model of perfection existed against which their own tentative attempts would be measured, they felt free to follow their own voices. The climate of collaboration—an equal partnership between teachers and children engaged in a complex, yet ultimately satisfying, process—supported their efforts.

Supporting the Struggle

The teachers also felt it was important to continually support those who were struggling with the process of creating a poem. Thus, when Jennifer complained that her poem wouldn't "come out right," Sheryl told her:

> Do you know that's a plague of every poet and every writer? Everyone who tries to write poetry has ... problems at one time or another trying to get down what is in their heads. Because oftentimes it's an image, a picture, or an idea. Then when you try to write that down ... you can't find the words to say what you are feeling or thinking. Don't get discouraged because I tell you when you first start to write sometimes it is very difficult ... but it will come—don't despair.

When Bryan became convinced that he would never get his limerick, "Caterpillerick," the way he wanted it, Sheryl told him: "Keep at it. Keep reaching out and reaching deep inside yourself too. You'll get it." How reassuring for children like Jennifer and Bryan to know that their frustrations were acceptable; shared by all of us who try to express ourselves in writing.

Sometimes, sensing general frustration with revising, Sheryl would bring the whole class together for a pep talk. One such session occurred in November after a day in which there was general grumbling about having to work so hard to create a good poem.

"You're finding that writing poetry isn't easy, is it?" Sheryl told the group. "It takes years and years of experience to write well and it takes a lot of willingness to do what?"

"Revise," responded one child.

"Yes, revise. That's a big key because you don't just slap a poem down and have that be it. What did we find out about Frost?"

"He writes beautiful poems," answered Angela, who had just finished a biography about Frost and was now deep into a book of his collected poems.

"They are beautiful, aren't they?" said Sheryl. "It just seems like they must have come out so easily. But do you know how many poems he wrote without revising? Anybody know? He wrote one poem that he didn't revise. ... So take heart ... you are not going to be able to sit down and write a poem in a first draft. ... You don't have to take every poem to a revised conclusion. They are always there if you keep them. They are always there to go back to." The group left this session with a more positive attitude towards poetry as something challenging to write yet with potentially rich rewards for both writer and reader.

It seems that sharing their own struggles as well as those of professional writers in conveying precisely what one's mind envisions assured the children that struggling was part of the process.

It also allowed them to openly feel frustrated and anxious about their work.

Indeed they sometimes did. Once I observed Carrie who had made several unsuccessful starts on a new piece, throw down her pencil and say, "I hate poems! I'm having a hard time working with them." Yet after taking some time out to talk with friends as well as Sheryl, she returned to her piece with renewed enthusiasm and wrote an unusual poem that compared snowflakes to children playing tag.

Similarly, Mandy had worked repeatedly with friends and both teachers, but she still felt dissatisfied with her "Milkweed" piece. She confided to me in exasperation, "I'm never gonna finish this poem!" Peggy, realizing her frustration, encouraged her to keep going because the poem had "wonderful possibilities." She showed Mandy which lines had potential. Encouraged, Mandy returned to work and eventually created a piece that described milkweed as "a fluttering flying bird" that "meets a cloud in the sky."

Offering Praise and Feedback

The kind of response Peggy offered Mandy with her "Milkweed" poem was very important. Not only did it help her get through some of her initial struggles with a piece, but it also showed her that her efforts were valued. This was true for the other children as well. Comments like "I love the way you started that" or "That's an unusual way to start a poem" or "That's so beautiful, it made my skin crawl" or "You have some good stuff in that poem—keep working on it" helped to communicate which aspects of their work were good, thus more purposefully directing their efforts.

Often the teacher's comments were focused and quite direct. They pointed out a particularly good line or a play on words, suggesting the child retain that element or even revise so as to build the poem around it. When Angie shared the second version of her "Seashell" poem, Sheryl told her, "You know, when you revised, you lost the best part of your original poem, the part that was unusual."

She pointed to the particular line in Angie's journal.

"Go back to your original and work on that idea."

Or when Shelly sought feedback on her "Autumn Leaves" poem, Peggy told her, "It would be good to expand the last line. Think about *how* the leaves crackle and crunch when you land."

The teachers also wanted the children to become reliant on their own ideas and those of their peers rather than constantly seeking adult approval and guidance. To this end they constantly endeavored to help the children make their own decisions on what

Classroom Environment

should be revised or retained in their poetry. If they thought a child was becoming too teacher dependent, they would deliberately step back and try to refocus their comments so as to support the child's own ideas.

This was not always easy. It was tempting to try to help a child "fix" things by suggesting specific ideas. Sometimes the children sensed this and tried to persuade a teacher to supply ideas, useful phrases or appropriate words. But Peggy and Sheryl knew the children would never develop independence if they were allowed to go on what Graves (1983) termed "writer's welfare."

They also believed the process of writing poetry was too personal for someone to dictate a poem's specific form or content to the writer. Yet sometimes in spite of themselves, they would become too directive. When they realized this was happening, they would try to step back and encourage the child to go it alone and rely on his or her own resources. As Peggy told Lesa who was requesting a good word for a particular line, "*You* need to just list several things first. You see, if I give them to you, then you're not going to be in that poem. You think of some ideas, then we'll start playing around with it as a group."

Ultimately, the children were encouraged to believe in themselves and their own ideas. The teachers would provide suggestions and encouragement. The final decision, however, as to what went in a poem was ultimately the writer's.

Freedom Within Limits: Establishing Expectations

Although both teachers encouraged interaction, experimentation, and divergent thinking, the environment was never chaotic nor could their attitude towards the children's activities be characterized as laissez-faire. Rather, a sense of order and common purpose was created through the articulation of clear, explicit expectations for both appropriate behavior and task completion. These guidelines were always general, presented as parameters within which children could exercise much self-determination. Nevertheless, they provided limits.

At the beginning of the year, these expectations were most often communicated in large group meetings called "planning time." Generally, during these meetings teachers would describe the nature and purpose of various activities that could occur that day, then discuss how such activities might be completed. Often specific examples were used for emphasis and clarity. Additionally, children were usually reminded that they would be held accountable for their work by reporting at the day's end.

As the year progressed, these formal teacher-directed planning sessions met less frequently. Usually, they were held on Monday to set the tone for the week, then held once or twice more during the week as needed. General daily expectations would be written on the board and children would be expected to refer to these guidelines as they pursued the day's tasks. Sometimes Peggy gave the fifth graders planning sheets that detailed suggested activities they might pursue that week.

In addition to direct statements as to what was expected the teachers used peer modeling as a means of communicating their expectations. For example, they would often ask children to share work in progress, thereby providing a peer model of expected response, as well as a source of new ideas for the other children. Both teachers also regularly recommended that children directly examine a friend's poetry journal to get a better idea of how things were done. This assistance transcended grade levels. Children sought help from a close friend or available willing peer, regardless of age.

This use of peer examples was not confined to work done solely by current class members. Anthologies of favorite poems, poetry notebooks, and illustrations of peer-written poetry, created by children from previous years, served as additional resources for transmitting expectations. Children would often pull out those old journals to examine them, commenting to a friend about the neat ideas or declaring, "I'm gonna write a poem like Eddie's 'Combine' poem."

The teachers did not automatically assume the children would fulfill tasks in a disciplined manner. Rather, they regularly monitored student activities providing encouragement, feedback, and sometimes direct assistance to help children follow established procedures. Sometimes monitoring took the form of subtle "checkups" that were designed to determine if children were keeping up with their work. For example, one day early in the year Sheryl was concerned that the sixth-grade boys hadn't had a particularly productive morning. That afternoon she decided to check and see what had in fact occurred.

"Hey, Ronnie, bring your poetry book over here," she said. "Let's see where you are with it. Brian, did you get today's poetry done? Do you have time to do it now?"

"I got it done this morning," Brian told her.

"Good, I'm glad you're not behind," Sheryl told him. "What I don't want you to get into is a position where you have to play catch-up and you become overwhelmed." She then turned to Jimmy R.

"Jimmy, did you feel good about what you did this morning?

Did you get everything done? Would you like to get to the point where you can come to share and have something to show? Where could you best accomplish that? Over here at a group table or over there where you were?"

"When I work in a group," said Jimmy.

"Okay, why don't you go there this afternoon?" Sheryl suggested.

At other times this monitoring took the form of praise for those who had successfully adhered to established expectations. Students who had toiled over multiple revisions or given particularly helpful advice to a friend would be complimented. The implications seemed to be that if one experimented and took risks within the agreed upon behavioral parameters, one's responses would be seen as appropriate.

Occasionally, more direct statements were necessary to convey the message that some children were not doing what was expected. This was usually done in a large group session. Teachers would discuss a problem (such as a generally unproductive morning), then describe possible consequences if the problem was not resolved. Thus, they might say, "You'll be discussing your own poems this afternoon so you'll need to be prepared to do some talking." At other times, specific comments would be directed to an individual or small group as when Peggy was helping a small group of children illustrate their poems. She turned to another table and said, "I think you may be talking about something that doesn't have anything to do with school." She was right. The group immediately resumed working on poetry.

Supporting the Journey

Jennifer's "August" could not have been created in a traditional environment. Most classrooms require children to conform to teacher-created boundaries of time, correctness, and behavior. Such boundaries can be intimidating, compelling children to hide their own ideas until they figure out what it is they're "supposed" to say and do.

In contrast, Jennifer had a place where she could feel free to experiment; to move in one direction, then deviate to move down a new, previously unexplored path, and she could take as much time as she wished for her wanderings. Such journeys might end unexpectedly in a dead end. Yet we believed these explorations— dead ends included—were essential for the children's growth into

Building a Community of Poetry Writers

poetry writers. Our task was to recognize and approve even the smallest, seemingly insignificant steps taken—and to provide the impetus for the journeys. We hoped this would help Jennifer and the other children find their way.

CHAPTER 10

Writing Poetry:
Children Help Each Other

What metamorphosis
Are you going through—
From a caterpillar
To a mysterious chrysalis?

With silk wings
To the naked eye
Stretch out that silk,
Butterfly.

ANNE
Grade 3

And find their own way they did. Although appropriate and timely teaching does not usually lead to immediate results, these interactions still leave their mark. Good teaching can nudge along natural development, providing the impetus that helps children put it all together. This is exactly what happened. In their own way, the children surprised us by what they had learned about writing poetry. Just as they began to appreciate good poetry, to comment on an artfully developed metaphor or seek out pieces with particularly pleasing images or rhythms to read together, so they began to help each other write pieces that reflected their awareness of these notions. Because the teachers had supported their initial attempts at writing poetry, providing a map for how to do it as well as an environment that encouraged experimentation, the children began doing this on their own. Many would still meet with a teacher to get help with a particular piece. Much of the writing and thinking, however, was done in the company of trusted friends who provided encouragement and suggestions for making a piece "sound more poetic."

Peer Writing Communities

Just as various small poetry reading communities developed, so did various writing communities. And just as the children sought out classmates like Carrie or Jimmy who could be counted on to keep a reading session going, they would similarly often seek out "good critiquers" like Aaron, Jennifer, or Stacie when they needed specific help with a poem in progress. But most eventually became committed to a regular group of friends to which they inevitably turned when they wanted assistance with improving a poem. Usually these were the same children with whom they shared published poetry.

As January skated into February, then into the slushy days of March, we were daily amazed by how the children were increasingly able to provide substantive help for each other. Of course there were times when they would get silly and mess around. But for the most part we were observing many instances of active and constructive assistance. Emphasis seemed to have shifted from the "turn taking" we'd observed at the beginning of the year to "sense making"—to a collaborative effort at refining a poem's meaning through precise word choice, reorganization of lines, logical thinking, and the like.

That the children had internalized what the teachers had modeled was clear from many of their statements. I would frequently hear echoes of Sheryl and Peggy as I watched the children talking together. Jennifer would tell Angela to "play with it" or Aaron would ask Mike H., "Now what do you want your reader to get out of this poem?" Sometimes such comments were prefaced by a statement explaining that a teacher's behavior was deliberately being imitated. I overheard Deon tell Angie, "I'm being Mrs. Reed now: what are you trying to say here?" Usually the children seemed unaware their statements reflected an adult model. They had made these comments and ideas part of their own critiquing repertoire, shaped to fit their personal needs and purposes.

Of course some groups were more productive than others; they stayed on task, provided more focused assistance, and moved each other beyond superficial ideas. Initially we thought the more productive groups were those formed by the sixth graders. As we observed more carefully and became attuned to the subtle interactions and seemingly casual comments made between friends, however, we realized that the fifth graders too had discovered how to help each other. What seemed to make the difference was not so much grade level as it was willingness to experiment with poetry. These children who participated regularly in teacher-led critiquing groups, offered comments in large-group sharing sessions and who read great quantities of poetry to each other were invariably those who worked well in the peer writing communities, regardless of age.

I did observe several children who regularly wrote alone or who seemed to deliberately detach themselves from a group to write. I was curious about this phenomenon, particularly since group work was such a prominent part of life in this classroom. As I casually questioned these children, I discovered several reasons for their behavior. Some children, like Jennifer and Jeremy, frankly preferred working alone on their own poems. Both told me they accomplished more on their own and thought the other children rarely gave them ideas that got at the true essence of what they wanted to say. Still, they would often join groups to help others with their pieces and occasionally sought help with their own.

Other children, like Jimmy, would cite "solo writing" as the best way to really concentrate on a poem. Generally a child like Jimmy would conceive the original idea for a poem in private, then share the piece with friends, soliciting suggestions for revision.

With other children, it was a matter of logistics. A few children were out of the room often for special tutoring, making it difficult for them to participate in the continuous, informal interactions that tended to meld a group together. These children tended to work on their own or move from one group to another on the basis of accessibility rather than shared purpose.

Despite these individual idiosyncracies, the children were not fragmented into insular groups that functioned completely separated from each other like cogs in a wheel that never manage to mesh. Often, Peggy and Sheryl would temporarily bring different children together to give them fresh ideas or to expose them to children who used more sophisticated critiquing techniques. Sometimes the children themselves moved between groups for similar reasons. Many seemed to know instinctively when they needed to expand their horizons and get a new perspective on their poetry. The dynamics were open and flowing. Children had a home base from which they could explore to get fresh insights, then return enriched, bringing renewed vitality to the interplay among group members.

The Nature of Peer Assistance

As the children became more aware of how to help each other, I discerned recurring patterns in the kinds of assistance they provided. Sitting among them, watching as well as sometimes participating in the ebb and flow of their conversations, I noticed that particular themes wove continually through their talk. These included providing honest praise and feedback, serving as an audience, supplying ideas, and clarifying meanings.

Providing Honest Praise and Feedback

Just as the teachers provided support for those who were struggling with initial drafts and ideas, peers began offering similar assistance. As they became used to each other and more familiar with the critiquing process, their comments became more focused, often addressing specific aspects of a poem as well as recognizing the writer's struggle to create it. I began hearing statements like "this is a good poem—the words just roll around in my head" or (in an awed voice) "I love your poem, you really showed me about spring."

One of the most common ways positive comments were offered was through what I termed "inventorying." When inventorying, children would review their poetry journal with a friend, labeling the contents, pointing out checkmarked poems, rereading favorites and identifying "beginnings" that held possibilities for further revision.

Ostensibly this was done to index a poetry collection. But comments like "This is your best one" or "Remember when we worked on this one?" showed it had another purpose. Inventorying seemed to reassure the children of past successes, allowing them to review what they knew and had control over before tackling new tasks. The presence of a friend who was similarly involved in the process provided additional validation that one's previous efforts were appropriate. This legacy of past satisfactions and successes then provided the impetus to work through new challenges.

Critical comments also became more focused, often specifying particular modifications. When Jenny S. read her "Time" poem to Stacie, her friend responded, "You've got some good ideas, but it doesn't have any rhythm. It does at first . . . then it drops off."

"Should I reline it?" asked Jenny.

"Yeah, that might help," Stacie told her.

Johnny and Jimmy were particularly good at constructively supporting other children's efforts. Johnny would often combine a suggestion for change with praise for another aspect of a person's poem. I often heard him say things like "That's good. I really like the part where you . . ." or "That's perfect, except for the last line, where you could . . ." I frequently observed Jimmy sitting quietly reading through a friend's poetry journal on request, then writing encouraging notes in the margin. The others usually found these ideas helpful and in turn began offering more focused comments themselves as a result of this modeling.

Some children, like Kellie, never did feel comfortable critiquing a friend's work. Even when directly solicited for help, Kellie rarely offered assistance as seen in the following incident with her friend Deon. Deon first asked for some general help.

"You guys, tell me how this poem sounds," she requested. She then turned to Kellie and directly asked: "Kellie, any comments?" Kellie looked at Deon's poetry notebook but offered no response.

Deon began to get a bit exasperated. "Kellie, just come out and say it."

Still no response. Kellie returned the book to Deon and smiled shyly at her but seemed unwilling to venture any kind of opinion.

"Okay," said Deon, finally. "Just tell me if you don't like it, like it, or medium like it."

At this point Carrie grabbed Deon's book and responded to her plea. Kellie looked distinctively relieved.

Peer approval and honest feedback was important. As children experimented with how best to express their poetic voices, they tried out their ideas with peers involved in a similar struggle. As a result the pieces evolved in an atmosphere of mutual trust and support, critical elements for creative expression.

Serving as an Audience

Poetry is meant to be read aloud. The words not only must convey meaning but also must appeal to the ear. It is through reading aloud that both these qualities become evident. Furthermore, poetry seems to almost beg for a reaction from the reader, even if it is just a shared laugh over a humorous rhyme or a request to read it again.

The children became intuitively aware of this. Often friends would gather to share each other's poems, making changes, then rereading them aloud to gauge the effect. For example, when Mike J. and Aaron were working together on Mike's "Green Predator" poem, Mike crossed out several words in his poem and added some new ones Aaron suggested. Mike then said, "Okay, let's read it, let's see how it sounds." His words seemed poetic, as if working with the poem had cast a spell on his everyday way of talking.

Another time I watched Carrie work intently by herself on a

Halloween poem, then move to the writing community of fifth-grade girls who were working at their usual table.

"Read it aloud for me," she told them. Dolly took the poem and read it with much expression, emphasizing the "scary" words.

"Oh, that's good!" the girls said, shivering. "Add more scary words."

They read the poem aloud again, stopping at various points to suggest ideas to make the poem scarier. Carrie's efforts had definitely been rewarded. For her and the other children, friends served as appreciative respondents for sharing the joy of a poem's sound or the emotion evoked by its words.

Supplying Ideas

Throughout the year children relied on their friends to provide ideas for topics. With time the ideas became increasingly focused. In one instance, for example, Dolly, Mandy, Robin, and Tiffany (all fifth graders) organized a topic brainstorming session. They began by dividing a small portable chalkboard into quadrants, then put each girl's initials in one quadrant. They then brainstormed possible topics for poems, including "cats," "love," "friendship," and "mystery." Each topic was written in a section until every girl had at least three ideas written under her name. A debate then followed in which they argued for the merits of one topic over another. Finally, a vote was taken. The group decided to each write a friendship poem, then compare the resulting pieces to get "different ideas for writing about friendship."

Usually, however, suggestions for topics were offered more informally. Sometimes children would exchange poetry journals with a friend, leafing through each other's book to get ideas from titles, indexes, or idea pages. Deon, for instance, suggested a book exchange to Kellie, telling her, "Let me get some ideas off your poetry book and you can get some off mine." Journals left behind by previous class members were scrutinized for the same purpose. I would frequently find children in a corner, surrounded by these journals, busily writing down ideas on scraps of paper or in their own idea pages. Sometimes the sixth graders would even retrieve their own journals from the previous year, finding topics they had used before that could possibly be reworked into a new piece.

Children also sometimes wrote poems on the same topic after hearing one read aloud by a friend. For example, after Jimmy R. read aloud his "Me and My Shadow" piece in a large-group sharing session, Mike J. used the idea to write his own shadow poem. Close examination of the poems reveals similarities in word selection, rhythm, and imagery, although each has its own voice. (The poems also reflect the children's familiarity with Livingston's "Street Song.")

Me and My Shadow	Shadows
Me and my shadow.	My shadow follows
Walking along.	me along
Crushing and crashing along	Me and my shadow
Me and my shadow,	Walking alone
Walking along	Just me and my shadow
	walking along.

JIMMY R.
Grade 6

MIKE J.
Grade 5

Friends were also valuable resources for generating poem titles. This usually entailed reading the poem to several children, asking them to generate possible titles, then voting on their choices. Increasingly the suggested titles were those that aptly captured a poem's meaning or made a reader curious about its content. When Jimmy wrote a poem about a roller coaster ride entitled "Feel of a Roller Coaster," his friends told him this title was too obvious and "revealed too much to the reader." He changed it to "Scared" so as to make a reader continue on to see why he was frightened. The poem eventually read as follows:

Scared

Round after round,
Nothing but fear
Peaks as you reach the big hill
Facing down the endless track.
A scream bottles up inside your throat,
Pops the cork,
Trickles out,
Becomes a piercing shriek,
Ending the journey of fear.

JIMMY
Grade 6

Similarly, when Jennifer asked friends to suggest titles for her poem that compared pictures in nature to those in an art gallery, they generated "Nature's Gallery," "Water Art," and "Pieces of

Art." After much discussion and a vote, they decided "Nature's Gallery" was the best choice for extending the metaphor in her piece:

Nature's Gallery

Carved wooden puddles,
Crystal canvas springs,
Splatter painted brooks.
Make nature's children believe
They too can become pieces of art.

JENNIFER
Grade 6

Friends also made suggestions regarding specific word choices. As with topics and titles, a viable list would be generated by the group from which the child would select one. Sometimes this was done by brainstorming as a group. At other times, the thesaurus would be pulled out and the merits of various words would be debated as they were read aloud. The ideas were usually recorded in the margin of one's journal next to the poem's various revisions for use in subsequent drafts.

Suggestions for words also grew more focused as the children became more aware of how word choice influenced meaning. Rather than offering a barrage of words, suggestions became more thoughtful, aimed at finding the "best" word. This change was aptly expressed by Brandon, who made the following comments in a large-group critiquing session near the end of the year: "You gotta be careful. When you look in the thesaurus, you can't pick out any word for your friend. You gotta find one that really goes with your poem or it don't sound right. You gotta make sure the words go together."

Friends also provided ideas for extending a poem. In response to a child's question of "What can I say next?" suggestions for new directions a poem could take were often offered. Sometimes this assistance was quite general as when Aaron told Bryan H. that he should "add more lines and tell more" in his sun poem. At other times this assistance was more focused and directed. For example, when Mandy requested help for her milkweed poem from Robin, Robin suggested she add a part to tell how the milkweed moved through the air, like "a butterfly," "a leaf," or a "floating feather." Mandy wrote these ideas down in the margin of her journal and carefully considered each possibility. She decided she liked both the alliterative qualities and meaning of "floating feather" and added it to her poem.

Similarly, Angie and Shawna helped Carrie extend the metaphor of dark winning a fight over day in her poem "Night." Although Carrie usually worked with Stacie and Deon, on this day she widened her search for new ideas. The first draft read as follows:

The Fight of Night and Day
(first draft)

Towards the end of day
Night steps out
Ready to fight
The sky turns darker.
Night pounces on day
They struggle
Night swats at day
But misses
Night was won.

Carrie was concerned that her line "The sky turns darker," was rather ordinary and didn't really help extend the metaphor.

"How can I make it say that the dark is starting to win?" She thought for a moment. "What about 'as night gains, the sky turns dark'?" she asked her friends.

"I like that line better than the line you had," responded Angie.

"How can it be stronger?" Carrie wanted to know. "I shouldn't put 'Towards the end of day' at the beginning. I should say that later when they're fighting. Am I making any sense? Come on, you guys, suggest something."

"How about 'It's towards the end of day when night steps out'?" said Angie.

" 'When night steps out on the shadow of day'?" suggested Shawna.

"Neat idea," I thought to myself.

"How about 'it is the end of day when night steps out'?" suggested Angie.

"Do you guys understand what my problem is in this poem?" asked Carrie.

"No, not really," Angie responded frankly. "I'm just trying to make suggestions."

"How can it be the end of day when they haven't fighted yet?" asked Carrie.

This question seemed to stump the girls. They sat thinking quietly for a few minutes. No one could immediately come up with a solution to Carrie's dilemma.

Shawna was also writing a nighttime poem (although hers described the beginning rather than the end of day). She suggested they work on hers to get ideas for Carrie.

"Okay," Carrie agreed. "Tell me the first line and title."

After reading Shawna's poem aloud the girls decided they liked Shawna's reference to "shadows dancing at sunrise" but felt her second line needed to be "more poetic."

"What about saying 'things fade at glimpses'?" suggested Carrie. "That means when you first look at something, it's like it isn't there, then it is. I still don't quite like it yet. What do you think, Shawna?"

" 'Glimpses.' I like 'glimpses,' " she replied. "What if I put 'shadows dancing, things fade at glimpses'?"

"That's good," said Carrie. "Except the problem is 'things.' That's too ordinary and doesn't sound very poetic."

"Would it be too weird to add 'upon walls' to 'shadows dancing'?" asked Angie.

"That's neat, 'shadows dancing upon walls.' I like that," responded Shawna enthusiastically.

I was amazed by the give-and-take I had observed among the girls. I'd observed college students who were unable to articulate their ideas or help each other as well. Friends certainly seemed to be a valuable resource for ideas in this classroom.

Clarifying Meanings

Children also helped clarify the intended meaning of a friend's poem. Because the teachers emphasized that meaning was critically important, the children soon became aware of how important it was to help a friend convey what he or she really meant.

Often the focus was on clarifying one word. For example, when Jimmy wrote a poem about a wind that "strips" and "tugs" the bark off trees, Johnny told him that "strips" describes a strong wind and "tugs" tells about a gentle wind; "Those two words don't really go together." The two boys generated many words, deciding that "terrorized" was the best match for "strips." Similarly Stacie questioned Teava about the meaning of her poem, "Crying," commenting: "A never-ending rainfall that never stops? Hmmm...that don't make sense. Do you cry all the time?

I don't think 'never-ending' is a good word to use." Stacie pulled out the thesaurus. After reading aloud several possibilities, Teava selected "streaming" as a word that more accurately described the flow of tears during a strong cry.

Sometimes the focus was on clarifying a whole line or even the ideas of the entire poem. When Deon asked for help on her "Wind" poem, which began

> The wind races across the foggy sky
> Blowing leaves scatter the ground
> The wind blows the tree branches
> And blows the tree prancing along.

Carrie asked how the sky looks with a strong wind. "Is it really foggy then?" she asked Deon.

Deon thought for a moment and decided that foggy days were generally quiet and eerie with almost a stillness about them. She crossed out "foggy" because she realized she was actually describing a wild, blustery day.

"I like 'races'," commented Carrie. "That's a neat way to describe a big wind. How can you tell about the leaves better?"

"What if I say something about the leaves and wind playing together?" asked Deon.

"Yeah," the other girls enthusiastically agreed. They asked her several questions to help her think about how the leaves play and move with a strong wind so that her meaning was really clear. Together they came up with "leaves play in the wind" and "spinning in spirals."

After several more drafts and conferences with teachers and her friends, Deon produced the following final draft:

Wind
(final draft)

> The wind races through the trees.
> Acorns run across the ground.
> Spinning in spirals,
> The leaves play in the wind
> Flashing their showy colors.

DEON
Grade 6

Ideas friends provided for clarifying and extending a poem's meaning lead to refinements that the writer, who was closely involved with the poem, could not always immediately see. Writers of course could freely accept or reject the advice offered. But because the suggestions usually arose from a listener's genuine confusion or puzzlement, his or her ideas were usually welcomed and used.

Children's Attitudes Toward Peer Assistance

I was curious about how the children really felt about all this help. Did they feel obligated to incorporate a friend's ideas even if they disliked them? I sensed not, since they so frequently sought each other's help. I wondered, though, if these conversations may have occurred because the children felt it was an expected part of their daily writing ritual. I decided the best way to find out was to ask.

"Do you think friends are helpful with poetry?" I asked.

After an enthusiastic chorus of "Yes!" several children offered individual comments.

"They give you ideas to work on a poem, new words and lines for it. They tell you if they like it," said Tammy, one of the children who had vigorously claimed earlier that she didn't like poetry.

I was surprised but excited by her comments. Maybe working with friends had helped Tammy become more confident about taking risks and trying new ideas.

Aaron agreed, "Yeah. Well, like, if you're thinking a line and you're trying to think of something else . . . lots of times they think of something better than you do."

"Friends help you move your lines around and make the meaning better," said Tiffany.

"Yeah," added Tammy. "You decide whether or not to revise by reading it over to yourself and your friends."

Becky, a fifth grader who had moved in at the middle of the year (and not to be confused with Becky, the sixth grader), added another perspective. "It was hard at first to do poetry 'cause I never done it before," she said. "But I'd ask them [the other girls] 'will you guys help?' And they did. And I learned how to do it better." Everyone nodded enthusiastically.

Although peer assistance was perceived as generally helpful, it wasn't always easy to accept, as revealed by a casual conversation I had with Jennifer and her friend, Jenny S. Because the girls worked so closely together, I was curious about how they responded to each other's suggestions.

"Well," said Jenny, "when I ask Jennifer for her opinion she always changes little things around here and there before she even tells me anything."

"Do you appreciate that?" I asked.

"Yeah, most of the time," she answered. "I know she's really trying to help me, but it's a pain sometimes." Jenny peeked out from under bangs to see if Jennifer was offended. She wasn't. In fact, she added her own insights about another incident where her suggestions were not positively received.

"That reminds me of when I was helping Teava with her poem," said Jennifer. "I'd just keep asking questions, and she'd just sit there and tell me my questions were too hard."

Jennifer didn't seem the least bit bothered by Jenny or Teava's remarks. It was okay if the receiver of a suggestion felt his or her own ideas were more appropriate, for it was understood that a poem was ultimately a personal construct. Friends could provide help but the writer was the final arbiter of what a poem should say and how it should sound.

Some children did initially feel threatened by another person questioning them about their work. Shawna was one of these children. When she first came to Ridgemont in December, she was quite reluctant to have anyone look at her writing, stating, "It's my poem, and I'll write it the way I want it."

I was curious as to why she felt that way. Did she really feel so strongly about the personal nature of her poems? Was she uncomfortable with people being critical of her? As I watched her working with the others and listened to her comments, it seemed to me that she felt overwhelmed by the abstract thinking and multiple possibilities that resulted when others made suggestions. This was tellingly revealed when she confided to Deon, "I don't want the teacher or these kids to read my poem. They get me all confused. I don't know how to do this stuff." Although Deon reassured her that everyone critiqued and revised and even confided that she'd written her current piece over "a whole bunch of times," Shawna remained initially unconvinced.

Nevertheless, as Shawna was drawn into the fabric of classroom life, she inevitably became an active participant in the critiquing process. I noticed her attitude was daily growing more positive. The change was most evident as I watched the evolution of her "Wind" poem. After reading the first draft, Sheryl felt the poem had potential and accordingly created opportunities for Shawna to share her poem with others. This continual, sustained attention to her poem was not easy for Shawna to manage. However, when the following revision was praised and eventually checkmarked, Shawna was ecstatic:

132

Wind
(checkmarked version)

The door slams
Behind us
From the pressure
Of the wind.
We force ourselves
Outdoors into leaves
Blowing in circles
Across the lane.

By the end of the year, Shawna was no longer avoiding critiquing sessions. In fact, she often actively solicited comments about her poetry, even progressing to the point of initiating a critiquing session with Angie in which they moved back and forth between two versions of the same poem, reorganizing lines and substituting words they decided "sounded better." Success with articulating her ideas in poetic form seemed to make a difference in transforming Shawna's attitude from defensive to trusting and appreciative.

This seemed to be true for the other children as well. Even children who because of their less outgoing personalities might be expected to be less willing to collaborate, often became active, enthusiastic participants once they'd experienced success as a result of working with friends. Revision was considered hard work, requiring much thought, considerable experimentation and infinite patience. Friends helped make the process easier.

Blackboard Critiquing: Children Help Themselves

By January, the rhythm and tenor of these groups was well established. More and more it seemed children rather than teachers orchestrated the events surrounding poetry writing. I still regularly observed groups of children meeting together with a teacher, but increasingly this occurred because the children requested it rather than because a teacher thought it was necessary. When they were stumped for an idea or felt something needed to be reconceptualized, and friends were unable to help, the children then turned to a teacher for assistance. The only exception to this pattern was the large-group critiquing sessions that the teachers continually scheduled on a regular basis. But even here, children were more likely to volunteer to share rather than wait to be drafted. The climate was increasingly one of collaboration and community in which all were partners in the challenge of writing poetry with the teachers acting as resource people rather than directors.

The children were becoming so self-reliant that they even began developing their own methods for helping each other. One, which we came to term "blackboard critiquing," evolved entirely from their initiative. For a long time I noticed that as the children began helping each other in more complex ways, changing lines from one part of the poem to another, generating long lists of words which were alternately tried in the poem, and similar strategies, they seemed to need to see what they were doing. Frequently a child would grab his or her friend's poetry book and write down ideas as they were suggested. Or the book would be placed between two children and together they would pore over it, pencils in hand, discussing various ideas for the poem. Originally, the teachers had not encouraged children to look at grammar or spelling in a poem they were critiquing but to focus on content instead. Just telling a friend one's suggestions, however, seemed more and more inadequate.

One day as I sat watching a sixth-grade small-group sharing session, Peggy gestured excitedly to me from the other side of the room.

"Come over here quick, you've got to see this," she whispered as I drew near. Together we tiptoed over to Robin, Dolly, Tiffany, and Mandy who had set up a small portable chalkboard, which they'd divided into four parts. In each quadrant they'd written a poem by one of the girls. As we watched, they moved to each poem in turn, adding and deleting words as various suggestions were offered.

We were astounded. Here was a clear example of the children taking ownership of a process, inventing something to meet their own growing needs. What a change from the aimless conversations, the constant reliance on a teacher's authority that we'd observed at the beginning of the year. Yet we wondered if this was a fluke, something that had been quickly improvised for the moment and then would be just as quickly abandoned. Much to our delight we soon saw other children imitating the technique. By March, both large and small chalkboards were frequently filled with marked off sections on which children helped each other with poems in progress, moving lines up and down in a poem, experimenting with the effect of various words, and the like.

Some groups even began devising coding systems. For example, Jennifer and Jenny decided to use an asterisk next to any line they decided to keep and a checkmark next to lines they thought might be deleted. This helped them "keep things straight" and enabled them to go back to the original ideas if they wished. Others used arrows, crossouts (so as not to erase the original), or initials (to remind them who had made which suggestions).

All these were advanced strategies requiring reversible thinking as the children moved back and forth among alternatives. Not having to retain the poem in one's memory seemed to facilitate such thinking. Seeing the words allowed the children to go beyond them to consider the meaning they conveyed.

Angela and Angie became particularly adept at using this technique to help each other. A session they had in January was a good example of how they went about it. On this day the girls first worked with Angie's "Weed" poem that originally read as follows:

Weed
(Revision 1)

A little weed grows in the cold shadows
While the sun
Just ignores the little spot
Where it was.

Together they changed word placement ("grows" was moved to the beginning of its line and "in the cold shadows" was moved to become the poem's first line), then relined it. The poem now read:

The Little Weed
(Revision 2)

In the cold shadows
Grows a little weed
While the sun
Just ignores
The spot where I found it.

ANGIE
Grade 6

After Angie had recorded the changes they'd made in her poetry journal, the girls began critiquing Angela's "Paintbrush" poem. Angela wrote her current draft on one side of the board, while on the other side Angie began writing some ideas to help her:

Paintbrush Angela's version (Revision 1)	Paintbrush Angie's version
A hand picks me up A hand swishes me in the paint I mess around the paper Until the hand Spoils the fun By washing me off	Down I go A hand swishes Me in colors Up I come Covering the paper with paint Until art is over and the hand spoils My fun by washing My bristles.

The girls began discussing both drafts. They moved back and forth between them to get ideas for refining what the brush was doing and experimented with words that would best convey the image.

"Why don't you begin by having the paintbrush go into the paint, then come back out of it?" suggested Angie. "That's how it really happens." She pointed to the lines describing this in her version. "And you've got 'hand' two times. That don't sound good. It's not a good repetition."

Angela partially agreed with her and made "Down I go" her first line. But after trying "Up I come," she decided the additional detail of the paintbrush coming back up wasn't essential to the meaning of her poem.

"Give me some words to tell how the paintbrush moves around the paper. I want it to sound really poetic," she told Angie.

They began discussing various possibilities, writing their ideas in a corner of the chalkboard. Angie's original suggestion, "Covering the paper with paint," was eliminated because both now agreed it wasn't "poetic enough." The same objection was made to "I mess around the paper" (Angela's original suggestion) and "the hand glides me across the paper" (generated in their discussion).

"Let's get the thesaurus," suggested Angie. "That might give us some good ideas for words." Soon words like "circles," "slides," and "skims" were written on the board. The girls stood back to read the poem and consider how each word in turn would affect its meaning.

"What about 'tickles the paper'?" Angela suddenly thought.

"That's perfect," agreed Angie. "That makes it more like a person." The third line of the poem became "I tickle the paper." Angela also crossed out "paint" in the second line and substituted

Angie's suggestion of "colors," again because she thought this was a more poetic description.

"I like your idea of saying 'bristles,'" she told Angie. "What about calling it 'hair'?" They decided to ask several other children which reference they preferred, eventually drawing Johnny, Jennifer, and Stacie into their session. The group eventually agreed that "hair" was probably the better word since it extended the personification more completely. They never used the formal literary term, but because of their experiences with poetry, they knew intuitively what Angela was trying to do.

Some experimenting with lining followed. Finally, Angela felt satisfied that she had said what she wanted:

Paintbrush
(Revision 2)

Down I go,
A hand swishes
Me in colors.
I tickle the paper
Until the hand
Spoils my fun
By washing the paint
Out of my hair.

ANGELA
Grade 6

Though Angela had retained many of the ideas and images from her original poem, collaboration produced additional ideas and refinements that Angela had not conceived on her own. Using the blackboard seemed to help both girls become more adventuresome. It allowed them to move freely between various ideas as they tested their viability in the poem. Because they also knew nothing was inviolate, ideas could be easily added or erased. They could be as playful and experimental as they wished.

Initially both teachers were reluctant to incorporate the blackboard into their own sessions. After all, this technique was something the children had evolved. They didn't want to turn it into a "teacher-owned" activity. Furthermore, they were concerned that when children saw a poem in writing, critiquing would begin focusing more on spelling and grammar rather than on the more important issue of meaning.

Nevertheless, Sheryl began using the technique during one group session when she discovered the children were having difficulty critiquing a long poem. After writing it on the board, she was amazed at the difference in the session. The children's revisions were more thoughtful and included suggestions for complex relining and revising the focus of the poem. Because the children had so much experience with critiquing and knew its essential purpose, spelling and grammar were not even mentioned. Soon both teachers felt comfortable incorporating the use of the blackboard into critiquing sessions when they thought it might be helpful.

How often do teachers incorporate methods or ideas developed by children into their teaching? Rarely, it seems. The fact that blackboard critiquing evolved from the children, then was adopted by teachers is further evidence of the atmosphere of trust and collaboration that permeated this classroom. A community of poetry writers was evolving.

Metamorphosis

Like caterpillars into butterflies, the children had metamorphosized before our eyes. No longer were they content with a first draft that contained little personal meaning or imaginative imagery. Nor were they willing to rely only on adult resources to help them with their pieces. They had come to see that writing poetry was not a process in which one followed set rules to put something down on paper. Rather, they understood that poets move among alternatives, becoming involved in recording an experience, then experimenting with different ideas for describing that experience until something pleasing to the writer has been achieved. They had learned to stretch their wings and fly on their own, in the company of other fragile new butterflies who were already drying their wings.

CHAPTER 11

Image to Image:
Illustrating Poetry

Carved wooden puddles
Crystal canvas springs
Splatter painted brooks.
Make Nature's children believe
They too can become pieces of art.

JENNIFER
Grade 6

As the year progressed, the classroom walls and bulletin boards became covered with the children's work. Poems illustrated with beautiful watercolor pictures of sunsets, intricate collage renderings of animal habitats, and brightly crayoned Halloween scenes adorned bulletin boards, doorways, and walls. In addition to all the children's writing, talking, and reading of poetry, another activity had become an integral part of class activities: illustrating their poems or poetry collections.

The children had access to paints, watercolors, collage materials, markers, chalk, inks, crayons, simple printing equipment, and other media to create their pictures. Stencils and calligraphy books provided models for lettering. All kinds of paper—from foils to tissue paper to special watercolor paper—were available along with wallpaper sample books. Even such things as sable paintbrushes and natural sponges were provided so the children could feel the pride of using fine equipment.

But how did they know what to do with all this, I wondered? Did the mere presence of all these exciting materials generate the explosion of creativity I saw occurring? As I watched the evolution of their work, I realized Peggy's unobtrusive, yet informed, helpful presence was what seemed to make the difference. Art was largely

139

her domain. The children might ask Sheryl or myself for our reactions to an almost completed project, but it was Peggy who made suggestions, stimulated divergent thinking, set out materials, and generally coordinated the work with art. Thus, the voice and perspective in this chapter are primarily hers.

Common Illustration Activities

Once a child's poem was checkmarked, the writer often chose to "set it up"—the class term for illustrating it. This was usually done on a large sheet of paper using whatever media the child believed best reflected the poem's mood or theme. Once the picture was made, the poem would be rewritten (often in calligraphy) and affixed to it. Sometimes a poem's content was such that it was almost impossible to illustrate with a picture. These might then be mounted using an abstract design for the background or triple mounted and displayed that way.

Children were never required to illustrate their checkmarked poems. In fact, sometimes teacher or child felt the poem should be left alone to allow the reader to envision his or her own images. In such cases, they reasoned, the illustration might spoil a poem's effect. Or the child might feel a poem was too personal to be placed on public display. But many children were so pleased by the combination of written and artistic images that this soon became a favorite class activity. Besides, it was fun.

The resulting illustrations were quite diverse. For example, Bryan used silver paint and collage materials, including sequins, to produce an unusual, visually compelling illustration for his poem, "Owl" (Figure 11–1). Johnny combined different wallpaper patterns with paint to show seaweed and multi-colored fish in "Tiger Fish" (Figure 11–2).

Once children had at least four poems with checkmarks, they were invited to make an anthology or illustrated collection of their poems. Sometimes these were organized around a theme. For example, Jimmy created an anthology of his rhythmical, rhyming poems and titled it *Reading in Rhythm*. Johnny collected and illustrated his animal poems. Often, however, children would just collect their favorites, illustrate them, then select an all purpose title like *All Kinds of Poems, Bite-Sized Poems*, or *Tiptoe to the Horizon* to describe the collection.

Sometimes several children would create a joint anthology in which a poem from each would be used to create a book. Often, these were organized around themes, such as favorite animals or humorous poems. Form was also an organizing theme. Thus, after

Building a Community of Poetry Writers

FIGURE 11–1 "Owl" by Bryan C.

FIGURE 11–2 "Tiger Fish" by Johnny

Jimmy, Brandon, Jennifer, and Johnny each wrote haikus, they created a joint collection appropriately titled *Haiku*. In other cases collaboration would be between writer and illustrator: one child would create a poem and another would illustrate it.

Some might perceive all this work with illustration as superfluous busy work, something to be assigned to fill an extra hour on a Friday afternoon or as a way to avoid "real," more academic learning. This was not true in Peggy and Sheryl's classroom. They believed that just as children need a way to concretely manipulate abstract mathematical concepts, so they need the opportunity to manipulate equally abstract literary elements. Illustrating a poem, in their opinion, causes children to look more closely at it, maybe seeing new dimensions or complex meanings that might have eluded them earlier. This was particularly evident when the children created an illustration for a poem, then made a new picture when the poem was included in an anthology. When we compared illustrations, we often noticed subtle variations in perspective or meaning (Figure 11–3, A and B). Occasionally they would even change a word or two of their poem because reillustrating helped them realize the change was "more like it [the phenomenon they were writing about] really was."

Illustrations also occasionally disclosed differences between the child's words and thoughts that were not always evident in conversations about the poem. For example, Jennifer, who usually wrote quite complex poetry, created a very literal illustration for one of her poems (Figure 11–4).

An illustration by Jeremy in particular showed us how a picture can reveal something quite different from words. Jeremy had written the following poem:

> The white snow
> And the
> Smooth ice
> Skate down
> The frosty
> Window
> Watching out for
> The heat of the
> Sun
> To melt it away.

As the teachers talked to him, listened to his ideas, and followed the progress of the poem's creation, they felt he understood the metaphoric reference. In creating the illustration, however, he spent

Milkweed

In a pod,
Seeds nap,
Waiting for a wind.
Whish!
There they go,
Gliding like silk butterflies,
To their new home.
By Jennifer Raeder. c-3

A

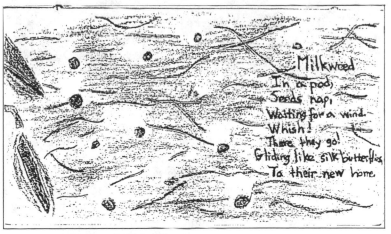

B

FIGURE 11-3 "Milkweed" by Jennifer

Look, a cloud
Shaping in the sky,
Shaping like a kitten,
Purring to the ground
To make a soft fog.

FIGURE 11–4 *"Cloud" by Jennifer*

considerable time working to get a small skating figure positioned just right on the frame: a completely literal image. His illustration was a complete surprise to the teachers. Neither knew what to say to him. Should they question him further about the poem's meaning? Should they suggest he do some rereading and rethinking about the illustration? As Peggy probed, she discovered it was merely the switch to the concrete medium of illustration that caused the change in perception. We learned a valuable lesson from Jeremy: never assume children understand without carefully examining every aspect of their response.

Helping Children Create Visual Images

Although these beautiful creations seemed to evolve naturally, I knew there was something happening to stimulate the children's thinking. I never saw Peggy give the usual art lessons with their emphasis on uniformity and technique. Yet, somehow she was imbuing the children with a sense of what was aesthetically pleasing, coupled with enough knowledge of artistic technique to achieve the effect they wanted. So, one day late in the year I decided to talk with her to discover how she accomplished this.

I had noticed she often shared picture books with the children to develop their sense of composition and awareness of different media. I was curious as to how she did this on a daily basis.

"I often begin by talking about Tomie dePaola and how he represents scenes and people in a simple way," she told me. "This seems to give the children courage to draw people, trees, and houses more representationally."

"Do you tell them anything specific or do you just give the books to them and let them browse?" I wanted to know.

"If someone wants to make a figure as realistic as possible I might show them specifically how to sketch, using a character in a picture book as the model," she continued. "I tell them to look at how arms bend, how shoulders meet necks, how upper legs shorten when a person is seated and how shadows give depth to a picture. This helps the children observe more closely and have some success with realistic drawing."

Peggy used Trina Schart Hyman's illustration in a similar way to show how things in nature, particularly trees, could be drawn.

"She draws trees like no other artist," said Peggy. "I show the children how you can actually feel the denseness of the forest by viewing a spread where trees extend beyond the page. Breaking the barrier of space defined by a piece of paper as Hyman does can bring a whole new dimension to an illustration."

She continued, "Hyman also often shows part of her subject, causing these to have more impact because they're shown up close. I like to point this out to children so they stretch their thinking about how to illustrate."

Soon the children began to assimilate these concepts. For example, Jimmy R. used the idea of extending a tree beyond the border of one page in his Haiku book (Figure 11–5).

Peggy also often shared McClosky's Time of Wonder for its atmospheric quality and contrasts.

"Many children write about fog and rain. This book shows how landscapes change when a curtain of fog erases distinct lines and

In leaf crisp forests
Deer bed down; when frightened they
Vault away soundlessly.

By: Jimmy Rowe

FIGURE 11-5 "*Leaf Crisp Forests*" *by Jimmy*

details," she said. "Our children also write about wind a lot. But when they try to draw wind they make lines to show the path of the wind or draw animated clouds with puffy cheeks and blowing lips. I show them how McClosky captures the way wind changes landscapes by rearranging the environment and altering color."

She pointed to the pages in the book in which McClosky depicts the impending storm. "See how the pictures gradually get darker as the storm gets closer?" she asked. "That's the sort of thing I try to show the kids."

Picture books were also used to show the finer points of illustration: borders, background, innovative cutouts, and the like. Peggy had a large collection of beautiful fairy tales in the room that she used to demonstrate the creation of borders, background, foreground, and similar concepts. Soon many of the children began experimenting with borders that they cut from wallpaper books or designed with watercolors. Others used pen and ink or bits of sponge to make borders and backgrounds for their pages (see Figure 11-6).

FIGURE 11-6 "T.V." by Jeremy

As the children became more secure and more willing to experiment with creative ways of representing images, Peggy felt they were ready to go beyond the boundaries of representational art. To this end books by artists who used more abstract techniques like Brian Wildsmith were presented. From such books the children could see how to capture something, not as a camera might, but in a free, impressionistic way. Thus, they would examine Brian Wildsmith's *Squirrel*, for example, to see how he used color in innovative ways.

"Do tree trunks have to be brown and black?" Peggy would ask them. "Not according to Wildsmith. You can use pinks, turquoises, yellows, blues—add whirls and swirls to make a tree like no other—extraordinary!"

How freeing this was to the children to realize they could move beyond the boundaries of what they defined as reality, drawing from the full spectrum of their imaginations for their work.

Children also learned how to use different media to convey just the right emotion or meaning for their poems. Peggy started the children off with watercolors. They not only seemed to enjoy this particular medium but many of them wrote about nature and weather—topics especially suitable for watercolors. Leonard Baskin's *Hosie's Aviary* and *Under the North Star* are two of her favorite books for showing the variety of ways in which watercolors can be used. For example, she would demonstrate how the wooden end of the paintbrushes could scratch the surface to create texture and detail, or she would show how fine-line markers could be used to add detail, thus sharpening and focusing the look of a watercolor picture.

Once the children became comfortable with a basic medium like watercolor or markers, Peggy tried to expand their horizons. She began pointing out the influence of media in other books—the primitive effect of woodcuts, the textured effect that collage seemed to generate, and the delicate feel of charcoal and colored pencils. "Why do you think Marcia Brown used woodcuts for a folk tale?" or "Why would an artist use soft blue colored chalk for a story about where butterflies go when it rains?" she would ask the children. A discussion would then arise on the interrelationship of text, media, and style. Usually she would then demonstrate how to use the materials, then leave them out along with the picture books in which they were used so the children could experiment on their own, using the work of professional artists as a resource for their ideas.

Soon Peggy began making some connections between art and text using illustrated poetry books. Valerie Worth's *Small Poems* series, illustrated with simple line drawings by Natalie Babbitt, was often a good initial example. Myra Cohn Livingston's *A Circle of Seasons* and *Sky Songs* with their bold striking pictures by Leonard Everett Fisher were also presented as models. Soon the children became as proficient at identifying the artist as they were at guessing the poet when Peggy held up a page to be enjoyed and studied. They also began incorporating the artistic styles into their own work.

When the children became interested in creating poetry anthologies, Peggy showed them how to make a book. Using squares of lightweight cardboard or cut up cereal or cat food boxes she would demonstrate various sizes and shapes as well as basic techniques for book assembling. Then using the picture and poetry books, again as models, she would introduce them to the concepts of composition, double page spread, endpapers, titlepage, and the like. Soon the children were launched into the world of publishing.

"I particularly have them examine book covers," she added. "I tell them that the cover is important for enticing someone to read your book and to project a sense of what's inside."

I noticed the children often took extra care of their covers as a result of this emphasis. Titles were carefully selected with votes taken to ensure a title reflected the collection's contents. Then stencils, cut-out letters, calligraphy, or other techniques would be used purposefully to extend the title's appearance and meaning (see Figure 11–7, A and B).

FIGURE 11-7 *Distinctive Covers. "Light Reflections" by Jeremy.*
"Pleasant Poetry" by Bryan H.

I wondered if the children ever felt intimidated by what they saw professional artists doing.

"No, not really," Peggy told me. "I just constantly encourage them saying, 'You can do this too. Just look at how they [the artists] have used color and space and this will make your illustrations better.'"

Most importantly, she told them, "Don't be afraid to take a chance by doing something you've never tried before." Fifth and sixth graders are very stodgy and tentative about their artwork. They are obsessed with making things look real and are easily discouraged when they can't. It took much encouragement from Peggy to keep the children trying new things.

Children who worked together were particularly inclined to copy each other's techniques and styles. In such cases Peggy would sometimes confront them, saying, "I think that was her idea. Why don't the rest of you come up with your own ideas?" Then she would suggest they experiment. She would bring over unusual paper samples, the calligraphy set, or a wallpaper book to get them going. When she noticed someone being innovative she might say, "Oh isn't that interesting? See what you can do when you experiment?" The combination of giving encouragement, providing alternatives, then praising experimentation, seemed to help.

She also refused to let them get by with mediocrity. An honest, thoughtful effort that didn't come out beautifully was perfectly acceptable, but a hastily created picture, done solely to get a poem displayed quickly, was not. Just as she would suggest a poem needed to be revised, Peggy would sometimes suggest a picture needed

more work and would quietly demonstrate some different possibilities. After some "huffing and puffing" (her term) the children
would usually rethink their pictures.

Each time something was tried and worked out successfully,
it was called to the attention of the group with emphasis on the
risk-taking involved in the creative process. All this support seemed
to help the children feel more comfortable with trying new things,

FIGURE 11–8 "Fish" by Jeremy

and eventually they began to do much more experimenting. For example, Jeremy tried combining techniques by first crumpling paper, then using marbleizing, collage, and paint to illustrate his haiku poem "Fish" (Figure 11–8). A rash of paper crumpling ensued after he shared his work and received acclaim.

Bryan H. used a brayer that was rolled through various colors of paint, then transferred to a piece of tagboard. Inside, strips of paper were arranged in a design and glued down with rubber cement (Figure 11–9).

If some of this experimenting didn't quite work as expected, Peggy and the class could usually figure out a way to rescue it. In fact, with imagination, disasters could sometimes be turned into gems. Sometimes the parts that were good would be cut up and saved, then mounted on new papers. Or Peggy would show a child how a solid background could mask fingerprint marks or a spill. Occasionally the spill or mistake could be incorporated into the picture with the simple addition of a few lines or collage materials.

FIGURE 11–9 *"Scissors" by Bryan H.*

"Even if I wasn't sure we could accomplish a rescue, I would always say, 'Oh, that's not so bad. Let's see if we can rescue it. If we can't, there are more supplies,' " Peggy told me. "I wanted them to feel it was okay to make false starts and use what they needed. Too many times children think they shouldn't waste things and that really stifles their creativity."

Through this continual sharing of art created by both professionals and the students, the children began developing an aesthetic sense and an ability to talk about art, which carried over to the construction of their own pieces. We began to hear them say things like "It looks kind of flat. Why don't you put some distance in your picture?" or "Why don't you change the way you put the poem on the page so it doesn't look like everybody else's. Maybe your poem could go over part of the picture." Often the children together would pull out the picture books they'd studied to examine a particular artist's technique again or to get new ideas. Inevitably a discussion would arise as to how those artists' techniques could be adapted to their own work.

Providing time for the children to share their pictures with the group was also a critical part of the illustration process. During sharing, a child who had created something unique or had solved a particularly troublesome problem would describe how the picture evolved. Maybe someone found a way to hide the hinges on their book, and he or she would show others how they did it. Or someone else would have discovered an unusual way to make a book cover: covering the cardboard with black construction paper, then using several colors of paint to make fingerprints all over the cover with white paint splattering over that to give a mottled, marbleized appearance. The others were encouraged to tell what they liked as well as any suggestions they had for improvement. It was up to the child who was sharing as to whether or not the suggestions would be acted upon.

Through all this demonstrating and encouragement, Peggy had to continually remind herself not to take ownership of an artistic composition. Indeed, she would sometimes catch herself saying, "Why don't you do this?" or "That's perfect. Why do you want to change it?" When this happened she would consciously try to pull back and make comments that encouraged the child to reflect and make judgments. Thus, instead, she might say "What do *you* think would work here?" or "How could you show the inside of a house? Get John Goodall's book [*Story of an English Village*] to see how interiors are drawn." or she might send them to a friend saying, "Ask Aaron how he handled that problem. He can give you some good ideas."

Building a Community of Poetry Writers

Image Making

It was evident that Peggy did very little whole-class demonstrating. Rather, she moved among groups and individuals working on particular projects, helping those who faced challenges that were personally important: whether that involved how to show the wind terrorizing trees or how to make a snake look like both a garden hose and itself so as to extend a metaphor. She would usually show several possibilities for solving the problem saying, "You could use collage here or maybe you might want to get a different effect with charcoal or chalk." The final decision would then be left to the child, paving the way for choice and experimentation. For Peggy, opportunities to share, experiment, collaborate, and, yes, even fail led to innovation and a heightened aesthetic sense. Anne, a student from another year's class aptly captured this emphasis in the following poem:

Art

A flick of a paintbrush
A splatter of paint
A smear of chalk.
A flick,
A splatter,
A smear,
Art!

ANNE
Grade 4

Although all this took a significant amount of Peggy's time, we believed it was worth it. The time spent working through the technical problems of illustration and picture/text integration was important. Not only did the children learn to think, to make choices, and to give and take constructive suggestions, they also learned how to get satisfaction from working hard to achieve an aesthetic goal. Pride in a finished work of art, knowing it often took intense individual effort to create, was a valuable attitude to learn.

PART IV

Learning About Poetic Elements

B y the end of the school year Sheryl and Peggy's teaching of poetry merged with their teaching of writing. When the children wrote, they saw themselves as part of a community of writers that included the poets who created pieces they read over and over again. When they read poetry together, they were aware of the struggle involved in creating a meaningful piece. Their own experiences as writers had made them aware.

This awareness was particularly evident when I examined the children's knowledge of how poets use various elements—rhyme, rhythm, lining, figurative language, and the like—to craft their pieces. Through both reading and writing poetry they were discovering the various tools poets use to make a poem "sound more poetic." Jason, a child from another year's class, expressed this idea perfectly in the following poem:

> To find the right key
> To unlock your poem,
> You may have to sort
> Through your key ring.

JASON
Grade 4

These understandings did not evolve sequentially. The children drew simultaneously from their reading and writing of poetry. They seemed to gather insights from the work of published poets that they used to help them with their own pieces. On the other hand, their struggle as writers helped them appreciate the work that goes into crafting fine poetry. Thus, it is necessary to look at both the reading and writing of poetry to get a sense of how such understanding evolved.

The children were never formally taught what are often termed the "skills" of poetry. There were never specific lessons on rhyme, metaphor, or iambic pentameter. The teaching was done incidentally as part of a larger conversation about what made a particular poem pleasing or enjoyable. When I asked Sheryl and Peggy what they were teaching about poetry, they were unable to articulate any specific principles. I was the one who—through observing, conversing, and participating in the melange of poetry activities—was able to discover recurring patterns and themes.

Although these elements have all been mentioned in previous chapters, weaving in and out of the discussion of other events and interactions, this section provides a clearer picture of how the children became aware of each element and gained an overall understanding of poetry. Each element is isolated from the others in order to examine it closely, but it is important to remember that the music of poetry is made by combining all of the elements into a harmonic whole.

CHAPTER 12

Making It Real:
Being True to Your Subject

Poetry is not something apart from life, but is a vital
and sustaining part of it, expressing every observation,
feeling, experience, wish and dream, emotion and idea
that is part of being alive

The Child as Poet: Myth or Reality
MYRA COHN LIVINGSTON

Poetry, according to Carl Sandburg (1970), is a "series of explanations of life." It can illuminate our experience, give us new insights,
and teach us about the human condition. It helps us find new
meaning for ourselves. Thus, it must reflect life—or at least life as
the poet sees it. To do this poets must be keen observers and
commentators on reality, although they may distort it, juxtapose
one vision against another, or describe it from different perspectives.

The teachers continually developed the children's awareness
of this connection between poetry and the world. They alluded to
it in published poetry, then helped the children to forge the same
connection in their own work. This idea needs to be emphasized
because initially many of the children perceived poetry as serious
gobbledygook whose meaning was accessible only to adults. This
same feeling was reflected in their own pieces. What one said didn't
matter as long as it sounded poetic. The teachers knew this perception would need to change if the children were ever going to
appreciate and understand good poetry.

Thus, when critiquing poems, the importance of one's poem
being true to life was second only to sense-making. Comments and
questions from both teachers helped children refine their pieces so
they presented real images. For example, Kellie, a sixth grader, came

to Sheryl for help with her poem about wind and leaves in the fall. Her early draft read as follows:

Fall
(Revision 1)

The leaves change colors
The breeze races through the leaves
Till they can't bear anymore
The leaves break off the branches
And

    S

      i

        n

          k to the ground
Collecting in the pile below

"What is a breeze? How strong is it?" Sheryl asked her. "Would it follow that leaves could bear no more with only a breeze? What *could* cause that to happen?"

"A big wind," responded Kellie thoughtfully.

"Okay," answered Sheryl. "Now, would leaves really collect in a pile below if blown off the branch? What would really happen to leaves then?"

Kellie thought carefully about the questions and eventually incorporated the responses they stimulated into her poem. The final draft reflected her awareness that her poem must not only include colorful language but must also reflect accurately how leaves really respond to a fall wind:

Fall
(checkmarked version)

When fall leaves
Can bear no more
Of the racing wind
They break loose
And take to the air.

KELLIE
Grade 6

Similarly, during the milkweed science unit, the children completed experiments, wrote books, and observed these plants in their natural habitat before ever writing poems about them. When they eventually began experimenting with milkweed poems, Peggy told them, "You have to look at it closely. Be the milkweed. Look at yourself from the point of view of the observations you've just made of the milkweed. *Then* write your poem." The resulting poems were notable for their accurate, imaginative depiction of milkweeds. Certainly their newly acquired scientific knowledge shaped the poems, but their ideas were expressed in a form that evoked the aesthetic dimensions of the phenomena they had studied.

Past and Future

Flying in the wind
A milkweed passes by.
The milkweed like a fluttering, flying bird
Meets a cloud in the sky.

MANDY
Grade 5

Sometimes milkweed grows
Tall as corn,
Short as dandelion.
Sun dried,
Pods burst open
And race in the
Wild, wild wind!

JENNY S.
Grade 6

Soon, the children were experimenting on their own to make their work more real. They altered various words or lines so that their poem's meaning was a true representation of reality as they perceived it. I watched Angie look up "cherry blossoms" in the encyclopedia, then decide the delicate pink color of these flowers made her simile inaccurate: a face made cold by a chilly winter day was not a "face like a cherry blossom." Similarly, Mike J. carefully considered the look and behavior of hunting dogs, focusing particularly on the way they run, while creating his poem, "Blue Tick Hound." Sheryl helped Johnny experiment with a cork in the fish tank to capture the exact sounds of fishing for his poem, "Fishing." They moved back and forth between the tank and his notebook, brainstorming various sounds until Johnny exclaimed, "I think we got it!"

The following are examples of pieces in which the writers were particularly aware of keeping true to their subject:

Making It Real

Blue Tick Hound

Blue tick hound
Races through the woods.
Running with the instinctive rhythm
of his breed,
His determined bark
leads us to a ringtailed catch.

MIKE J.
Grade 5

Getting Dizzy

Spinning around
Marbleized sights
Catch your eye,
Flashing,
Again and again
You start to get dizzy.

MIKE H.
Grade 5

Fishing

"Ssssss"
Sings the line,
"Snap,"
Speaks the bait.
"Plop,"
Answers the water.
Silently,
Bobs the bobber.
"Splash,"
Flips the fins.
"Sizzle,"
Fries my fish.

JOHN
Grade 6

October

Birds sing a last summer song
Grapes mount upon October

Leaves deepen darkly
Milkweed seeks a new home.

DEON
Grade 6

Cough Drops

Pop one in your mouth
And let the heat go
Through your head
And down your throat
Like a bit of the sun.

MATT
Grade 6

Sand Pile

In a
Pocket-sized
Desert
Tiny creatures
Crawl and search
For shelter
Among
Miniature weeds.

AARON
Grade 5

Ronnie's "Wolves" Poem

Ronnie had become intrigued with wolves after reading *Julie of the Wolves* and decided to write a poem about them. "Wolves" is a good example of a poem that was changed primarily in response to the writer's desire to stay true to his subject. Ronnie's first draft read as follows.

Wolves
(first draft)

They're silent
in the snow
staring at the deer that
play in the mushy snow

waiting for the right moment
then they attack the sickest
one of the herd.

"I'd like for you to think about what really happens here," Sheryl told him when he asked her for help with the poem. "What do you really know about wolves and deer? How can you show it in your poem?"

"It's not about around here. It's about Alaska," replied Ronnie.

"Do they have deer in Alaska?" responded Sheryl. "What are deerlike animals called in Alaska?"

Ronnie thought for a moment. "Caribou," he replied.

His friend, Johnny, offered another suggestion. "I can't picture the wolves. They don't just stand. Somehow they move around or something. Maybe you need to make your first line tell more how they really are. What are some good words to tell about the wolves?"

Ronnie thought for a minute but couldn't seem to think of any ideas.

"Well," continued Johnny, "how do you feel when you have no friends, when the other kids shove you around, then walk away?"

"Lonely . . . all alone," replied Ronnie.

This seemed to be a catalyst for Ronnie. He put "all alone" at the beginning of his poem and began working on it again, deleting and adding various words to make the meaning clearer. He became so engrossed that he stayed after school to talk about it further with Sheryl. The revised poem read as follows:

Wolves
(Revision 3)

All alone
The wolves and the caribou
Stand quietly
Then death sneaks up
On the slowest one

"Now, get a picture of the caribou," she told him. "If they're frightened, do they stand?"

"No, they go everywhere," responded Ronnie.

"How could you say that poetically?" asked Sheryl.

"Shocked with fright? Afraid with fright? Looking around with fright?"

"Think about those ideas," answered Sheryl. "Think about what really tells how the caribou and wolves feel here." She continued asking questions to stimulate his thinking.

"What would the air be like in Alaska? How would it feel?"

"It would be all fogged up with the breath of the caribou and wolves," answered Ronnie.

"Okay, think about how you would say that in a poetic way," suggested Sheryl.

Ronnie left school that afternoon in a thoughtful mood. I felt sure he would spend time thinking about his poem during the long walk home. I caught up with him several days later and asked if he'd worked any more on his poem. He showed me the latest version. I was stunned by the change. Ronnie had truly captured the stark, barren feel of Alaska and animal survival. I asked him what had influenced the change.

"Well, I went back to *Julie of the Wolves* and a book I had on wolves and read all about them again," he responded. "Then I saw a TV special on timber wolves. I found out more about how wolves survive, how they kill, how they signal and show friendships. Then I just got in the mood to write it." The following is his final draft:

Wolves

Arctic air is fogged with wolf breath,
Caribou run without fear.
Death sneaks up on the herd.
And a weak one falls.

RONNIE
Grade 6

Making It Real

In Lilian Moore's *I'll Meet You at the Cucumbers* (1988), Amanda and Adam, two major characters (who also happen to be mice), converse about the power of poetry.

"Do people like poets?" asked Adam.
"I don't know," said Amanda. "But they need them."
"Need them?" Adam was puzzled.
"Yes, poets are very helpful."
Amanda was thoughtful for a moment. Then she said, "I think it's the way poets see things—as if everything were new. Then we read the poems and we feel, 'Yes, that's the way it is.'"

This is exactly the attitude we wanted the children to adopt. Poets must be able to present their vision of reality in a way the reader will recognize. It is this ability to represent the essence of something in a new way that distinguishes fine poetry. As Peggy continually stressed, "Good poetry should be something that goes to the heart of the matter." The children soon learned to search for this quality in published poetry and to strive for it in their own pieces.

CHAPTER 13

Wordcrafting:
Selecting the Best Word

Words spin together tightly,
    Threaded with punctuation.
When a dictionary of terms
    Passes by my mind's eye,
The web of my thoughts
    Catches the choicest of words
To make the connection complete.

JEFF
Grade 4

The words in a poem are like colors in a painting. A poet knows the nuances, textures, even the effect a word can have, just as the painter is sensitive to the subtleties of a color. When the words of a poem are put together with care, they make a vivid image for the reader just as a painting does for the viewer. Thus, the subtle nuances of meaning, the sound of a word, and the relationship between a particular word and the total poetic image must be carefully weighed. This is particularly important for poetry because it is so compact. Poets pare down their pieces, cutting out every unnecessary word, substituting the perfect one where originally there were three or four, so as to distill their thought to its essence. Thus the poet must select just the right shade of meaning for the context.

Appreciation

Sheryl and Peggy continually developed the children's awareness of the importance of judicious word selection in poetry. In the large-group sharing sessions, they often commented on the ability of a particular poet to select the perfect word to convey an intended meaning. Usually this was done as part of a general conversation about what made a particular poem seem memorable or sound good. For example, after reading Elizabeth Coatsworth's "Swift Things Are Beautiful," the group together marvelled at the vivid images the poet had created by contrasting unusual descriptions of swift and slow things like "a runner's sore feet" or "the pause of a wave that curves downward to spray." Or when reading Carl Sandburg's "Summer Grass," they enjoyed Sandburg's personification of the grass as it "aches and whispers" for rain and "pours out wishes to the overhead stars."

Sometimes a poem was read aloud specifically for enjoyment of its interesting words. This occurred when Sheryl shared Marcia Lee Masters' "April" with the group. She decided to read it to them, she said, "because it lingers in my head. The words will just come back to me for no reason at all." She began reading aloud:

It's lemonade, it's lemonade, it's daisy.
It's a roller-skating, scissor-grinding day;
It's gingham-waisted, chocolate flavored, lazy,
With the children flower-scattered at their play.

It's the sun like watermelon,
And the sidewalks overlaid
With a glaze of yellow yellow
Like a jar of marmalade.

It's the mower gently mowing,
And the stars like startled glass,
While the mower keeps on going
Through a waterfall of grass.

Then the rich magenta evening
Like a sauce upon the walk,
And the porches softly swinging
With a hammockful of talk.

It's the hobo at the corner
With his lilac-sniffing gait,
And the shy departing thunder
Of the fast departing skate.

It's lemonade, it's lemonade, it's April!
A water sprinkler, puddle winking time,
When a boy who peddles slowly, with a smile remote and holy,
Sells you April chocolate flavored for a dime.

"Well, what do you think?" she asked the group.

"I like all the different words she put in there," said Jimmy. "She talks about April in a lot of ways."

"Yes," answered Sheryl. "Who would ever think of talking about April as a roller-skating, scissor-grinding day, or gingham-waisted? It talked about it [April] in so many ways, 'children flower-scattered at their play,' sun is like what? First time I had ever heard the sun compared to this."

"Like a watermelon. That's neat!" Carrie responded.

"I like the part about the sidewalks looking like a jar of marmalade, with the sun on them," said Jennifer.

"Yes, what a way to say it," marvelled Sheryl. "Rather than just saying the sun shone on the sidewalk, she says 'the sun like watermelon, / And the sidewalks overlaid / With a glaze of yellow yellow / Like a jar of marmalade.' Any other interesting things about the words in this poem?"

"I like how she said about the mower," said Jennifer. "Read that part over."

Sheryl read the requested part again. As she did, I noticed several children swaying slightly to the poem's rhythm:

It's the mower gently mowing,
And the stars like startled glass,
While the mower keeps on going
Through a waterfall of grass.

"I like that," Jennifer continued, "because that's what we have in springtime."

"Do you have a picture of April that is somewhat different from any of the other poems you have ever read about spring or certain months in spring?" Sheryl asked the group.

Everyone nodded.

"That's one of the things poets do. They try to use unusual words and combinations of words to tell us something in a new way."

The teachers also often explained the meanings of words that were not part of the children's vocabulary. When reading Masters' "April," Sheryl told the children about gingham material, then asked them to speculate as to why the poet selected that particular word to describe April. Another time she explained the word "caravan" as a prelude to discussing Worth's metaphor of caterpillar feet as a "caravan of bristles" in "Caterpillar." Again, these interactions helped children perceive the importance of word selection in poetry.

Soon the children began commenting on word selection themselves without prompting from a teacher. For example, after hearing Moore's "I Never Saw the Sea," the children were so intrigued by her description that they spontaneously began discussing the poet's word choices.

"I like the way she says it 'splinters the water,'" commented Becky after Sheryl had finished reading.

"How does that look, 'the sun splinters the water'?" Sheryl asked the group.

"It's the waves all streaky," answered Ronnie.

"Like pieces of glass," offered another child.

"I like it how she said she didn't know the sea could do that stuff," said Bryan, "That was neat how she said it. Read that part again."

Sheryl read the poem again. "Did you ever think about the ripples and waves in the sea as being wrinkled? Do those words help you look at the sea in a different way?"

Word selection was always looked at as part of the larger purpose of heightening enjoyment and appreciation. The teachers wanted the children to become sensitive to poetry as something deliberately crafted, to show them that poets select words carefully to create the vivid images and beautiful sounds that evoke a response from a listener.

Making It Their Own

As the children became attuned to how carefully poets use words, they began experimenting with their own pieces. Initially their efforts were relatively unfocused. They knew searching for just the right word might make their piece "sound more poetic," but they would often just select a word at random, usually based on their perception of it as a big word (i.e., not part of their normal speaking vocabulary).

A thesaurus was usually consulted to generate the list. All the possibilities would be written down the side of the page, then a word that seemed unusual or "big" would be selected for the poem. When Lesa was looking for a word to describe the color of the sky in her poem about fall, she looked up "blue" and "bright" in the thesaurus, then wrote all the suggested words next to the poem. After examining the list, she chose "fluorescent" because, she told me, "it's a big word and probably has deep meaning."

In another instance, I watched the fifth-grade boys try to help Aaron find a good word to describe heat in his "Sandpit" poem that compared the school sandbox to a desert.

" 'Ghastly heat' in the last line don't sound good. You need another word to make it poetic," Mike told him.

Aaron pulled the thesaurus off the bookshelf and looked up hot. "What about 'roasting heat'? 'thermal'? 'broiling'? 'torrid'?"

"Yeah, 'torrid,'" exclaimed Mike. "That sounds good."

"How about 'scorching'?" suggested Aaron.

"Yeah, 'scorching,'" agreed Mike again. He seemed receptive to any suggestion to help Aaron get something down.

"I like 'scorching,'" said Aaron.

"Okay. Okay. Just put that down," Mike told him.

Though these children seemed to realize that wordcrafting was important to poetry, they didn't yet understand that selecting a particular word could focus and extend a poem's meaning. The teachers were encouraged by the children's awareness of word-crafting, but hoped they would become more purposeful in choosing words for their poems. They unobtrusively tried to help. In addition to discussing how professional poets use words, they would fre-quently point out the importance of word choice in the children's own work. I often heard Sheryl give advice like the following: "You have to watch for words that don't fit. Do my words say what I want them to say? Do they really mean what I'm trying to get across? Remember when we talked about words earlier this year? We called them *specific words*. You choose the best word to express a specific meaning." The children would be encouraged to experiment with using specific words in their own work, playing with how they sounded in relation to one another as well as how they conveyed the meaning of the poem.

Soon, when children generated a list from the thesaurus, the teachers would try to help them discover which really was the best word. When working with Aaron on his "Sandpit" poem, Peggy helped him find a word other than "little" to describe this small-scale environment. Together they tried different words in the poem, finally deciding "pocket-sized" (to describe the terrain) and "min-iature" (to describe the weeds) were most effective. Similarly, when Johnny wrote his "Kitten" poem, his friends helped generate a list of words for how a cat moves that included "zips off," "rush," "scurry," "leaps," "dash," and "tear." He then asked Sheryl which one she thought would work best.

"Does 'scurry' really fit a cat?" Sheryl asked him. "What do we think of that scurries?"

"Mouses," he replied, "Hmmm...that word don't work for a cat."

"What about 'dash' and 'tear'?" Sheryl probed again. Together they tried different words in the poem, finally deciding that "leaps" best described the cat's movement after it had attacked a dangling string.

Stimulated by what they'd read as well as all the talk surrounding their own writing, most of the children soon began selecting words that were not only unusual but were also appropriate to the poem's meaning. As before, these words were often initially generated through the thesaurus, but now a list was scrutinized more critically or used only as a springboard to select a word that really captured what the child was trying to express. When Angela was working on her "Sunrise" poem, in which she tried to create a personification of the sun eating the night, she looked in various sections of the thesaurus to find an appropriate word to describe its movement. She wrote "steps," "peeks," "sneaks," and "tiptoes" in the margin of her poetry journal, then asked her friend Angie for help in selecting the best word. "Why not put 'the sun *tiptoes* to the horizon'?" advised Angie. "That's most like what an animal does." (See Chapter 16 for a copy and a more detailed discussion of the poem.)

In another instance, Johnny was trying to find the right word to compare the wind on a fall day to a painter. He too used the thesaurus for help and generated words like "painting," "brushing," "coloring," and "decorating." But none of them seemed quite right.

"What does the wind do to the leaves?" Peggy asked him.

"Captures them," he replied. "Oh, that's good! That's just what they say a painter does!" He changed the line to read "capturing a fall day." The poem eventually read as follows:

Autumn Masterpiece

The wind brushes
Warm colors
On a turquoise sky,
Capturing a fall day.

JOHNNY
Grade 6

Similarly, Bryan searched in the thesaurus for a word to describe a caterpillar's feet as it crawls up a branch. After much searching, then experimenting with different possibilities, he discovered "suction-cupped," which did indeed aptly capture what he was describing:

Caterpillar
(Revision 3)

On suction-cupped feet
The caterpillar crawls up

To a high, high branch
So softly
For his dinner.

BRYAN
Grade 6

A few children reached the point where their search for words could be characterized as experimental. These children actively played with variations of words, viewing the thesaurus more as a helpful tool than an ultimate authority. Rather than using the first word that seemed right, these children experimented with many different words as they manipulated the meaning of their poems. When Jennifer created a poem about a unicorn inside a miniature glass snowball, she generated several possibilities for a word, selected one, then several weeks later generated a whole new list for the same word when her subsequent revisions subtly changed the meaning and focus of the whole poem. When Jimmy was seeking just the right word to describe the quickness of a fox as a leaping fire, he systematically wrote in a series of words, changing other lines as he tried each one until he decided on the ones that described both a fox and the flames of a fire so as to complete the metaphor:

Fire Fox (first draft)	Fire Fox (checkmarked version)
It's a flame	It's a flame
It's a fox	It's a fox
Maybe a fire fox	Maybe a fire fox
He jumps and flips	Lunging and leaping
But the fire just won't	Panting with
go out	determination
JIMMY Grade 6	JIMMY Grade 6

Jim P's Basketball Poem

One of the most complete examples of how a poem's meaning evolved and was substantially modified by changes in word selection was Jim P's "Basketball" poem. Jim's poem is only one of many that showed how children in this class were choosing their words more carefully. Although Jim made many other changes in this poem, those dealing with word selection will be highlighted to clarify how far he had come in his understanding of wordcrafting. The following is the poem's first draft:

A motionless
Boy looks
At the net
He waits
Sweating
He wonders
If he is going
To make it in.
He bounces it
Crouches
He tosses
It.
The ball swirls and swirls
It goes in
The crowd
Gets wild
The team
Carries
Him all
Around.

After examining the first draft, Jim independently decided that "stares" was a better word than "looks," and "he sweats" made the poem sound more personal than "sweating." To determine the most appropriate word for how the ball really sounds as it goes in the basket, he selected "swoosh" because, he told me, "that's how the ball really sounds." He also changed "goes in" to "sinks in" to describe exactly how the ball enters the basket. The poem now read as follows:

A motionless boy
Stares at the
Net.
He sweats,
Wondering
If he can make it
He bounces the ball
He tosses it.
The ball swirls and swirls
SWOOSH

The ball sinks in
The crowd gets wild.

Jim then submitted his poem to a critiquing group of fellow basketball players that included Aaron, Jeremy, Johnny, and Mike J. They suggested he change "He sweats" to "Sweating in anticipation" so "you get the idea that everyone was waiting for something to happen." The group then talked extensively about the procedure a player uses to shoot a basket generating words like "concentrates" and "bounces the ball" to describe the steps. Jim wrote these in the margin of his notebook then added several to his poem, although he was adamant in turning down those he thought didn't fit.

Eventually, he showed his poem to me. "Hey, Amy, did you see I got a new title for my poem?" Now it's called 'One Point Behind'."

"Why did you change it?" I wanted to know.

"Okay. It's like you're at the foul line. It's the end of the game, and you've got so many seconds left. And when you're behind, you get all sweaty and nervous and stuff. Making it say 'One Point Behind' tells you more about what's happening. Just saying 'Basketball,' that's kind of plain."

"You crossed out a lot and tried a lot of different things in this poem," I said, noticing that some words were almost illegible and there were several rips and tears in the paper because it had been vigorously erased and written on so many times.

"Well, some of it didn't sound right," Jim told me. "When you write a poem you try out a lot of ideas when you write it. I'm trying to do a lot of that by myself now."

Jim had also completely reconceptualized the meaning of his poem. Rather than having the ball go in the basket and the crowd carrying the boy all around, he had decided instead on a less than happy ending in which the ball falls away from the basket and the game is lost. When asked why he made the change, Jim told me:

"I've read a lot of basketball poems. I read one that a kid in another class did, and they were always happy endings. I thought of making mine different. I had it happy for a while, but this is better."

I agreed. To me, a poem about losing the game had a greater emotional impact.

A subsequent critiquing session focused specifically on how to precisely describe the ball's movement in relation to the basket. Eventually the word "travels" was selected, although Jim insisted he could come up with a better one. As the group sat thinking, he had a brainstorm.

"You know how the sun orbits the earth?" he asked the group. "Doesn't the ball orbit the rim of the basket just like that?"

"Yea, that's great. That's it!" The group enthusiastically agreed. They substituted "orbits the rim" for "travels the rim," then Jim added "hesitates" and "falls" to describe how the ball moved. Following is the checkmarked version of Jimmy's poem:

One Point Behind

Motionless,
A boy stares at the net,
Sweating in anticipation.
He bounces the ball,
Concentrates,
Shoots,
And follows through.
The ball orbits the rim,
Hesitates,
Falls,
The game is lost.

JIMMY P
Grade 5

Wordcrafting

An awareness of how precise word choice affects meaning in poetry was internalized by many of the children. They appreciated the ways professional poets used this tool and successfully experimented with it in their own pieces. They skillfully coordinated word meaning with their overall poetic image. Although the words had to be physically present on the page for them to do this, they still were moving towards more abstract understandings of how meaning is precisely conveyed and emotion evoked by careful crafting of the words. Most importantly, they were learning that words could shape the feelings and meanings that they were trying to express.

CHAPTER 14

Music Making:
Rhyme and Rhythm
in Poetry

It doesn't always have to rhyme,
But there's the repeat of a beat, somewhere
an inner chime that makes
you want to tap your feet
Or swerve in a curve;
a lilt, a leap, a lightning split.

It Doesn't Always Have to Rhyme
EVE MERRIAM

Rhyme and rhythm are the music of poetry. The words in a poem have an infinite variety of sounds. There are short, brittle sounds, soft rolling sounds, the sibilance of many S's, and the long liquid sounds of flowing O's. Orchestrating these along with meaning is not an easy task. Sometimes poets must feel much like composers. In music, a slight change in rhythm affects the melody. These changes, in turn, require an adjustment in the lyric. The same is true for poetry. Your many revisions finally produce a beautiful chiming sound but then—the rhythm is off. Adjust that and then somehow the meaning doesn't quite work. But when everything comes together in an harmonic, melodic whole, the effect is a wonderfully pleasant musical experience for the listener.

The children's understanding of rhythm and rhyme was woven into previous discussions about their work. But it has not been the focus. Here we will trace the evolution of their awareness of sound in poetry.

Rhyme

Rhyme is one of the first things children seem to be aware of in poetry. "If it rhymes it's gotta be poetry," they invariably say. Conversely, it seems they think if it doesn't rhyme, it isn't poetry. Our children were no exception. Even though the teachers had stressed that poetry didn't really have to rhyme, we had a sneaking suspicion they didn't truly believe us.

This was certainly evident in the children's initial pieces. At both grade levels they seemed compelled to use rhyme with little or no thought to meaning. Essentially, the poems were nonsense as the following pieces reveal:

> The colors shine
> In my mind
> Bringing joy
> to the boy.
>
> ROBIN
> *Grade 5*

> If Sally and Kelly
> Could ever get along
> And marry King Kong
> And bong a song
> to get along.
>
> TIFFANY
> *Grade 5*

The teachers continually tried to show the group that poetry didn't always have to rhyme. In the large-group sharing sessions they read aloud many examples of published free verse helping the children discover how, for example, rhythm or imagery could make a piece a poem. Soon we realized they were beginning to develop an awareness of the distinction. As Lesa, a fifth grader who had originally been fond of rhyming, sing-song poems, commented in late fall: "Poetry doesn't always have to rhyme to be good. In many books the poems don't rhyme, and they're still good poems. You can say things better when you're not always trying to rhyme." This was a victory in our eyes! Although many of the children still preferred poems that rhymed, they gradually seemed to realize that rhyme was not essential in order to characterize something as poetry. Yet the teachers didn't

178

want to overdo it. Rhyme is a particularly pleasing component of poetry and is not something to be eliminated entirely. But they wanted the children to realize that rhyme was subservient to meaning: a poet must focus on meaning first, then, if desired, use rhyme to extend and complement meaning.

To further develop this awareness of rhyming's subservient role, Sheryl and Peggy would stress the interrelationship between rhyme and meaning in poems they read aloud. After an initial reading of a poem, the children would be asked first what they thought it was about, then how the poet "made it sound like a melody."

As the year progressed, more subtle elements like internal rhyming and assonance were discussed. A good example of how these distinctions evolved occurred during Sheryl's reading of John Ciardi's "Catbird." After reading the poem aloud once, she could tell the children had enjoyed the rhythm and rhyme. Many were repeating the words to themselves and each other. Repeated requests were made to read it again. After doing so, Sheryl asked, "Now he used common, everyday words, but why were these words so effective?"

"The place he put them and the way he used them, like 'a fat bird, a cat bird'," answered Johnny.

"Yes, the way he used them," responded Sheryl. "If he'd just said 'a fat bird was sitting on a stump' . . . "

"It would be boring," said Stacie.

"A fat bird, a cat bird, what is he doing with that?" Sheryl asked the group.

"Rhyming," answered Bryan.

"He's rhyming," Sheryl agreed. "That's called internal rhyme. It's not at the end of lines but inside, close together within a line."

Similarly, when reading Merriam's "Summer Rain," which has lines like "A tangle, a tickle" and "A trickle, A silver dot freckle," Sheryl helped the children see how Merriam used words like "trickle" and "freckle" together to create an "almost rhyme."

These same ideas were then applied to the children's own writings. Both teachers reassured the children that rhyming was not essential in poetry but, rather, was something that might be used to enhance a poem only after the meaning was clear.

"It's very hard to write rhyming poems," Sheryl told them. "I want you to be able to do that eventually. But you need to get feeling and meaning into it first."

Soon the children themselves began commenting on rhyme's subservience to meaning when they helped each other revise. The following conversation is a good example. In this incident, Robin was sharing one of her latest poems with a small group.

"This is the one about pebbles. I want you guys to help me with it," she told them. She then read her poem aloud:

> Pebbles that shine
> They're certainly fine
> You can't find them in a coal mine
> They won't even stay in a line.

The group was silent for a moment after she finished reading. Then Johnny, in his usual forthright manner said, "That don't make sense."

"Like you don't mostly find pebbles in a coal mine. Mostly what you find is coal. These two lines [the last ones] don't go good," Aaron told her.

"You mean it don't fit in with the rest?" she asked.

"It's just...I think you're trying too hard to rhyme," Shelly suggested.

"What happens when you try to rhyme?" asked Sheryl who happened to overhear the conversation.

"Sometimes it don't make much sense!" responded Aaron.

"Yeah, you're right," responded Robin thoughtfully, although she seemed a bit frustrated.

"Here's another one like it," Sheryl told the group. "Shelly, read yours. The rest of you see what you think."

Shelly read her poem aloud:

> Sand so fine,
> Pebbles that shine...
> Water that grabs the shore
> Glistens at night
> in the moonlight
> Grasping for more and more.

"That's a good poem!" Johnny exclaimed. "She's got rhyme, and she's got some meaning."

After the nonsense rhyme stage, most of the children went through a time in which their pieces were essentially devoid of rhyme. It was almost as if they were scared of it. They seemed to be so conscious of creating a meaningful piece, that they couldn't contend with yet another element like rhyming. This was fine. We wanted them to see meaning as central. We were confident that eventually they would use rhyming in purposeful ways.

Our intuitions were right. Gradually the children began incorporating rhyme into their pieces. Usually they would first create a rough draft in which the emphasis was on conveying an image, capturing a particular feeling, or some other sense-making purpose. The use of rhyme was then considered for subsequent revisions. Often a series of rhyming words would be generated, then those words that seemed to fit well together would be selected. Bryan, after creating an initial draft that compared snowflakes and butterflies, generated a list of words with long I sounds, then experimented with various combinations to create the following poem:

Snowflake

Fluttering from the sky
Like a winter butterfly.
Moving left, moving right
In the coldness of the night.

BRYAN C.
Grade 6

Similarly, Teava experimented with rhyme along with rhythm to create her "My Red Mood" poem. After an intense blackboard critiquing session in which a small group gave Teava suggestions for words they associated with red that also rhymed and provided rhythm, she created the following poem:

My Red Mood

Red is the heat from a hot, blazing fire,
A soft furry sweater awaiting a buyer.

Red is the sweet smell of roses in spring
Red are my cheeks that the winter winds sting.

Red is a feeling that rings deep inside
When I get angry and want to hide.

Red is a sunset waving good-bye.
Red is the sunrise shouting, "Surprise."

TEAVA
Grade 6

The following poems are additional examples of those which similarly evolved from small-group critiquing sessions:

Dunkin'

Grab the ball,
Hold it high,

Jam it in,
While passing by.

MIKE J.
Grade 5

Kitten

He was a furball, black and white
He made me sad one lonely night.
He slipped away into the dark,
The only sound, a lone dog's bark.

JOHNNY
Grade 6

Sunday morning french toast
I'll eat, you be host.
Spread the butter, spread it thick;
Pour the syrup, pour it quick,
Sprinkle cinnamon, sprinkle it brown
Smell it while I gulp it down.

JEREMY
Grade 5

Of course all the children did not write poems with succinct meanings and clever rhymes. Indeed, some wrote essentially free verse the entire year. Or they might use rhyme for one poem, then not use it for a while. This was fine. We didn't want them to use rhyme all the time just because they'd figured out how to do it appropriately. Rather, we wanted the children to use it purposefully, when it seemed to fit a particular poem. Rhyming, we hoped, would become one more resource in their poetry writing repertoire.

A few children did experiment with the more complex kinds of rhyme that had been introduced in a sharing sessions. For example, Johnny used internal rhyme, or what he termed "a different kind of rhyme," in his haiku poem. His first draft of the poem read as follows:

A green milky stack
Wearing bunches of yellow
As her spring hat.

Although the poem was a haiku in the technical sense that it had almost the proper number of lines and syllables, Johnny felt it needed more. After looking up synonyms for "wearing" and generating a list of rhyming words for "yellow," he experimented with different word combinations, eventually creating the following checkmarked version:

Hello Spring

Thin bodies of green
Sport caps of yellow, yellow.
Hello, Hello, Spring!

Similarly, Jennifer experimented with various elaborate rhyme schemes, to write the following poem in which she experimented with assonance and rhyme:

Tears

A wrinkle
A sprinkle
Tears tickle my cheeks.

A gleam
A stream
Tears streak my cheeks.

After a downpour
A yawn
I sleep.

JENNIFER
Grade 6

Jimmy experimented with some internal rhyme in his cat poem that he left untitled. The poem had originally begun "he tiptoes slightly across the room." After several revisions and conversations with friends, the line was changed to read as follows:

He rip toes, tip toes
Across the room

The relining was done deliberately to enhance the rhyming.

Alliteration and Onomatopoeia

The patterned repetition of a series of consonants, or alliteration, is also a sound in poetry. Children seemed to particularly enjoy this element. Consider the popularity of tongue twisters like "She sells seashells by the seashore" and nursery rhymes like "Hey, Diddle Diddle" and "Sing a Song of Sixpence," and you will probably agree that alliteration creates a musical quality in verse that children love.

The children became more sensitive to the ways professional poets use this device and experimented with it in their own writing. Shortly after listening to and talking about poetry that used alliteration, the children began commenting on how it contributed to a poem's aggregate sound and meaning. Thus, after hearing Rutherford's "Lone Dog," Bryan commented, "She made the dog sound real lonely by the way she repeated the sounds." Similarly, after reading "Summer Rain," the group shared a mutual appreciation for Merriam's musical phrases like "speckles the spotted rain" and "the rainingest rain." Everyone repeated these phrases over and over, allowing them, in the words of Becky, "to roll around our tongues and out of our mouths."

With all this exposure to alliteration, it was natural for the children to begin experimenting with it in their own work. The use of alliteration gradually began appearing in poems written by children at both grade levels. Deon commented that she deliberately changed the line "blowing leaves scatter the ground" in her "Wind" poem to "blowing leaves spinning in spirals" in an attempt to sound more poetic. Similarly, Tammy, a fifth grader, changed the word "knocking" to "scratching" so her "Halloween" poem used more alliteration:

> Ghosts, witches, goblins and spooky things
> Scratching at your bedroom window.

Johnny, with Jimmy's help, experimented with various alliterative patterns in his "Rain" poem:

Rain
(rough draft)

> Pitter, patter
> Coming down
> Washing cars
> And watering plants.

Once the boys thought of "puddles up potholes" to describe the rain's effect, it was easy to change the first lines so they were alliterative. With some additional reconceptualization the final poem was created.

Rain
(checkmarked version)

Pouring rain
Puddles up
Potholes
Showers down
Dusty cars
And saves
Thirsty plants.

JOHNNY
Grade 6

In a similar manner, Brandon deliberately added the word "sweet" to his haiku poem to heighten the alliterative effect of the "s" sounds.

A brook moves slowly
Carrying signs of spring
Into sweet summer.

BRANDON
Grade 6

Sometimes the teachers would offer advice as to how alliteration could be used to enhance a poem's sound. When Angela was working on her poem about ice cream, Sheryl asked her to read her poem aloud. They then focused on specific lines.

"What parts do you like the best?" asked Sheryl.

" 'Tongue, tongue, tongue, tasty,' " said Angela. "I like how it sounds with all the *t*'s."

"Do you remember what I said about alliteration?" Sheryl asked her. She pulled Jarrell's *The Bat Poet* off the shelf and read aloud some of the parts that contained alliteration. They moved back to Angela's poem.

"Hmmm...tasty what? An ice cream is a tasty what?" asked Sheryl. "If you're going to carry through the alliteration, you need to add what? Why don't you think about it or go around and ask some of the kids?"

Angela left, returning about ten minutes later.

"Stacie suggested 'tasty tingles' and Kelli said 'tasty taste,' " she told Sheryl.

"Those are good ideas," replied Sheryl. "And well … ice cream is a real …"

"Treat!" exclaimed Angela. "I'll play with those and see which one I like best."

Here is her checkmarked version of the poem:

Ice Cream Cone
(checkmarked version)

Drip
Drip
Drip
Down the side
lick
lick
lick
Up the side
tongue
tongue
tongue
The tasty treat
crunch
crunch
crunch
The cone I eat.

ANGELA
Grade 6

The children developed an awareness of onomatopoeia, the use of words that represent a sound, in much this same way. Again the work of professional poets stimulated the children who began to experiment with this device in their own work. Because onomatopoeia was much easier to integrate meaningfully into a poem than some of the other elements, more children felt comfortable using it. The following are typical poems in which this device was used:

Wind

The wind terrorizes the branches
Whip, nip, rip

It wipes off the leaves
Slip, snip, strip
And munches on the trunk
For the fun of it

JIMMY R.
Grade 6

Watch out!
A roaring wave
Chasing you across
the beach
Splash!
The roaring wave
Shrinks
Never to be seen again

JEREMY
Grade 5

Mr. Early
in the morning
wakes me with his
   Cockle
     Doodle
      Doos
Cockles me out of bed
And into
   my
     shoes.

ANGELA
Grade 6

Rhythm

Rhythm gives a poem its pulse and movement and weaves the words together into a connected whole. It's also often the first thing about poetry to which children respond. Listening to babies' rhythmic babble or watching young children who feel compelled to move to their various play rhymes, you realize that rhythm is one of the most basic elements of poetry.

Peggy and Sheryl frequently urged the children to listen for the rhythmical, musical quality in poetry. "Think about how words play against each other, sound with each other, slide from one to another, bounce against each other," they continually said. Accordingly, when sharing the work of professional poets, they would often discuss how words functioned to provide a rhythm for the poem. For example, during one sharing session I heard Peggy ask the group, "What besides its meaning makes a poem go around in our head after we walk away from hearing it? What about the rhythm? So how a poem reads, the way it moves, the rhythm, that feeling of a beat, has something to do with how we react to it."

In another instance after reading Van Doren's "Dance Song Six," the children were asked to think about the effect of the following lines:

> Here we go round like raindrops.
> Raindrops here we go round.

"Does the rhythm help you decide things about the poem?" Sheryl asked the group. "Did the rhythm of this poem make you think of any way that it might be [like] a ballet?"

Several children nodded in agreement.

"It makes you think, doesn't it, of the smoothness and flow of the words and the smoothness and flow of ballet," continued Sheryl.

Another time later in the year, Sheryl made similar connections while reading Merriam's "Autumn Leaves."

"Listen to what she [Merriam] does with leaves. It starts out in a very ordinary way. But look what she does. She catches us up in it by her use of words to make it sound like autumn leaves really sound."

She read the poem aloud, emphasizing the sounds of words like "skittery" and "flittery."

"See if you can play with words in your own poetry," she told them. "Play with patterns and sounds of words, like 'skittery' and 'fluttery,' [or] 'hustle by, rustle by.' What do you think those mean?"

Soon, just as with the other poetic devices, the children began responding appreciatively on their own to the rhythm of a poem. When Coatsworth's "Swift Things Are Beautiful" was read, Stacie commented that she "liked how the poet made it go fast when she talked about swift things and slow when she talked about slow things." At other times, children would tap their feet or snap fingers to a particularly rhythmic poem.

As a result of the attention given to rhythm in the sharing sessions, the children began to recognize when their own poems lacked rhythm or where one line broke the rhythm of the entire piece. They soon learned one way to solve this problem was to pare away unnecessary words, "using their scalpel," so that the resulting piece possessed a rhythmical, musical quality.

Initially, however, children were rather indiscriminate in their use of the scalpel. They would eliminate all the "little" words (like grammatical constructions such as articles or conjunctions) or remove *ing* endings. Following a rule rather than improving the style seemed to be their rationale at this point. For example, when Angie helped Michelle with her "Winter" poem, her first comment was, "This poem needs work. You've really lost your rhythm here." She then indicated the words to be cut by placing an "x" over them as follows:

Winter
(rough draft)

x
~~Cold and wintry day~~
x
Chattering my teeth

x
Slapping my cold hands
x
on my face

Making my cheeks cold
x
and red.

MICHELE
Grade 6

The poem is probably improved by these changes, but the cuts were not made thoughtfully. Angie was just following a rule she had internalized without considering how meaning was affected by the changes.

To help them, the teachers would often read a child's poem aloud to establish a sense of when the rhythm didn't quite work, thereby disrupting the flow of the poem's sound. Sometimes they would suggest the scalpel be used. With the teachers explaining why cutting out unnecessary words made a poem better, the children eventually understood how to do this deliberately and thoughtfully on their own. This occurred when Jeremy was working on his "Breaking" poem about breakdancing. He read it aloud to Peggy and some of his fifth-grade buddies.

" 'Breaking to the beat with hightops on your feet'," he read aloud.

"I like the rhythm," commented Aaron. "It's got good rhyming that makes the rhythm better. Do you think you should keep the word 'with' in?"

"That's a good question," interjected Peggy. "How would your lines work if you said 'breaking to the beat, high tops on your feet'?"

After reading both possibilities several times to himself Jeremy decided the group was right and erased "with."

Eventually, many of the children were able to carefully select words for their revisions so as to create a rhythm that functioned consistently within the total meaning of the piece. Rather than randomly cutting lines and words, they became increasingly aware of revision that simultaneously enhanced rhythm and extended meaning. Thus, for example, Tommy changed the second line in his "Bacon" poem from "grease pops on the stove" to "popping grease" because it not only sounded more like a poem but also "made a picture in your mind." Similarly, Carrie changed the lines "Snowflakes play tag" to "Tag is the game snowflakes play" because "it had more rhythm to it and went better with the rest of the poem." It seems that exposure to good models, and then having the opportunity to experiment with rhythm in their own pieces gave the students the support they needed to integrate rhythm *and* meaning. Eventually, rhythm in poetry seemed as natural to them as the rhythm required for rope-jumping, basketball dribbling, and breathing (Livingston, 1982).

Jimmy's Unicorn Poem

The evolution of Jimmy's "Unicorn" poem is representative of how the children began integrating elements of rhythm and rhyme along with meaning in their poetry. The idea to write such a poem came from Jimmy's rich knowledge of folklore, fairy tales, legends, and myths as well as his active imagination. Following is an early draft:

Unicorn
(Revision I)

I wish to see a unicorn
To feel the curving of his horn,
Then feel its silk like skin
But my dream is hopeless
For unicorns are works of my imagination.

Jimmy liked the rhyming of "unicorn" and "horn" in his first two lines, but he was dissatisfied with the last three lines because he thought they didn't sound poetic enough. Somehow the rhythm wasn't yet right. He was frustrated. "This poem needs better rhythm, but it's got to make sense too." I encouraged him to keep working on it.

He began experimenting with various ways to change these lines. Realizing the first two lines were each eight syllables long, he began playing with different ways to have the others follow the same pattern. Soon he created, "To touch his silver, silken skin" and "To dream a dream of him again." I asked him about the "silver, silken skin" line.

"That's got a good rhythm," he told me. "Also, the words 'silver' and 'silken' go good together because they start the same."

I noticed he'd also changed "wish" to "seek" in the first line.

"Why did you do that?" I asked him.

"Well, 'seek' sounds more like olden days and that's when unicorn stories take place," he replied. And it sort of rhymes with 'see.' "

Later I noticed he changed it back to wish. "It sounded too much like a book," he told me.

I found this comment intriguing. Jimmy obviously had tried to use more sophisticated alliteration, yet when the poem lacked the tone he wanted, he abandoned it in favor of his original thought. Jimmy seemed to have a strong sense of his own poetic voice.

He now concentrated on the last two lines, first changing "hopeless" to "shattered," then rejecting it as not quite workable for the rest of the poem. He also crossed out "imagination" because "it's got too many syllables and messed up my rhythm." Eventually the whole last line was discarded as unworkable.

He then began to seek the advice of peers and teachers.

"How would you really like to see a unicorn?" Sheryl asked him.

"Free—not belonging to anyone," answered Jimmy. Then, thoughtfully, he whispered to himself, "wildly free." He added this phrase to the last line of his poem.

When he showed me a subsequent revision, I noticed he had essentially added a new line by changing the words in the first line around. I asked him why.

"Mrs. Reed read us a bunch of poems where the poet repeats lines and words to get rhythm," he replied. "I tried it in my poem, and it sounds good."

Finally, satisfied he had successfully integrated rhythm and rhyme with meaning, he created this version:

Not Mine, Not Yours

I wish to see a unicorn,
To feel the curving of his horn,
To touch his silver, silken skin,
To dream a dream of him again.
A unicorn I wish to see,
Not mine, not yours, but wildly free.

JIMMY
Grade 6

Jimmy had created a symphony.

Music Making

Through repeated encounters with reading poetry, the children became attuned to its rhythmical, musical qualities. In turn, they began to create pieces on their own that revealed they recognized the importance of these elements, even though they weren't always capable of using them in sophisticated ways. Both reading and writing contributed to their awareness. Their understandings were also contextually based, rooted in the larger purposes of evoking emotion or creating an imaginative image. No directives like "Thou shalt write a three line haiku with a certain number of syllables per line" were given. Nor were the children expected to adhere to tight, formal rules of rhyme or meter. Rather, we encouraged them to offer honest, unclichéd visions of their world. Rhyme and rhythm were viewed as tools that could add to the effect of that vision.

CHAPTER 15

Image Shaping:
The Look of Poetry

Poem clouds
Pelt words,
Lightning letters
Flash across a piece of paper,
While thundering metaphors
Sound throughout my poem.
A wild wind
Scatters ideas
Forming a line pattern
Appealing to the eye of the storm.

"From the Eye of the Poet"
SETH
Grade 4

One of the least discussed poetic elements is the visual image a poem creates: how the words are written, how many are placed per line, the spaces between the words and between each subsequent line, and the meaning of the whole poem in relation to its indentation and punctuation. Some poets use print creatively to emphasize particular letters or words as when "splash" is written in capitals to denote the loud sound a wave makes as it crashes against the beach in a storm. Other poets create a visual image that mirrors their meaning. Myra Cohn Livingston's poem "Building" is written in the shape of a skyscraper, and Eve Merriam's "Showers, Clearing Later in the Day" is written entirely in exclamation points and asterisks. Although how a poem looks is not usually the driving force for its creation, it can nevertheless have a significant influence on its meaning and effect.

The children gradually acquired a sense of the various factors that influence how a poem looks. We weren't quite sure how this happened since the teachers never presented any formal lessons on the topic, and the poetry was usually read aloud and not seen by the children.

Occasionally, however, during the large-group sharing sessions, they pointed out instances in which a poet had used an unusual shape or series of line patterns. Arnold Adoff's poems were particularly appropriate for this. After his visit at Ridgemont the previous year, the children had closely examined his poetry and became fascinated with his intriguing, unusual line patterns. As a result, his techniques were often imitated, particularly by Johnny who often tried to line pieces in Adoff's style:

Milkweed Meal
(checkmarked version)

Aphids,
Scaly insects,
Delicious food
Ladybugs
Love
To snack
Upon.

JOHNNY
Grade 6

Other times the teachers would point out how a poet used a certain number of words per line or varied the spacing to achieve an unusual effect. This was always done after the teachers had discussed other aspects of a poem since lining was considered a means to an end rather than the major focus of a poem.

The children rarely made verbal comments on their own about a poem's written form, even during their conversations with each other. For the most part they got a sense of how poetry looks through closely examining the work of many poets. They then experimented with line and shape in their own pieces. Trying it out on their own when they had a need to make their own poems look more poetic seemed to make the difference.

Most children passed through the initial stage of paragraph poetry (see Chapter 7) in which their pieces looked more like prose than poetry. Seemingly, they had little idea of even the basic concept of poetic form, much less any notion of lining and spacing or how the placement of words could serve a deliberate purpose. With more experience examining the work of professional poets, their pieces moved from paragraph form to that which more closely resembled the way conventional poetry looks. They became more aware that poets use space differently from prose writers and that the visual effect of one's piece is important.

The children became more aware of relining as a possible tool, but initially they had little idea of its relationship to meaning. Often they would write a poem that approximated conventional form (a few words per line, capitalization at the beginning of each line, etc.); then they would move a word up or down a line. Sometimes the only change would involve rewriting the same line in a different visual pattern. The following poems by Johnny and Mike are typical of this kind of revision.

Rain
(Revision 3)

The rain falls on
The roof pitter patter pitter patter
plop plop
repeats the rain.

Mike H.
Grade 5

Rain
(checkmarked version)

The rain falls
On the roof.
Pitter, Patter
Pitter, Patter
Plop, Plop
Repeats the rain.

Mike H.
Grade 5

Wind
(rough draft)

The wind whistles
Through the branches
Like a train
Through a tunnel
Invisible to the eye

Johnny
Grade 6

Wind
(checkmarked version)

The wind whistles
Through the branches
Like a train
Through a tunnel—
Invisible to the eye,
Captured by the ear.

Johnny
Grade 6

When I asked the children why they made these changes, they usually replied that they wanted their pieces to look like "real" poetry. There was no sign that they were aware of how changing line patterns could affect meaning. As with their initial revisions for rhythm, rhyme, and wording, they seemed to be following a rule.

The teachers tried to help by encouraging the children to

experiment or "play with" various line patterns. Sometimes they would subtly suggest changes that would help make their pieces more closely adhere to conventional poetic form. For example, when Angie asked for advice on her "Seashell" poem, she told Sheryl, "This don't make sense. The last two lines aren't right."

"Maybe . . . particularly the way you lined it. Why don't you reline it? Maybe you won't have to change anything else then," Sheryl suggested.

In another instance Jennifer was encouraged to "use the scalpel" to cut out unnecessary words, thus allowing her to combine two lines.

"Is there any way you can make one line out of the first two lines, 'a friend in the sky, a friend in the night'?" Sheryl asked Jennifer. "Think about ways you could combine those first two lines and see what you can get. How could you put all that in one line—and mean the same thing?"

"Sky night," answered Jennifer.

"Almost," Sheryl urged her to keep thinking.

"Night sky," said Jennifer.

"'A friend in the night sky'," replied Sheryl, "see what I mean? You combined that and got a lot more mileage out of your words. You even made a stronger statement."

The teachers stimulated the children's thinking by challenging them to "consider the possibilities for reorganizing the lines yet still retaining the meaning." Or they might say, "This poem seems backwards to me. Could you rearrange things so they go together better?"

Many of the children gradually became more aware of the subtle relationship between lining and a poem's meaning. This was particularly true for those who regularly participated in teacher-led critiquing groups and examined professional poetry on their own. I noticed a more deliberate manipulation of words and lines with these children. They moved lines and words around to make a meaning clearer or to create a stronger visual effect. Many did this on a rather limited basis. One line might be moved from top to bottom, or two lines would be combined, or every other line would be indented to emphasize a unique rhythm. Their actions were definitely more deliberate than those I'd observed earlier in the year.

By January I was observing many instances in which the children included relining as a natural part of the revision process. Thus, Johnny, on the advice of his friends, relined his "Bat" poem in the following way:

Bat
(Revision 1)

Hanging on a porch
In the midday light
Waiting for night
To talk the day away
The cuddled shape.

JOHNNY
Grade 6

Bat
(Revision 2)

Hanging on a porch
In the midday light
The cuddled brown shape
Waits for night.

JOHNNY
Grade 6

"My new version sounds better because the rhyme and meaning go together now," he told me excitedly.

Similarly, when Ronnie was writing a poem about fog, his friends suggested he move the word "then" to a line all by itself so it would stand out and make a reader continue reading:

Fog
(Revision 2)

Fog cuddles you in its
   mysterious gray blanket
Waiting for the sun to
   penetrate
Then it will vanish into
   daylight.

RONNIE
Grade 6

Fog
(Revision 3)

Fog cuddles you in its
   Mysterious gray blanket
Waiting for the sun to penetrate
Then
It will vanish into daylight.

RONNIE
Grade 6

Brandon experimented with relining until satisfied that his final version had just the right rhythm for the topic, "Jets."

Jets
(rough draft)

Jets flying across the
sky leaving their
white streak calling
card across the sky

BRANDON
Grade 6

Jets
(Revision 2)

Calling cards of white
Streak the endless sky
Fluff out, fade
Then disappear into the
blue like the jets
that created them.

BRANDON
Grade 6

Jets
(Revision 3)

Calling cards of white
Streak the endless sky
Fluff out,
Fade,
Then disappear
Into the blue
Like the jets
That created them.

BRANDON
Grade 6

Brandon's rough draft is evidence that we still occasionally had children who wrote paragraph poetry, even near the end of the year. Yet when we looked more carefully at the process and refrained from commenting on the use of this form, we discovered this was often done as a rough draft, as was Brandon's purpose. Jim P. wrote several revisions of his "Owl" poem in essentially paragraph form— then wrote the final version in meaningfully lined poetic form when he was satisfied with everything else. The slashes were added just before the last revision to indicate where line breaks should be in his final version. It is interesting to note that in the final process of relining, he dropped the word "he" out of several lines. Evidently the relining process helped him perceive a more concise way to give the effect of an owl waiting, then suddenly bearing down on its prey:

Owl
(revision)

The owl sleeps/in the day/
But at night/he hunts
He screeches/he swoops down/
feeds upon whatever he finds.

JIM P.
Grade 5

Owl
(relining)

The Owl sleeps
In the day
But at night

198

Learning About Poetic Elements

Hunts,
Screeches,
Swoops down,
Feeds upon
Whatever he finds.

JIM P.
Grade 5

Aaron did a similar thing with his "Sandpit" poem:

Sand Pit (rough draft)	Sandpile (checkmarked version)

Sand Pit
(rough draft)

A small desert in
the middle of nowhere.
Tiny creatures crawling
for food.
And miniature cactuses
Take over the land.

AARON
Grade 5

Sandpile
(checkmarked version)

In a
Pocket-sized
Desert
Tiny creatures
Crawl and search
For shelter
Among
Miniature weeds

AARON
Grade 5

Some children became quite skillful at manipulating multiple lines within one poem or even manipulating whole verses. Deon experimented with shifting the lines in her "Witches" poem to "make it sound better and emphasize the rhyme."

Witches
(Revision 2)

On my broom
With my cat
I fly around
The moon
Knocking
On windows
With my
Pointy hat.

DEON
Grade 6

Witches
(Revision 3)

Black against the moon
She rides with pointy hat
As she hunches on her broom
With her cat.

DEON
Grade 6

199

Witches
(Revision 4)

As she lurches on her broom
She rides with pointy hat
Black against the moon
With her big black cat.
She swoops down, down, down
To rattle windows
All over town.

DEON
Grade 6

When Jennifer revised her "Snowball" poem (about a unicorn within a crystal snowball) in late March, she experimented with various ways to reline by changing lines from one verse to another, revising fourteen times. She then asked Sheryl for her opinion and was told to follow her own intuition. Returning to her work, Jennifer took elements from each of her last five revisions and wrote a new one. She then experimented with this fifteenth revision, manipulating lines and verses. She finally was pleased with the effect of her sixteenth revision, the final draft. The most complex relining strategies occurred between revisions nine and ten. Her changes in these resulted in the best revisions and line patterns for her final draft.

The Unicorn and the Snow
(Revision 9)

I am the unicorn
Reaching for a storm
In a snow crystal.

I expect the snow
In my glass ball.
Underneath, the snow pauses.

The snow around me,
Upside down,
Plays in circles.

JENNIFER
Grade 6

The Unicorn and the Snow
(Revision 10)

In a snow crystal,
Reaching for a storm,
I am the unicorn.

Underneath, the storm pauses.
In my glass ball,
I expect the snow.

The snow around me
Plays in circles
Up-side down.

JENNIFER
Grade 6

The Unicorn and the Snow
(Revision 16, checkmarked version)

In a snow crystal,
Awaiting a storm,
I play the unicorn.
At the bottom
Of my glass ball,
The storm rests.

Up-side down
The snow surrounds me
And plays in circles.

JENNIFER
Grade 6

She even wrote notes to herself to keep things straight, saying things like, "If I use this line here, I have to change what that line says." She then drew arrows to the appropriate lines.

Jennifer was not typical, but her work is evidence that children *are* able to manipulate abstract ideas if what they are working with holds personal meaning for them.

Those who adopted the blackboard critiquing strategy became particularly willing to experiment with relining. Writing the piece on the board provided a concrete referent for the abstract task of manipulating both lines and meaning. Although the children were developing the ability to think abstractly, they still seemed to need a concrete representation of the process.

Angela's "Kitten"

Angela's "Kitten" is a good example of the extent to which children became aware of relining as a way of refining the meaning of their pieces. In late April, Angela decided to go back to an earlier poem she'd written because Sheryl said that she had "captured some marvelous feline attributes." At the same time she had advised Angela that the last stanza wasn't quite as strong as the first two. The original read as follows:

Kitten
(rough draft)

He's nothing much but fur
And two round eyes of green,

201

Image Shaping

He has a giant purr
And a giant meow.

He darts and pats the air
He cocks his head and ear,
When there is nothing
For him to see or hear.

He runs around in rings
Chases his tail
With sideways leaps
He springs.

    Probably because Sheryl had commented on the third stanza, Angela decided to begin with that. She rewrote it several ways, experimenting with different ways to make the rhyme "sound good" but still retain meaning. First she did the following:

He chases his tail
With sideways leaps and springs
And runs around in ring.

This was crossed out and a new version was attempted.

With sideways leaps and springs
He chases his tail
And runs in rings

Angela drew arrows from her original to her new version to remind herself about the particular changes she was making.

    Finally, she decided to once again change the order of her lines while simultaneously combining parts of lines two and three of stanza three. Again, she did this to emphasize the rhyme:

He chases his tail
In rings
With sideways
leaps and springs

    Next she focused on the second stanza. Deciding line two, "He cocks his head and ear," should occur first in the sequence of events she was describing, she made it line one. "Then darts and pats the air" was moved to the end of this stanza.

    "A kitten first listens, then moves and pats the air with its paws," she told me. "I wanted to make it like they really do it."

Now moving to the first stanza (in the margin of which she had written a note to herself saying, "get better words here"), Angela generated several synonyms for "giant" to describe the size of the kitten's meow because she decided repeating "giant" was not a good idea. Writing "loud," "trumpet-toned," "powerful," and "booming" in the margin of her book, she experimented with each in turn until deciding that "trumpet-toned" was the meaning she wanted.

Her checkmarked version read as follows:

Kitten

He's nothing much but fur
With two round eyes of green.
He has a giant purrrrr
And a trumpet-toned meow.

He cocks his head and ear
When there seems nothing
For him to see or hear,
Then darts and pats the air.

He chases his tail
In rings
With sideways
leaps and springs

Angela's poem still lacked a steady rhythm but she felt ready to move on to something different. This was fine. Angela had worked hard on her poem and was satisfied with it. She knew her work on the relining had helped her come closer to her goal of creating a rhyming poem that accurately described a cat's movements.

Image Shaping

Alec, one of Sheryl's more recent students, wrote "Frost" in long, slim thinness; a form that reflected his sense of the waning days of autumn.

Frost

Silent
Silvery,
Frost
Slips in
When I

Sleep.
My cold nose wakes me.
My cold toes shake me.
Frost whispers to me
Winter,
Winter
Winter.

ALEC
Grade 4

Alec, like many of the Ridgemont children, had internalized the notion that strong as the image, words, or rhythm may be, the way a poem presents itself on paper also influences the reader. He knew that this time he had captured a look that closely resembled his image of impending winter.

Yet to say that Alec and the others will continue to combine the elements of poetry and line pattern in such a satisfyingly appropriate way is an overstatement. They are but beginning to try on the shoes of poetry—some choices will be beautiful but not serviceable, or practical but not attractive. As they grow, those elements that once fit and were once well loved will be set aside for those that better serve their developing taste and allow for growth.

And so it is and will be with a child who has been taken to a shoe store bursting with selections, where someone cares to offer choices and helps at the appropriate time with the fitting of the shoes. By sharing many kinds of poetry Sheryl and Peggy presented the group with a variety of possibilities for fitting their poems into a meaningful shape. They then provided guidance as to the best fit. But the ultimate selection was, of course, left to the children.

CHAPTER 16

Image Making:
Using Figurative Language

Wind crimps
New fallen snow
Like fresh ideas
For a poem
Buckling onto my paper.

CHELSEA
Grade 4

The impulse to make metaphor is a fundamental aspect of human intelligence. Our entire conceptual system is essentially metaphoric in nature, allowing us to understand one thing in terms of another (Lakoff and Johnson, 1980). Through these connections we create relationships that challenge our accepted version of reality and provide us with fresh perspectives and new insights.

Children seem to make metaphors instinctively. They mix dream and reality, fact and fiction, making impossible combinations of ideas in their haste to capture everything they experience (Langer, 1951). Thus, they will put a bucket on their head and label it a hat or tear up a piece of paper and solemnly hand you a "dollar" (Gardner and Winner, 1979). They also delight in metaphorical images created by others; the moon "as the North Wind's Cooky" (Lindsay, 1986) or snow that "makes bushes look like popcorn balls" (Allen, 1957), for example, are completely acceptable and appealing to them.

Thus, one would assume that poetry with its particular element of figurative language (metaphor, simile, personification) would hold strong appeal for children. Unfortunately, this is generally not the case. In fact, as children grow older, figurative language is one of the most disliked poetic elements. As Terry (1972) discovered in her national survey, "Students frequently found poems containing the poetic elements of imagery and figurative language unenjoyable and difficult to understand. Because of the presence of these [metaphorical] elements, the meaning of the poem becomes less obvious."

Some researchers have concluded that this lack of affinity for figurative language is due to children's immature intellectual development. Cognitive psychologists like Piaget (1952) assert that the capacity to deal with ambiguity, double meanings, and abstract comparisons does not develop until adolescence. His research suggests that children are incapable of comprehending the abstract associations of figurative language. Others contend that children may lack the experiential background necessary for relating metaphoric images to what they know about reality or they may use personal experience inappropriately, completely ignoring the author's intention or clues provided in the text (Skelton, 1963).

Other researchers disagree with these conclusions and suggest instead that intermediate-grade children have the potential to both understand and appreciate figurative language if properly supported in their efforts. They contend that the critical factor may well be the way students are introduced to figurative language rather than the language constructions themselves (Smith, 1973; Redmond, 1978; Folta, 1979). For example, when the figurative language of a poem is discussed, teachers often emphasize discovering the "right" interpretation rather than allowing children to explore multiple interpretations of the images. Or children are required to memorize a definition along with some examples and are then asked to complete a fill-in-the-blank workbook page. These worksheets encourage the creation of clichéd, superficial metaphorical constructions in that they limit children to describing what "love is" or "happiness is" rather than allowing them to explore the images in a way that is personally interesting. Rarely are they encouraged to forge a connection between their own experience and the abstract image created by a poet. Such a connection is critical for the comparison to be understood and appreciated. When this connection is missing, children turn away from figurative language.

Learning About Figurative Language

Sheryl and Peggy introduced the elements of figurative language as a natural part of a general discussion about a poem. Their emphasis was first on enjoyment—what made the poem intriguing, interesting, or vivid. Then they would try to intensify the children's enjoyment by exploring with them how a poet orchestrates figurative language to create particular effects.

The discussions focused on similes and metaphors and, to a lesser degree, personification. After a general discussion of the poem, the group looked more closely at what was being compared, so as to understand how this comparison helped them view the phenomena differently. They soon became adept at noticing when a poet was "comparing things," but few used the terms "metaphor" or "simile." Those who did generally used "metaphor" indiscriminately for both.

The following large-group discussion that developed from the reading of Eve Merriam's "From the Japanese" shows how these understandings often evolved. The poem has subtle imagery and is not one the teachers would use initially with children. It is the kind of poem that provides a fresh challenge after many previous experiences with poetry and figurative language. As usual, the poem was first read aloud:

> The summer night
> Is a dark blue hammock
> Slung between the white pillars of day.
> I lie there
> cooling myself
> with the straw-colored
> flat round fan
> of the full moon.

"Read the first part again," several children said to Sheryl. They seemed fascinated by Merriam's image but were also puzzled as to her meaning.

"What do you think it means—'The summer night / Is a dark blue hammock / Slung between the white pillars of day'?"

"I think the poet is in a hammock and she's writing about the night," said Johnny.

"Yeah . . . it's talking about how this poet is in a hammock at night," added Brandon.

Several children nodded, agreeing with Johnny and Brandon, others looked puzzled, while still others looked downright skeptical.

Sheryl noticed the looks and asked the group, "Well, what do you think? Does anybody have a different idea?"

Becky tentatively raised her hand, "I think it's talking about day against night."

"What do you mean?" asked Sheryl.

Stacie broke in, "Like it's between the end of one day and the beginning of another. You know, one day is one white pillar, and the next day is the other pillar. The hammock is like the night. You know, it's dark."

I heard several children say "Ohhh...yeah." Awareness dawned on their faces.

"Why do you think the poet called it a dark blue hammock?" asked Sheryl?

"Because dark blue is like the night's color. Lots of people say it's black but it really isn't always. White is for the day," answered Deon.

"That's a really different way to show it, isn't it? Would you have thought to show it like that? That's an interesting metaphor," Sheryl told her group.

The children differed in their ability to discern what the poet was trying to say with a metaphor. Some were only able to see things literally: they knew the poet was comparing but had little understanding of the purpose of the comparison or how it related to a more abstract, complex meaning. For example, when Sheryl read aloud Thurman's "Breaking Ground" (a poem comparing a plant breaking through the ground to morning breaking through night and spring breaking through winter), Matt saw the poem as merely about "a seed coming out of its shell." Similarly, when Peggy organized a group of fifth graders to discuss "Warning," a poem about a middle-aged woman longing to be as spontaneous as a child, Tiffany insisted the speaker was a child. She maintained this stance even when others showed her lines that indicated the woman was addressing her children. Brandon and Johnny's comments that "this poet is sitting in a hammock at night" during the reading of Merriam's "From the Japanese" is another example of such thinking.

Other children consistently sought to discover what they termed the "deeper meaning." Becky, for example, disagreed with Matt's comments about "Breaking Through": "I had a different view of that, I was kind of thinking it was comparing spring and the day to a seed breaking through the ground. You know how everything has to fight through to get out...when they're first beginning. All three verses have this alike." In the discussion of "Warning" Earnie, in contrast to Tiffany, understood the allusion to an adult "thinking about the future and how she wanted to change." Stacie's comments about the poet's metaphorical use of hammocks and pillars in "From the Japanese" showed her understanding went far beyond the literal level.

A discussion about Frost's "The Road Not Taken" was particularly helpful in showing us how differently children can interpret the same poem. It's also a good example of how a teacher can accommodate and resolve divergent viewpoints. After reading the poem aloud to the sixth graders, Sheryl asked them what they thought Frost was trying to say.

"Well, he came to a fork in the woods and . . . ," Ronnie's voice dropped off.

"Did he have a big decision to make at that point?" Sheryl asked.

"Yes," answered Ronnie.

"Why? What was he doing?" Sheryl asked again to keep him thinking.

"He took the road that didn't go very many places," Ronnie said thoughtfully.

"Okay," said Sheryl. "What do you mean it doesn't go very many places? You said something different. The first hadn't been used as much. What decision do you think he comes to? Let's hear part of it again:

> I shall be telling this with
> A sigh somewhere ages and
> Ages hence
> Two roads in a woods and I,
> I took the road less traveled by
> And that has made all the difference.

Suddenly Becky broke in. "It sounds like he is talking about his life on ahead. It sounds like when you take a road or when you grow up you take different directions on what you want to be and stuff."

"Wow!" I thought. She really had cut to the heart of this poem. Surely this would be the focus of the rest of the discussion. Becky had neatly summarized some of the poem's ideas in her own way. But fortunately I was wrong. Sheryl kept on probing for other children's opinions.

"What road do people usually choose?" she asked. "Do they usually choose the road less traveled by?"

A chorus of "Nos!" greeted her question.

"They go on a road that most people use," said Jennifer.

"They want to be like their friends," added Stacie.

"What else?" Sheryl persisted, "You are saying it's like coming to a decision instead of actually a road. What do you think?"

"Maybe that's the road he lives on," said Bryan.

"Okay," responded Sheryl. She wanted to accept Bryan's idea as valid at this point, but I could tell by her expression that she didn't want the group to get too far off the track. So she added, "But you are thinking of actually living on a road; Becky is saying she thinks it has more to do with decisions in life or any other decision you come to. You have to make a decision and you are choosing from . . ."

"Two roads," Becky finished the sentence.

"Maybe he thought if he took the other road he might like it or something," Bryan continued.

"Well, he looked down it, remember," said Sheryl. She read the relevant lines. 'I looked down as far as I could to where it bent in the undergrowth.' It was attractive to him. Why did he choose the one less traveled by?"

"Maybe he was feeling sorry for it, and he wanted to. . . ." Bryan's voice dropped off. He seemed to be considering both possibilities. The one seemed clear and concrete—yet inadequate. The other required him to make an intuitive leap that he couldn't quite yet do.

Sheryl tried to help, "Let's just think in terms of what Becky said about decisions—making decisions instead of actually traveling down a real road. What does 'the road less traveled' mean when you are talking about decisions people make?"

"Well, usually people don't make that kind of decision," said Johnny.

"Why?" asked Sheryl. "Why is the less traveled road not usually taken? What does 'the road less traveled' mean when you are talking about decisions people make?"

"Maybe he had been down that one too much," suggested Matt. "[Maybe] he wanted to go down the other one." Matt's comment revealed that some of the children were still pursuing the interpretation of a literal journey down a real road.

"Possibly, but listen to this," Sheryl replied as she read part of the poem aloud again.

> I kept the first for another day
> Yet knowing now
> I doubted if I should ever come back.

"There he was. He couldn't travel both and be one traveler."

"Maybe he didn't want to do what other people do . . . see what other decisions might do for his life. That's a decision people don't usually make," said Jennifer.

"Yes, why do you suppose they don't take the road less traveled by?" Sheryl again asked the group.

"Because they don't know what it will bring them?" asked Becky.

"Possibly," responded Sheryl.

"Maybe they're unwilling to take chances. It's a harder way to go," offered Bryan.

"People like it when it's easy," added Stacie. "And he chose to take a chance."

It seems that children had differing abilities to make connections between an abstract idea and its concrete referent. Yet the teachers tried to refrain from making value judgments about these differences. This may not be evident from a mere written description, but facial expressions and body language made it clear that they were receptive to various ideas. Although the teacher might direct the discussion in a particular way to help the children consider alternatives, the individuals felt free to present their own viewpoints.

It was impossible to detect who was more able to discern an abstract relationship. Some children demonstrated unusual insights with one poem, then offered only a literal interpretation for another. Sometimes the whole group was able to make the abstract connections in a metaphorical allusion as in their discussion of Hughes' "Mother to Son." Similarly, most easily recognized the comparison of a toaster to a "silver jawed dragon" in Smith's "The Toaster," but few understood the imagery of e.e. cummings.

Maybe, I hypothesized, the difference was due to how closely the poem mirrored personal experience. A mother giving advice to her son and a description of a toaster are closer to the everyday lives of these children than e.e. cummings' language and unusual connections. When asked, however, the children could never articulate what made the difference.

Making It Their Own: Using Figurative Language

Once the children began developing an awareness of how professional poets use figurative language, they began experimenting with it themselves. As with the other poetic elements, they initially used these ideas rather literally, following a rule they'd figured out. In the case of figurative language, it was that poets "compare things." So they would write a poem in which one thing was compared to another. Little attention would be given to the uniqueness of the image or how the rest of the poem functioned in relation to the metaphor. The following are typical poems that exemplify this level of understanding.

Rain

Rain is like thunder
That can't stop itself
Then it stops to rest.

DOLLY
Grade 5

Windmill

As the windmill
Spins and spins
It cuts the wind
Just like cutting a pie.

JIMMY R.
Grade 6

Winter

Winter snow falls in my
mitten, like rain on
A cloudy day falling in
A puddle.

DEON
Grade 6

As they became more knowledgeable about figurative language, they began experimenting with how to select just the right words, then manipulate rhyme, lining and phrasing so as to maintain the metaphor throughout the poem. The teachers urged the children to extend and "stay with" their comparisons. When Jeremy was trying to compare lightning with a train that moves "as fast as a silver bullet," Sheryl guided him toward words that could describe both lightning and a train.

"What colors do you associate with both lightning and a train?" Sheryl asked him.

Jeremy thought for a minute. "Silver," he replied. Then he exclaimed, "That describes a bullet too, so I'm making it work for all three things!"

They began talking about lightning—what it does, how it moves through the sky, how it sounds.

"Some images work for lightning but not a train," Sheryl said. "It's good to find words that work for both."

Jeremy decided "strikes" and "whistling" would work for both

images. He added this to his poem so that the second and third
lines read:

> Whistling through a moonlit night
> Silver lightning strikes ahead.

"We need some way to end this," said Sheryl. "What could
the lightning be doing that a train would do too?"

A small group of children generated several possibilities:
"looking for an end," "searching," and "attracted to its destiny."

"I like 'searching,' " said Jeremy.

"Okay, put that down," answered Sheryl. "Now, searching for
what? What would both lightning and a train search for?"

Again, the group generated several possibilities including "a
home," "a target," "its end," "its journey," and "its destination."
Jeremy wrote these down in the margin of his notebook, then went
off in his customary fashion to finish the poem alone. He returned
with the following:

Midnight Express
(checkmarked version)

> Fast as a speeding bullet
> Whistling through a moonlit night,
> Silver lightning strikes ahead,
> Searching for its journey's end.

> JEREMY
> Grade 5

"That's so poetic!" Johnny exclaimed to him. "You compared—and
that's really poetry."

Johnny was so impressed in fact that he wrote his own poem
that compared a train with a natural phenomena, in this case, wind.
You can hear echoes of Jeremy's ideas here, although Johnny has
created his own unique imagery:

Wind
(checkmarked version)

> The wind whistles
> Through the branches
>   Like a train
> Through a tunnel—
> Invisible to the eye,
>   Captured by the ear.

213

The children also experimented with personification. Many found this easier than metaphor and could more frequently sustain the comparison throughout the piece. After hearing Smith's "Toaster," Earnie elected to create his own personification poem using the pencil sharpener as his subject, comparing it to a monster eating its prey. Selecting "chews and spits splinters of wood" as a good description that fit both a monster and a pencil sharpener, he next considered the problem of how to end his poem. "You've made your point," he overheard Peggy tell another child. "That's it!" he gleefully told me. "That's a good play on words, you know, point on a pencil and making a point with words. Do you get it, Amy?" I assured him I did. After several relinings and word changes, Earnie's poem read as follows:

Pencil Sharpener
(checkmarked version)

A sharp jawed monster
Awaits a long-leaded meal.
With its mouth of metal,
It chews and spits splinters of wood,
Makes its point,
Then satisfied, it rests.

Earnie
Grade 5

Following the enthusiastic class reception of "Pencil Sharpener," Earnie wrote another personification poem that I found astounding.

Balance Scales
(checkmarked version)

Twin brothers sit side by side
One no higher than the other
Until one is filled with hate
And sinks lower than the better brother.

Earnie
Grade 5

What a tribute to the climate of openness, trust, and support these teachers had created!

Following are some additional poems that use figurative language in an unusual or complex way.

Nature

Nature is outside
Waiting for a newborn
To see the sun rise,
To hear the wind blow
To fight the harsh world.

JIMMY
Grade 6

A Leaf

This light green vessel
Skims sunspecked waters.
Rolling rapids rip this graceful ship
From calm waters
Forcing it to its destiny of doom.

AARON
Grade 5

Green Predator

A green rope
    Twists through the wet weeds
And under a low bush
    Hunting for a victim.

MIKE J.
Grade 5

Spring

Spring is on
the street
Playing tag
with the kids
While summer waits
Around the corner
To take a swim.

ANGELA
Grade 6

Hippity Hop

I hippity hop
Hopscotch

Under the trees
While the leaves
Hippity Hop
Hopscotch
On me.

MANDY
Grade 5

Night

In the moonlit night
Stars wink silent eyes
At the dark earth
Night fades...
Stars fade...
Morning comes.

JEREMY
Grade 5

A gashog tears into a driveway,
Slides to a stop.
Like magic
A giant mouth slowly opens
And swallows the beast.

BRYAN H.
Grade 5

As the shades of evening come down
Night gives word to day,
Saying, "lights out..."
But the world says, "No!
It's time to play."

JIMMY R.
Grade 6

Angela's "Sunrise"

The evolution of Angela's "Sunrise" poem is a good example of how many children were eventually able to stay with a metaphor, consciously using particular words, line patterns, and other elements to accomplish this goal. Angela was a sociable critic who also sought response to her work from a variety of sources. Thus, although the evolution of "Sunrise" is fairly typical, this example has more references to idea solicitation than an example of a poem by a child like Jeremy or Jennifer, who were more solitary workers.

Angela got the original idea for her poem from an ordinary event in her life: an early Saturday trip to Columbus in October. As the sun rose that morning, she became intrigued by the interplay of shadow and color and jotted down her initial impressions. Later that day she created the following rough draft:

Sunrise

The sun is slowly rising
Over the horizon.
A bird chirps its song
While the other birds join in.
As the sun rises higher,
The world wakes
To sun rays in
their windows.

Angela initially asked her mother and sister for reactions. Both agreed the line "While the other birds join in" just didn't quite fit. Angela decided to eliminate it, later stating that "it didn't sound poetic." Her teacher indicated that the poem "had possibilities" so Angela decided to work on it further.

The poem was next submitted to several friends who focused mainly on refining the words. After looking through the thesaurus, they suggested Angela change "slowly" to "gradually," "higher" to "greater," and "rises" to "grows." These selections "made the meaning better" in their opinion. When I asked them what they meant by this comment, they told me, "These words are better for telling about how the sun moves." At one point, Angela crossed out the last four lines herself (she later decided to keep them).

The poem was then taken to a critiquing group, led by Sheryl. The group first talked extensively about the phenomena Angela was trying to describe; what really happens, what the sun looks like at that time of day and other issues to ensure that she "remained true to her subject."

"What is it you're trying to say in this poem?" Sheryl asked her.

"Just about the sun and how it looks when it comes up in the morning," answered Angela.

"Well, how does the sun come up?" Johnny asked her. "The word 'gradually' is kind of ordinary. Can you think of some others?"

Using the thesaurus, the group generated many words, in-

cluding "explodes," "pops up," "sneaks," "peeks," and "creeps."
Angela wrote the ideas in the margin of her notebook.

It was at this point that a major reconceptualization occurred.
"I like 'sneaks' the best," she said thoughtfully. "Oh, you know what?
I could make the sun be like an animal that eats up the day. You
know how it's like day is eating up the night in the morning."

The group agreed this was an appropriate comparison and
that "sneaks upon the night" was a good way to convey the metaphorical image of the sun eating night as analogous to an animal
eating something. As they talked, Bryan who was casually passing
by the table commented, "Well, if you're making it sound like an
animal [eating another], why not use 'preys'?" Angela loved this
idea and added it to her poem so it read:

preys
The sun ~~sneaks~~
Upon the night.

After some experimentation with relining, the poem read as follows:

Sunrise
(Revision 3)

The sun preys
Upon the night
As it steps across the horizon
The sun grows greater
At the crack of day.

Angela once again sought help from her friends. They weren't
much help this time. At one point, Deon told her, "I got this from
Mrs. Reed: What are you trying to get across to your reader? Just
think about your readers so they understand." This admonition,
unfortunately, provided no specific help.

Mainly, I overheard Angela muttering to herself as she played
with various lines and word patterns.

"Crack is like what you do with an egg...that don't sound
right," she said. And later, "I don't like 'steps,' I like 'peeks over the
horizon' better."

"What about 'tiptoes' instead of 'peeks'?" suggested Angie.
"That kind of is what an animal does."

"That's good!" exclaimed Angela and added it to her poem.
It now read as follows.

Learning About Poetic Elements

Sunrise
(Revision 3a)

The sun preys
Upon the night
~~peeks~~
As it ~~steps~~ across the horizon
tiptoes
The sun grows greater
At the crack of day.

At this point Angela temporarily abandoned her poem. Perhaps she needed some time away from it to get a fresh perspective. It wasn't until December that she returned to it, reexamining her ideas and experimenting with a few revisions. One was to describe the sun as "devouring the night like a big gumball." This was soon abandoned because Angela decided it was not a helpful comparison, "Gumballs don't eat things." She also eliminated the last two lines because, as she had considered earlier, "they don't sound good." The poem now read as follows:

Sunrise
(Revision 4)

The sun preys
Upon the night
As it tiptoes across the horizon.

Angela then decided she needed help constructing an ending for her piece and initiated a blackboard critiquing session with Angie and Becky just before Christmas vacation. Her friends suggested that Angela describe the sun's colors. Generating "pink," "yellow," "red," and "blue," they decided "yellow," although not unusual, was the most appropriate color. They also experimented with several other words substituting "peeks around" for "preys" (later rejected because it broke the rhythm) and adding "swallows" to describe what the sun does to the night.

Angela still needed an ending, so the girls brought Sheryl over to help. After reading the poem thoughtfully aloud, Sheryl pretended to eat with large chewing motions, imitating the idea of the poem's comparison.

"What am I doing?" she asked the girls.

"Biting," they replied.

"Big biting, big biting," responded Angela thoughtfully.

"Does that fit with your metaphor?" Sheryl asked the girls. "What about your title?" (The girls had changed it from "Sunrise" to "Devouring the Sun.") Can you think of a title that goes along with eating and the beginning of day?"

"Breakfast!" exclaimed Angela. "That's perfect!" She wandered off to finish her poem alone. The poem finally evolved into the following:

Breakfast

The sun preys
Upon the night
As it tiptoes to the horizon.
Big, yellow bite; by big, yellow bite,
The sun swallows the night.

Angela had taken a simple, everyday experience, and turned it into an image that was fresh and imaginative. This was not accomplished independently; her initial ideas were nurtured and affirmed by an environment that valued them.

Image Making

These children were not given prescriptions or rules for using and appreciating figurative language. Nor were they required to complete worksheet images constructed for them by adults. Peggy and Sheryl firmly believed that formulas and gimmicks could too easily supersede the necessarily rigorous process of creating something original as well as cause the group to underestimate the discipline and skill required for creating and appreciating good poetry. The children's personal poetic voices were recognized and respected. Images, words, and ideas that were false or beyond their experience were neither presented nor encouraged. The result was a growing appreciation for how poetry can give us a fresh view of the world through an imaginative juxtaposition of images.

PART V

Final Reflections

CHAPTER 17

Endings and Beginnings

Poems are floating inside my head
Like dandelion fluff, dancing
through the air.

Jumbling together,
Sending a message to my hand.

JAMIE
Grade 5

It was finally June. Time to pack up the art supplies, science materials, and poetry books until another fall. Time to say good-bye to the sixth graders who were nervously anticipating the transition to junior high and to quietly hug the fifth graders whom we would see again next year. And it was time to savor the memories of the year, to realize how far we had all come.

We thought back to the tough beginnings of our journey together: the silences that separated all of us after a poem was read; the writing that was initially devoid of feeling and meaning, the lack of interest in pursuing ideas. Now we watched as children like Jimmy, Johnny, and Ronnie eagerly pulled poems from Sheryl's poetry file, finally settling down to read some Shakespearean sonnets to each other. We helped children like Robin, Mandy, and Dolly put finishing touches on their anthology collections—treasures to be taken home, shared with parents, then placed proudly on bedroom bookshelves. And we sat quietly alongside to listen as Jennifer, Angie, and Jenny S. squeezed in one final critiquing session to polish Jennifer's haiku poem about summer flowers.

We realized anew how much the children had surprised us. We had not immediately recognized their slow and easy development into avid readers and writers of poetry. In contrast to their initial lack of interest children now often chose poetry above any other activity. Peer reading and writing communities had developed as everyone began taking some risks in their responding, sharing, and writing. Many of the children were making meaning in their writing most of the time. Some often took their journals home at night to write more. Most importantly, the talk before school, at lunch, during recess, and after school was frequently about fine books and poems, favorite authors and writing. It was a good feeling.

Beyond the good-byes and reflections on a satisfying year, Peggy and Sheryl were already looking forward to next year, to a fresh start with new confidence that all children can learn to love poetry if only given the opportunity and support. I discovered this as we sat down for one last afterschool talk at the Plaza Truckstop Restaurant.

"Would you have done anything differently this year?" I asked.

Sheryl thought for a long time, then responded. "I wouldn't change a thing I did, or thought or agonized over, or learned in spite of myself this year. I look over my shoulder and feel encouraged by the clear path behind me. I can go on more confidently now because I am convinced that children who are invited into poetry, surrounded by fine books of poetry, given time and space to become obsessed with it, then supported in their experiments with it will find it a joy."

Peggy nodded slowly but added, "I'm starting to think about next year . . . about how I can inspire even better poetry writing and illustration."

"Are there some things you would add?" I wanted to know.

"I'd like to do much more with going out of doors," she said. "Perhaps I'll start many days by having the children go out in small groups to do some collecting, observing, recording, note taking, sketching, and painting. This seems like a natural way to get better work while also involving the most reluctant students. Also, instead of having the children make many small poetry books, I might encourage them to create individual ongoing collections of artwork, poetry, observation records, and other kinds of writing. I think I'll do more with class collections where everyone contributes their artwork and poetry to a group anthology. This motivates the kids to participate because no one wants to feel left out."

Both teachers vowed to do more with particular poetic elements. "I'd like to delve more deeply into the use of figurative language with my kids," Sheryl commented. "I'd like to encourage them to use more metaphor and simile as they write about more abstract subject areas."

"Word play will become an important part of writing in my classroom," added Peggy. "I'll be using Eve Merriam's and X. J.

Kennedy's work to encourage this. I'm convinced some unusual poems will evolve from this."

The two chatted on about their plans for next year—and beyond. It was clear that although they were celebrating the accomplishments of the year just completed, they were already carefully thinking about ways to make next year successful. As I left the Plaza that day to begin the long trip home down Route 33, I couldn't help but mull over these comments. "What a strong sense of dedication and purpose these teachers have," I thought.

The teachers weren't the only ones excited about what had occurred this year. I thought back to the conversation I had had with the children that same afternoon. Sitting among them, tape recorder casually at my side, I had recorded one final class discussion. When I asked them why poetry had become such an important part of their lives, they told me that something about it had touched them on a personal and emotional level. Johnny said, "Poetry has rhythm and deep feeling to it—that's why I like it. Some stories have feeling to them, but it's just not the same as how poetry does it." Earnie had the same idea when he commented, "It's rhythmical and it shows things. It's a way to express your feelings. "It's just my favorite thing to read." Carrie stated emphatically, "I prefer to read books first, then save the best [poetry] for last!"

Aaron said it best. Grabbing the tape recorder's microphone out of my hand, he spoke into it: "I want to tell all those kids out there that once you get into poetry, you'll really like it...really!" Everyone agreed that he was absolutely right.

It was the ending of a year but the beginning of a future in which we were sure poetry would continue to be a central part of all our lives.

Appendices

Peggy and Sheryl's Favorite Poetry Books

Suggested grade levels are indicated in parentheses.

ADOFF, ARNOLD. *All the Colors of the Race.* Illustrated by John Steptoe. New York: Lothrop, Lee & Shephard, 1982. (3–6) (Hardback)
Poems of a child's feelings about her mixed heritage.

———. *Eats.* Illustrated by Susan Russo. New York: Lothrop, Lee & Shephard, 1979. (2–6) (Hardback)
Fantasy poems about food such as pizza, apple pie, hamburgers, Twinkies, chocolate.

———. *Greens.* Illustrated by Betsy Lewin. New York: Lothrop, Lee & Shephard, 1988. (2–6) (Hardback)
A poetry book about all things green: vegetables, crayons, dandelions, etc.

———. *Outside, Inside Poems.* Illustrated by John Steptoe. New York: Lothrop, Lee & Shephard, 1981. (4–6) (Hardback)
A book of poems about a boy and baseball.

———. *Sports Pages.* Illustrated by Steve Kuzma. New York: J. B. Lippincott, 1986. (2–6) (Hardback)
Poems about sports showing the feelings associated with winning and losing.

AMON, ALINE. *The Earth Is Sore: Native Americans on Nature.* Illustrated by author. New York: Atheneum, 1981. (4–6+) (Hardback)
Poetry and prose from early speeches of Native Americans about living in harmony with nature.

BAUER, CAROLINE FELLER, ED. *Snowy Day Stories and Poems.* Illustrated by Margot Tomes. New York: J. B. Lippincott, 1986. (2–6) (Hardback)

————. *Windy Day Stories and Poems*. New York: J. B. Lippincott, 1986. (2–6) (Hardback)
In the two books above, Bauer shares folktales, recipes, an assortment of facts, some activities, and many poems about snow and wind.

BEHN, HARRY. *Crickets & Bullfrogs & Whispers of Thunder: Poems & Pictures by Harry Behn*. Edited by Lee Bennett Hopkins. Illustrated by Harry Behn. New York: Harcourt Brace Jovanovich, 1984. (3–6+) (Hardback)
Some of the best of Harry Behn's poems on nature, holidays, fantasy, and the child's world grace the pages of this collection.

BOBER, NATALIE S., COMP. *Let's Pretend: Poems of Flight and Fantasy*. Illustrated by Bill Bell. New York: Viking Kestrel, 1986. (3–6) (Hardback)
An anthology of poems to fuel the imagination of childhood.

CASSEDY, SYLVIA. *Roomrimes*. Illustrated by Michele Chessare. New York: Thomas Y. Crowell, 1987. (4+) (Hardback)
Poems that describe rooms and spaces for each letter of the alphabet from "attic" to "zoo."

COLE, JOANNA, COMP. *A New Treasury of Children's Poetry: Old Favorites and New Discoveries*. Illustrated by Judith G. Brown. New York: Doubleday, 1984. (K–6) (Hardback)
An enjoyable selection of poems divided into categories such as: Celebrate the Time, Inside Myself, A Different Way of Seeing, etc.

COLE, WILLIAM, ED. *Poem Stew*. Illustrated by Karen Ann Weinhaus. New York: J. B. Lippincott, 1981. (2–6) (Paperback)
What poets have to say about things to eat all in a stew of poems.

CUMMINGS, E. E. *Hist, Whist & Other Poems for Children*. Illustrated by David Calsada. New York: Liveright, 1983. (4–6) (Hardback)
This challenging collection of twenty poems invites young people to stretch their perception of poetry.

DE REGNIERS, BEATRICE SCHENK, EVA MOORE, AND MARY MICHAELS WHITE, COMPS. *Poems Children Will Sit Still For: A Selection for the Primary Grades*. New York: Citation Press, 1969. (Primary+) (Paperback)
This book contains 106 short, rhythmical poems for beginning listeners.

DE REGNIERS, BEATRICE SCHENK, EVA MOORE, MARY M. WHITE, AND JAN

CARR, SELECTORS. *Sing a Song of Popcorn: Every Child's Book of Poems.* Illustrated by Marcia Brown, Leo and Diane Dillon, Richard Eglieski, Trina Schart Hyman, Arnold Lobel, Maurice Sendak, Marc Simont, and Margot Zemach. New York: Scholastic, 1988. (Pre-K–6) (Hardback)
A celebration of poems, 128 in all, that bring to children a rich variety of poets, poems, illustrators, and illustrations.

DICKINSON, EMILY. *I'm Nobody! Who are you? Poems of Emily Dickinson for Young People.* Illustrated by Rex Schneider. Owings Mills, MD: Stemmer House, 1978. (Upper Grades) (Paperback)
The mixed media illustrations are softly done to match the lovely poetry in this book. There is a glossary of Victorian language in the back of the book.

DUNNING, STEPHEN, EDWARD LUEDERS, AND HUGH SMITH, COMPS. *Reflections on a Gift of Watermelon Pickle and Other Modern Verse.* Glenview, IL: Scott, Foresman, 1966. (Upper Grades) (Paperback)
A collection of poems to stimulate deep thinking. It would be nice to have one for each child to follow along or read together.

ESBENSEN, BARBARA JUSTER. *Words with Wrinkled Knees.* Illustrated by John Stadler. New York: Thomas Y. Crowell, 1986. (All Ages) (Hardback)
Esbensen piques children's curiosities in twenty-one poems about words that reveal the essence of the animals they identify. Animal names will be looked at in a new way. Children will see "elephant" as a heavy word, "spider" as a silken one, "crow" as a noisy one, etc. Children will want to write their own words-as-animals-as-words poems.

FARBER, NORMA, AND MYRA COHN LIVINGSTON, SELS. *These Small Stones.* New York: Harper & Row, 1987. (All Ages) (Hardback)
A special look at the world of small things, real and imagined, provides children with a balance of fine poets, subjects, and dimensions of thought. This specialized anthology could be a window through which children look at other specialized collections organized around certain subjects and see the possibilities for writing or selecting their own poems to go along with a book or a theme of study. An excellent project for a group of children or class would be collecting and selecting poems written by their peers and teacher to create their own group or class anthology.

FISHER, ROBERT, ED. *Ghosts Galore: Haunting Verse.* Illustrated by Rowena Allen. Boston: Faber & Faber, 1986. (Upper Grades)

Peggy and Sheryl's Favorite Poetry Books

(Paperback)
Scary poems that children love!

FLEISCHMAN, PAUL. *Joyful Noise: Poems for Two Voices*. Illustrated by Eric Beddows. New York: Harper & Row, 1988. (Upper Grades) (Hardback)
A collection of poems to be read by two voices or two groups of voices describing the characteristics and activities of several insects. A good book to get children involved in reading poetry aloud.

FROST, ROBERT. *Birches*. Illustrated by Ed Young. New York: Henry Holt, 1988. (Upper Grades) (Hardback)
The poem "Birches" is illustrated beautifully on buff paper. The entire poem is reprinted at the end of the book.

————. *You Come Too*. Illustrated by Thomas W. Nason. New York: Holt, Rinehart & Winston, 1978. (Upper Grades) (Hardback)
In a selection of poems meant to be read to, or by young people, Frost invites them to entertain ideas, to view the world from a fresh perspective, and to expand their imaginations.

GIOVANNI, NIKKI. *Spin a Soft Black Song*. Illustrated by George Martins. New York: Farrar, Strauss & Giroux, 1985.
A choice collection of poems about trips, fears, basketball, and friends.

GREENFIELD, ELOISE. *Honey, I Love*. Illustrated by Diane and Leo Dillon. New York: Thomas Y. Crowell, 1978. (4–6+) (Hardback)
Poems of Black America that all children will love.

HILL, HELEN, AGNES PERKINS, AND ALETHEA HELBIG, EDS. *Dusk to Dawn, Poems of the Night*. New York: Crowell, 1981. (4–6) (Hardback)
A subject that would fit perfectly into science and other writing activities.

HOBERMAN, MARY ANN. *Bugs*. Illustrated by Victoria Chess. New York: Viking Press, 1976. (K–6) (Hardback)
Through her interesting and informative verses, Hoberman presents children with bugs from the unusual to the ordinary. This is a great book for connecting poetry and children's fascination with bugs.

————. *Yellow Butter, Purple Jelly, Red Jam, Black Bread*. Illustrated by Chaya Burstein, New York: Viking Press, 1981. (K–6) (Hardback)
This tall, thin book of humorous and rhythmical verses about real and imaginary experiences of people and animals is a delight for children to hear read aloud and to read themselves.

HOPKINS, LEE BENNETT. *Creatures.* Illustrated by Stella Ormai. New York: Harcourt Brace Jovanovich, 1985. (1–6) (Hardback)
A rhythmical journey into the realm of imagination where the traveler may encounter the gentle fairy folk or a great huge horrible horrible, and many other mild-mannered to ghoulish creatures. Contemporary and traditional poets are represented in this collection. It speaks to and expands the fantasies of childhood.

————. *Pass the Poetry, Please.* New York: Harper & Row, 1987. (All Ages) (Hardback)
Good resource book about poets and poetry.

————, COMP. *Dinosaurs.* Illustrated by Murray Tinkelman. New York: Harcourt Brace Jovanovich, 1987. (All Ages) (Hardback)
Hopkins has compiled an anthology of poems about dinosaurs, many of which were written for this book. This anthology would provide a poetic dimension to a study of prehistoric times or dinosaurs.

————, ED. *The Sky Is Full of Song.* Illustrated by Dirk Zimmer. New York: Harper & Row, 1983. (2–6) (Hardback)
Poems for the seasons. A perfect read-alone poetry book for all ages.

————, SELECTOR. *A Dog's Life.* Illustrated by Linda Rochester Richards. New York: Harcourt Brace Jovanovich, 1983. (All Ages) (Hardback)
Dog poems that all dog lovers will sit still for. The pen and ink illustrations complement the text.

HOPKINS, LEE BENNETT, AND MISHA ARENSTEIN, SELECTORS. *Poems You'll Like: Potato Chips and a Slice of Moon.* Illustrated by Wayne Blickenstaff New York: Scholastic, 1976. (2–6) (Paperback)
A book jam-packed with poems of many different subjects, forms, and moods. This is an excellent choice for multiple copies or for each child to own.

HUGHES, TED. *Season Songs.* Illustrated by Leonard Baskin. New York: Viking, 1975. (Upper Grades) (Hardback)
Deep poems about the seasons that invite young people to ponder over them, wonder about them, and return to them again and again, especially if a seasoned reader has read them aloud over and over, and invited and nourished their responses.

————. *Under the North Star.* Illustrated by Leonard Baskin New York:

Viking, 1981. (Upper Grades) (Hardback)
Difficult but tantalizing poems about animals of the North Country. Leonard Baskin's watercolors enhance this collection for older and experienced poetry lovers.

KENNEDY, X. J., AND DOROTHY M. KENNEDY, COMPS. *Knock at a Star: A Child's Introduction to Poetry*. Illustrated by Karen Ann Weinhaus. Boston: Little Brown, 1982. (2–6) (Hardback)
These fresh and exciting poems will stimulate children's interest in reading and writing poetry. The book is divided into four parts, and each part is divided into subsections. Explanations by the authors can be found at the beginning and scattered throughout each subsection. A rich resource for the classroom.

KUSKIN, KARLA. *Dogs & Dragons Trees & Dreams: A Collection of Poems*. Illustrated by Karla Kuskin. New York: Harper & Row, 1980. (K–6) (Hardback)
Kuskin's most popular poems have been reissued in this book with notes on poetry writing and appreciation. Fun, fancy, and feeling dance through this lively group of poems.

LARRICK, NANCY. *Bring Me All Your Dreams*. Photographs by Larry Mulvehill. New York: M. Evans, 1980. (3–6+) (Hardback)
Dreamy poems to spark discussion and encourage the imagination. A "meet the poet" section is in the back.

————. *Cats Are Cats*. Illustrated by Ed Young. New York: Philomel, 1988. (All Ages) (Hardback)
A rich collection of forty-two poems about all kinds of cats. The illustrations by Ed Young capture the personalities of cats and bring them to life in soft earthy tones. Children will want to read these poems and revisit Young's drawings over and over again.

————, ED. *On City Streets*. Photographs by David Sagarin. New York: Evans, 1968. (3–6+) (Hardback)
This anthology of poems about the city was chosen with the help of children. It contains many intense thinking poems by poets such as Langston Hughes, Walt Whitman, and William Carlos Williams. It includes a first line index. This is a good read-aloud and discussion book.

————, ED. *Piping Down the Valleys Wild*. Illustrated by Ellen Raskin. New York: Delacorte, 1968. (All Ages) (Paperback)
This large collection of poems presents to children of all ages a wide variety of poets, subjects, and types of poems. A wise

choice for multiple copies in the classroom or for ownership by each child.

LIVINGSTON, MYRA COHN. *Celebrations*. Paintings by Leonard Everett Fisher. New York: Holiday House, 1985. (1–6) (Hardback)
Children will enjoy hearing read and reading Livingston's sixteen holiday poems and will delight in Fisher's smashing illustrations.

————. *A Circle of Seasons*. Paintings by Leonard Everett Fisher. New York: Holiday House, 1982. (2–6) (Hardback)
When spring pokes fragrant fingers in the ground, the circle of seasons renews itself again. Children will be fascinated by Livingston's poem of three verses for each season that ends with a repeat of the first verse of the poem. Fisher's abstract paintings speak boldly of the seasons.

————. *Earth Songs*. Paintings by Leonard Everett Fisher. New York: Holiday House, 1986. (3–6+) (Hardback)
Livingston and Fisher have extended an invitation to explore our fascinating planet Earth, "little O," through the vision of poet and painter.

————. *Sea Songs*. Paintings by Leonard Everett Fisher. New York: Holiday House, 1986. (3–6+) (Hardback)
The moods, mysteries, and myths of the sea are explored by Livingston and Fisher in poem and painting.

————. *Sky Songs*. Paintings by Leonard Everett Fisher. New York: Holiday House, 1984. (3–6+) (Hardback)
The collaboration of poet and artist provides children with a fresh look at the sky and those things that pass through the sky. From poem to poem and painting to painting, the moods of the sky change.

————, SELECTOR AND ED. *I Like You, If You Like Me*. New York: Macmillan, 1987. (3–6+)
Livingston has provided 134 pages of delightful poems of friendship to share with children and to be shared among children. Friendship is a subject about which children might want to write.

MCCORD, DAVID. *One at a Time*. Illustrated by Henry B. Kane, Boston: Little, Brown, 1974. (K–6) (Hardback)
This large, illustrated collection of McCord's poems is a celebration of a child's world. With their strong rhythms, delightful sounds, and captivating subjects, McCord's poems, once heard, invite themselves into the house of memory.

MERRIAM, EVE. *Halloween ABC.* Illustrated by Lane Smith. New York: Macmillan, 1987 (4 +) (Hardback)

Merriam's rhythmic poems about Halloween, each introduced by a letter of the alphabet, cast a spell of delight upon the reader. The dark-toned, eerie illustrations by Smith catch the essence of each poem. This is a book to be shared with children both visually and by reading it aloud.

————. *Jamboree: Rhymes for all Times.* Illustrated by Walter Gaffney-Kessell. New York: Dell, 1984. (2–6) (Paperback)

This is a rhythmical, sensory, poem-laden book about weather, seasons, animals, children, grown-ups, spaces, and places. This is a choice book for each child to have a copy.

MOORE, LILIAN. *I Feel the Same Way.* Illustrated by Beatrice Darwin. New York: Scholastic, 1968. (K–4) (Paperback)

Moore's poems celebrate the world of young children. Her twenty poems speak of things children imagine and do and the way they view nature.

————. *Think of Shadows.* Illustrated by Deborah Robison. New York: Atheneum, 1980. (K–6) (Hardback)

Moore invites children to explore light and dark, shade, shadow, and moving mist in her theme book about shadows. This book could add an interesting dimension to science themes such as: night, dark and light, shadows, etc.

PRELUTSKY, JACK. *Rolling Harvey Down the Hill.* Illustrated by Victoria Chess. New York: Greenwillow, 1980. (2–6) (Paperback)

This is a book of funny poems and funny illustrations. Some of the poems have refrains that are fun to say together.

RILEY, JAMES WHITCOMB. *Little Orphant Annie.* Illustrated by Diane Stanley. New York: Putnam, 1983. (1–6) (Hardback)

This one poem book could be dramatized or used for choral reading. Children enjoy the dialect, the rhythm, and the subject of this poem.

RYLANT, CYNTHIA. *Waiting to Waltz: A Childhood.* Drawings by Stephen Gammell. Scarsdale, NY: Bradbury Press, 1984. (Upper Grades) (Hardback)

Rylant's poems are about growing up in Appalachia. Children can read these poems and perhaps reflect on their own times past.

WORTH, VALERIE. *All the Small Poems.* Illustrated by Natalie Babbitt. New York: Farrar, Straus & Giroux, 1987. (3–6 +) (Paperback)

The four books of Worth's small poems are brought together in this paperback edition. Worth uses few words to create her powerful images of such ordinary things as a safety pin, crickets, sidewalks, a hose, etc. This is a great book to share with children. They might want to try to create their own small poems.

The Research Process

When we share our ideas about poetry and the results of this study in workshops across the country, many people express curiosity about my research procedures. "How did you determine which children you would observe?" they ask or "How do you select the events you record from all the often overwhelming possibilities?" Ethnographic research is exhausting, sometimes confusing, and requires a faith that somehow the patterns will emerge. Inevitably they do if the researcher is willing to carefully watch and listen. This chapter is provided for those readers who are curious about how the study was carried out.

Ethnographic Observational Research

Ethnographic research is not undertaken to prove something—a theory, a cause/effect relationship, or a generalization. Rather it is a process of discovery, of learning about a particular phenomena under scrutiny. The task is to describe the culture of a particular group, identifying specific cultural patterns and structural regularities within the processes of continuity and change (Heath, 1982). To accomplish this task, the ethnographer identifies key incidents or recurring events, describes these events, positions them in the wider social context, and writes descriptions so others can see the generic within the particular (Erickson, 1977). This process enables the researcher to arrive at an understanding of events and how they relate to the social context.

Hymes (1982) identifies three approaches an ethnographic study might take: comprehensive, topic-centered, and hypothesis-generating. Each is concerned with capturing and exploring social phenomena in a particular manner. This study primarily employed a topic-centered perspective, focusing on a particular aspect of the social group under study. An hypothesis-generating approach, in which phenomena are studied within a general theoretical framework so as to generate hypotheses, was also used. It was thought that combining these two approaches would lead to understanding particular responses in one context and thus permit tentative hypothesizing about response, in other contexts.

Research Cycle

This study was composed of three interactive phases that reflect its ethnographic perspective. During the first phase (August to October), the major focus was entry into the setting and the collection of contextual data. Tentative research questions were identified to provide a general framework for what to observe. Interviews with teachers and children were conducted in conjunction with direct classroom observations. These were supplemented by my comments, which were designed to make tentative links between my observations and theory. Audiotaping was introduced to ensure accurate recording of contextual data, particularly the occurrence of teacher-student and student-student interactions. A preference survey was also given to discern the kind of poetry these children enjoyed at the beginning of the year.

This general observation phase led to the selection of various elements of response and context that seemed to merit closer scrutiny or were puzzling to me. Phase two (late October to February) was thus characterized by purposeful, focused observation of specific phenomena. Audiotaping of typical child-child and teacher-teacher interactions continued. Both teachers and students were interviewed, using open-ended questions dictated by the particular event under scrutiny. Videotaping was introduced so as to capture subtle nuances of particular classroom occurrences. The preference survey was again administered in February to measure midyear poetry preferences. These activities were all guided by the initial research questions that were refined and modified as new understandings emerged.

The final phase (March-May) focused on verification of data through additional observations and interviews. Primary emphasis was on ensuring that enough data was available to confirm or disconfirm trends that had arisen from the primary analysis. Near the conclusion of this phase, emphasis shifted to examining the developmental changes occurring over the course of the year. Figure A–1 (pages 240–41) depicts this cycle.

Role of the Researcher

Many studies using an ethnographic perspective require the researcher to assume a participant-observer role. This role allows the

Inquiry Cycle

STAGE ONE

Problem Framing, Planning,
and Collection of Initial Contextual Data:
July–September 1984

ROLE: OBSERVER

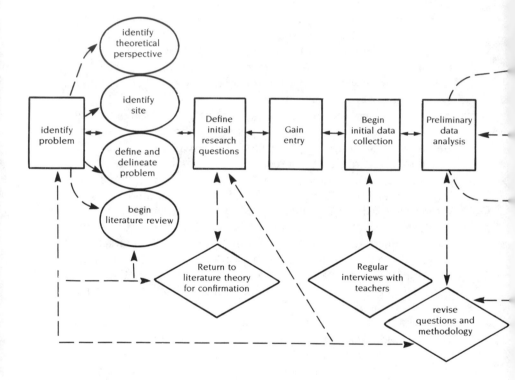

FIGURE A–1

Inquiry Cycle

STAGE TWO	STAGE THREE
Purposeful Data Collection and Preliminary Data Analysis: October 1984–February 1985	Final Data Collection, Verification, Analysis March–May 1985
ROLE: PARTICIPANT OBSERVER	ROLE: ALTERNATE OBSERVER/ PARTICIPANT OBSERVER

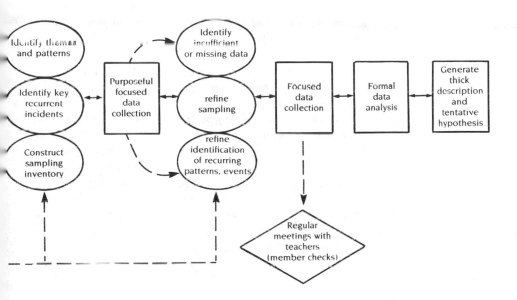

researcher to become an integral part of the social system so that the researcher's ability to view the situation from an insider's perspective is enhanced. Assuming a natural role in the group's ongoing activities, in turn, minimizes disruption, thus helping maintain the natural flow of classroom events.

At the beginning of the study my role was that of an observer: I sat quietly among the group during whole-class sessions or worked unobtrusively at areas in which small-group interactions occurred. Although tentative interactions with the children based on general topics of mutual interest were initiated, the main purpose at this point was to gather information on the general context as well as how response to poetry shapes and is shaped by this context.

Eventually, I assumed the more active role of participant-observer. Within this role I alternated between acting as a peer-group member and teacher aide. In the role of peer-group member, I exchanged views on pets, hairstyles, break-dancing, baseball games, and the like. As a teacher aide, I responded to questions, participated in small-group response sessions, and provided ideas for written and oral responses. These activities allowed me to directly observe children's responses. Additionally, I could verify initial conclusions concerning teacher behaviors by actually trying them out for myself. Throughout this phase, I endeavored to ensure that my active presence did not significantly affect the naturally occurring flow of events in this classroom.

Eventually (in March) I reassumed a primarily observational role. This was done to allow for objective analysis and to help ensure that a wide range of behaviors was being observed. It was initially difficult to assume this role since children were accustomed to using me as a source for help, verification, and support. Actually, a period in which I moved between observer and participant-observer ensued before the role of observer could be reassumed.

Data Collection

Data was collected through several methods. These included field notes, audiotaping, informal interviews, formal interviews, videotaping, collection of written materials and a questionnaire on children's poetry preferences. Each will be briefly described in terms of how the particular technique provided relevant data for the study. Table A–1 shows an abbreviated example of how data collection was guided by the research questions. (The complete example can be found in McClure, 1985.)

Relationship Between Research Questions
and Methodology: Context for Response

Research Question	Methods of Investigation	Form of Data
1. What environmental factors support children's response to poetry?	field notes	transcribed notes
	audiotaping	transcripts
	interviews with teachers	transcripts
	videotapes	tapes
2. What specific classroom occurrences inhibit or facilitate response to poetry?	field notes	transcribed notes
	audiotaping	transcripts
	informal interviews—teachers, students	transcripts
	videotaping	tapes
3. What teacher behaviors seem to support and nurture response to poetry?	field notes	transcribed notes
	audiotaping of teacher/student interactions	transcripts
	informal interviews of teachers and students	transcripts
4. What relationships are apparent between peer interactions and response to poetry?	field notes	transcribed notes
	informal interviews with children	transcripts
	still photography	slides
	collection of works	poetry journals
	audiotaping of peer/peer interactions	transcripts

Field Notes

Rough descriptive notes were made at each visit. These were kept in spiral-bound notebooks (a total of four), which I carried with me whenever I visited the class. These notes (over seven hundred pages) provided a general record of everything I saw occurring in the classroom as well as the context within which the events occurred. The notes were transcribed as soon as possible (usually the same night after an observation), then filed. At the time of transcription, notes were amplified as additional details not recorded on site occurred to me. Additional theoretical, methodological and personal notes, using double bracketing and red pen for highlighting purposes, were added. Notes were also made concerning the context and time where taping was used. In this way transcriptions of audiotapes, when completed, could be filed contingent to the descriptions that accompanied them.

Audiotaping

As it was often difficult to capture the exact content of a conversation through field notes, audiotaping was also used. Twenty-seven tapes were made, providing an oral record of large- and small-group events as they occurred. This helped me capture nuances of conversation as well as a better sense of the context surrounding particular events. Audiotaping also proved valuable in supplementing my presence. Because I couldn't be everywhere at once, a tape recorder could run continuously in one area while I took field notes in another. This had the additional advantage of documenting children's responses when no adult was present.

I found the use of a microcassette recorder particularly helpful. This was kept in my pocket and used during spontaneous interviews and conversations when I became aware that it would be impossible to simultaneously ask questions, listen, and take field notes. At first this equipment seemed intrusive as the children were quite fascinated by it. But the novelty soon waned, and I found its use valuable for spontaneous recording, particularly when children began voluntarily seeking me out to share their latest revisions and thoughts.

Interviews

Both teachers and children were interviewed informally to obtain an insider's perspective against which my observations and analyses were checked. Their views on the same subject were also often compared to get a fuller picture of events from many points of view. Children were asked their views of general classroom procedures, the nature and purposes of events related to poetry, and their understanding of the response process (e.g., How did you write this poem? Where did you get your ideas? What steps did you go through?). Teachers were also asked to address these issues and were questioned as to their perceptions of ongoing classroom events and their understandings of specific responses.

As the study progressed, these conversations became less like interviews and more like spontaneous dialogues between people with a shared interest in the topic. Children began initiating discussions, (e.g., "I wrote a poem yesterday I gotta tell you about.").

Other children who had contributed something to the event would add their perspective. Teachers also initiated discussions about various occurrences (e.g., "Did Tommy tell you about his poem? We had a good critiquing group yesterday.").

Most of these comments were summarized in field notes. In the case of poetry writings, notations were often made directly on a copy of the poem to facilitate later analysis of the relationship between process and product. Sometimes these conversations were recorded on audiotape. This was particularly done in the latter half of the study. By that time children had become so skillful at describing the process that only audiotaping could capture their full explanations. These tapes were later transcribed and filed as near to the writings or descriptions of the response event as possible.

I also scheduled formal interviews with the teachers approximately every three weeks. These tended to occur more frequently at the beginning and end of the study and were usually taped. The purpose was to confirm or disconfirm my observations as well as to further understand each teacher's theoretical orientation to poetry and response. The focus in August and September was on what goals they had for the year and on educating me about the classroom structure. Interviews from October through February focused mainly on the responses of individual children and changes noted in these responses and the classroom environment. By March, the primary emphasis shifted to verification and modification of my tentative conclusions, although discussion about response events still occurred.

Videotaping

As the study progressed it became evident that a fuller picture of response and its relation to context might be obtained through the use of videotaping. The actual events to be videotaped were selected purposefully from those that I determined were regularly occurring. The teachers verified the significance of these events, adding one more. The completed list included art sessions, large-group oral sharing, and small-group critiquing sessions (with and without teachers present).

Although I tried to minimize the intrusiveness of this equipment, videotaping proved to be the most intrusive of all methods. This was due to the bulkiness of the equipment as well as its novelty. Furthermore, the normal seating arrangements for taped activities had to be adjusted to accommodate problems of lighting, cord lengths, accessibility to microphones, and similar technical requirements. This encouraged behaviors like elaborate ducking around

245

the camera, "clowning," and such queries as "Are we gonna be on T.V.?"

Despite these problems, subsequent viewing of the tapes revealed that once children became involved in the activity being taped, they generally ignored the camera's presence. When comparing behavior from videotaped episodes with similar events in field notes and transcripts, little disparity was found. The same children talked, saying similar kinds of things. Those noted as inattentive in untaped episodes were similarly inattentive when the tape was running. Additional evidence as to the extent of obtrusiveness could be discerned through children's comments. Often, after a taping session, as the children were leaving, someone would pass by the equipment and state, "Oh, I forgot that was on."

Collection of Children's Written Work

Because the written response process was so complex, the children's writings were photocopied to preserve the various revisions and thought ramblings that lead to the completed product. Sampling of these materials was initially purposeful to facilitate understanding of various emerging patterns and themes. Later, these materials were sampled randomly to confirm or disconfirm previously identified conclusions.

The major sources for these materials were the children's poetry journals. Virtually entire poetry journals of students in the purposeful sampling group were copied to trace the students' development through the year. The poetry journals of students in the randomly sampled group were photocopied in a similar manner, although not as extensively. For other children, examples of an entire poetry cycle, the journal index, or a poem containing an interesting example relevant to the study were copied. Thus, although some children's work was studied more thoroughly than others, written samples were collected from virtually every child.

Poems written for other subjects and purposes were also collected. For example, sometimes children wrote a quick poem or referred to poetry in some way in their reading dialogue journals. These were photocopied and filed for later analysis. Additionally, poems were sometimes included in the class newspaper. These were photocopied to gain a sense of which poems were considered "excellent" by class members.

Another source of written response was the student-constructed anthologies of published poetry. These books were photocopied, or the selected poems were listed in the field notes.

Preference Survey

A simple questionnaire was constructed and administered to the children at the beginning, middle, and end of the school year. Questions were patterned after those used by the teachers with their previous classes and were open-ended, designed to elicit diverse, thoughtful responses about the children's poetry preferences and attitudes toward poetry.

Specifically, the questionnaire asked students to list their favorite poets and poems and tell why these were their favorites. They were then to list their favorite kinds of poetry as well as their favorite activities in conjunction with poetry. Children were encouraged to write as many responses as they could to take advantage of the questionnaire's open-ended nature.

Sampling

In qualitative research, sampling occurs throughout the inquiry process. Thus, decisions as to what will be sampled are made continually and are guided by the initial analysis that, in turn, modifies the research questions and data collection procedures. Sampling decisions are also guided by the theoretical framework of the study.

The particular events, participants, and processes selected for closer scrutiny were chosen based on their observed representativeness. The decision as to what was considered representative was based on data gathered during the initial phase in September. Once the particular contextual and response items to be sampled were identified, sampling inventories were constructed. These guided the systematic collection of data over the next three months. At the conclusion of this time, field notes, audiotapes, and other data were reviewed. The subsequent preliminary analysis suggested a need for minor modification of the sampling inventory. As a result, new items were added, and others deleted. The revised inventory then guided subsequent data collection.

Several types of sampling were used in the study, including time, event, participant, and process. Each will be discussed so as to provide a comprehensive account of how data was systematically collected.

Time Sampling

In qualitative research the time one visits a site can affect the nature of the data one collects. Schools are different at the beginning of the year than at the end. Similarly, the morning routine in a class can be quite different from that which occurs in the afternoon (Bogdan and Biklen, 1982). Thus, a researcher should sample widely from different times of the day as well as different days throughout the year.

As it was not practical for me to visit the school site each day, the particular dates and times of my participation varied depending on the events occurring on particular days. At the beginning of the year, however, I visited on a variety of days to ensure that the events I observed were typical rather than unique to a particular day. Normally I was present for the equivalent of two days per week throughout most of the school year (from September to late April). I visited once a week during May.

Generally, observations lasted all day. This was necessary because events relating to poetry occurred formally or informally throughout the school day. As the year progressed and data collection procedures were refined, I could sometimes vary this procedure, perhaps visiting one day and one afternoon or two afternoons, for example. Sometimes scheduling conflicts prevented maintaining this balance, but I sought it constantly.

Event Sampling

Event sampling specifies a locus of observation but does not usually specify the length of time an observation should occur. Rather, length is determined by naturally occurring boundaries related to the event within the ongoing classroom context (Evertson and Green, 1986). Which critical events were to be sampled was determined by examining the interaction between my theoretical assumptions about events and the information gathered during the initial observation phase.

Once the specific significant events for this study were identified, a systematic process was used to more precisely define the sampling units as well as identify the boundaries of their occurrence. First, field notes and transcripts were reviewed. Next, Corsaro's (1984) concept of an "interactive episode" was used to guide the initial definition. According to this definition, interactive episodes are defined as:

> those sequences of behavior which begin with the acknowledged presence of two or more interactants in an ecological area and the overt attempt(s) to arrive at a shared meaning of ongoing or emerging activity. Episodes end with physical movement of interactants from the area which results in the termination of the originally initiated activity. (Corsaro, 1984)

Corsaro's definition was then extended to account for specific episodes that were applicable to the present study. Two categories were developed. The first included episodes related to published poetry. This category was subdivided further into specific events including partner sharing, small-group sharing with peers, small-group sharing with teachers, large-group sharing with teachers, and poetry sharing activities occurring outside the immediate classroom context. The second category was comprised of events occurring in relation to the children's own writing. This was subdivided into specific events identified as partner critiquing with peer, partner critiquing with teacher, small-group critiquing with peers, small-group critiquing with teacher, and large-group critiquing with teacher. Each category is listed and defined in Table A–2.

Participant Sampling

Initially, those children who willingly approached me were sampled for their responses to poetry. But as the rapport between us developed, more purposeful sampling evolved. Children at both grade levels, with varying number and quality of responses, were identified. I then followed the development of these children through the school year, collecting their oral responses, written work, and poetry preferences. Their interactions with teachers and peers were also observed and taped.

I should stress that the selection and subsequent monitoring of this sampling group was somewhat complicated by the erratic nature of the poetic responses. A few children who had been making numerous responses of high quality would suddenly become disinterested. Others identified as initially uninterested in poetry would suddenly join critiquing groups, sharing sessions, or otherwise display a new interest. Rather than viewing these changes as disruptive to data collection, I chose to view them as indicative of developmental trends. Thus, the subjects chosen for focused analysis remained unchanged. Responses from the sampling group were supplemented by a less systematic collection of responses from all class members. These were compared with data collected from the sampling group to clarify and strengthen analysis.

Random sampling of participants was also used to further enhance analysis. In February, a random numbers table was used to select children from both classes. They were observed systematically so that their response patterns could be identified. The results were then compared with those obtained through purposeful sampling as a means of confirming or disconfirming results. Table A–3 lists members of the purposeful and randomly sampled groups.

Sampling Inventory: Event Sampling

I. Events Occurring Around Published Poetry

Event	Definition	Number of Incidents Recorded
Partner sharing with peer	Begins with acknowledged presence of two peer interactants, each carrying books of published poetry. Selected poems read aloud in a turn-taking procedure. Event ends with participants leaving area and pursuing a different activity.	32
Small-group sharing with peers	Identical to partner sharing, but more than two participants involved.	34
Small-group sharing with teacher	Begins with acknowledged presence of two or more peer interactants and adult. Selected poems read aloud in turn-taking procedure. Some comment and discussion occurs. Group membership may change. Event ends when participants leave area and pursue different activities.	2*
Large-group sharing with teacher	Begins with acknowledged, organized presence of whole class. Poetry to be shared may be selected by teacher or students. Teacher-led interactive discussion ensues. Event ends with physical movement of interactionants from area.	40
Poetry sharing outside classroom context	Any event occurring outside the physical classroom boundaries in which poetry is quoted, discussed, or written.	7

*This category was subsequently dropped due to the low number of observed incidents.

Process Sampling

Besides sampling across time, events, and participants, sampling of response processes was also used. These included the processes children went through to create both written and oral responses.

The process of written poetic response was collected in the

II. Events Occurring Around Children's Own Writings

Event	Definition	Number of Incidents Recorded
Partner critiquing with peer	Begins with acknowledged presence of two peer interactants carrying poetry journals. Examination of writings occurs. Event ends when other interactants are acknowledged or participants physically leave the area.	54
Small-group critiquing with peers	Similar to partner critiquing except that more than two interactants involved. Ends when majority of participants physically leave area or poetry journals closed and new material used.	63
Partner critiquing with teacher	Begins with acknowledged presence of one child and one adult interactant. Child has poetry journal. Teacher and child jointly discuss poetry in journal (usually one poem is focus). Event ends when the presence of one or more additional child is acknowledged.	31
Small-group critiquing with teacher	Event begins with acknowledged presence of not less than two but no more than six children and teacher. Not all children necessarily bring poetry journals In a turn-taking sequence, members present poems to be examined. Focus frequently shifts from partners to whole group to partners. Event ends when participants physically leave area.	33
Large-group critiquing with teacher	Event begins with acknowledged organized presence of whole class. Children bring poetry journals. Teacher-led interactive discussion ensues in which individual poems are critiqued. Event ends when participants physically leave area.	29

Note: Although events were observed throughout the year, formal counting included only events recorded from September through April.

form of a Poetry Cycle. This was defined as beginning with the conception of a poem through the various revision stages to the point where it was checkmarked and ready to be illustrated. These were relatively easy to sample as the written records in the poetry journals provided documentation of events that occurred when the

Sampling Inventory: Participants

Purposeful

Name and Grade	Description
6th Grade	
Jenny R.	High achieving female
Johnny	Middle achieving male
Angela	Middle achieving female
Jimmy R.	Middle-low achieving male
Angie	Middle-low achieving female
Matt	Low achieving male (classified EMR)
5th Grade	
Aaron	High achieving male
Robin	High achieving female
Mandy	Middle achieving female
Jimmy P.	Middle achieving male
Missy	Middle achieving female
Melanie	Low achieving female

researcher was not present. This written record also served as a prompt for both children and teachers, helping them recall various aspects of the response process.

Similar attempts were made to sample the poetry reading process, but because few permanent records captured these responses when the researcher was not present, it became apparent that sampling poetry reading cycles would be impossible. Therefore, these responses were gathered through other means.

Data Analysis Procedures

The analytic-inductive method of data analysis (Miles and Huberman, 1984) was used to test tentative hypotheses against new data, then increasingly refine these hypotheses to create a cogent description of poetic response and the context that nurtured it. The use of such procedures meant that data analysis occurred through-

Random

Name and Grade	Description
6th Grade	
Carrie	High achieving female
Stacie	High achieving female
Jenny S.	Middle achieving female
Deon	Middle achieving female
Ronnie	Low achieving female
5th Grade	
Farnie	Middle-high achieving male
Lisa	High achieving female
Mike J.	Middle achieving male
Tommy	Middle achieving male
Tiffany	Middle achieving female

out the entire research cycle, directing the collection of data as well as the subsequent interpretations arising from it.

In late December, all data collected to that point was reviewed and tentative pattern codes (categories and hypotheses derived from the initial research questions) were assigned. Once these codes were identified and defined, I assigned them to various units of data. They were then triangulated through both teachers and children.

Subsequent analysis (January through March) focused on verifying, refining, modifying, or disconfirming the patterns and themes that had been identified. Generally, analysis confirmed what had been hypothesized from the early data. Rather than observing many new patterns of response, it was more common to observe more children working with poetry in ways I had previously identified. New patterns and themes that did emerge were commonly the result of children deepening their understandings of poetry or experimenting with more complex aspects of previously identified responses. I never viewed the identified patterns as inviolate, however. Rather, I continually strove to remain skeptical so as to preserve the validity of my conceptualizations.

In late March the data was once again reviewed and coding was refined to facilitate analysis of the contextual factors. Analytic summaries, which served to link the data conceptually or demonstrated how specific data related to the themes were written, then filed with the related data. This process was repeated in June with the response data. Again, analysis seemed to confirm rather than disconfirm the identified patterns. Changes seemed to suggest responses were becoming more complex and sophisticated rather than different. The subsequent analysis reflected this.

Trustworthiness

Qualitative researchers must be careful to consider the validity or trustworthiness of their findings. They essentially work alone in the field—defining the problem, designing instruments, collecting and analyzing information, then writing it up (Miles and Huberman, 1984). The potential for observer bias is great. As a result, researchers must use several strategies to guard against such problems. Several suggested strategies were used in this study. They included prolonged site engagement, triangulation, and member checks. Each will be discussed as to its contribution to the overall trustworthiness of the study.

Spending an extensive amount of time at the site helps overcome any distortions created by the presence of the researcher. Subjects can adjust, reassuming any behaviors that might have temporarily ceased in the presence of an outsider. Prolonged site engagement can also help the researcher understand what aspects are typical as opposed to those that are actually atypical or irrelevant. Planning a minimum of twice weekly visits over an entire school year seemed to facilitate representativeness of my data.

Triangulation involves the use of different methods, data sources, and informants to corroborate a finding. This study triangulated data in several ways, including using multiple interviews on the same phenomena, tapping multiple data sources to investigate an event or series of events, and the like. Thus, for example, when reconstructing a child's poetry writing cycle, the child who wrote the poem would be interviewed as to his or her perceptions of the various stages. Additionally, peers who critiqued the poem and the teacher who offered suggestions or observed the process would be questioned. Because I also observed parts of the cycle, I could offer still other insights. Triangulation of sources also guided data collection and provided a basis for judging evidence. Puzzling or seemingly contradictory elements were explored through other sources, as a way to confirm or disconfirm conclusions. Thus, for example, participants in large-group sharing sessions were observed, videotaped, and interviewed as to their perceptions of what occurred. This helped clarify observations and solidify interpretations.

The trustworthiness of the data as well as the viability of interpretations arising from it can be further validated by presenting findings to different members of the social group under study. Initially, informal member checks were conducted with both teachers from the beginning stages of data collection. Unfortunately, it was immediately clear that they modified their behaviors and perspectives as a result of these discussions. Although these changes were subtle, I felt they were a cause for concern. Thus, I had to use a more indirect approach, questioning them so that I understood their thoughts and actions, then mentally comparing their responses with the understandings I had constructed from other data. More direct member checks were again attempted late in the study as corroboration was more critical and influence on data collection was minimal.

References

ALLEN, JOHN, AND JOHN ANGELOTTI. 1980. Response to Poetry. In David Mallick (ed.), *New Essays on the Teaching of Literature.* Sydney, Australia: Association for Teaching of English

ALLEN, MARIE LOUISE. 1957. "First Snow." In *A Pocketful of Poems.* Illustrated by Sheila Greenwald. New York: Harper & Row.

AVEGNO, SYLVIA. 1956. Intermediate-Grade Children's Choices in Poetry. *Elementary English* 33: 428–32.

BARNES, DOUGLAS. 1976. *From Communication to Curriculum.* New York: Penguin Books.

BASKIN, BARBARA; KAREN HARRIS; AND COLLEEN SALLEY. 1984. Making the Poetry Connection. In P. Barron and J. Burley (eds.), *Jump over the Moon: Selected Professional Readings.* New York: Holt, Rinehart & Winston.

BOGDAN, ROBERT, AND SARI BIKLEN. 1982. *Qualitative Research for Education. An Introduction to Theory and Methods.* Boston: Allyn and Bacon.

BRIDGE, ETHEL. 1966. *Using Children's Choices of and Reactions to Poetry as Determinants in Enriching Literary Experience in the Middle Grades.* Unpublished doctoral dissertation, Temple University.

BRITTON, JAMES. 1982a. Poetry and Our Pattern of Culture. In Gordon M. Pradl (ed.), *Prospect and Retrospect: Selected Essays of James Britton.* Portsmouth, NH: Boynton/Cook.

———. 1982b. Reading and Writing Poetry. In Gordon M. Pradl (ed.),

Prospect and Retrospect: Selected Essays of James Britton. Portsmouth, NH: Boynton/Cook.

COFFIN, ROBERT P. TRISTRAM. 1960. "Crystal Moment." In *Collected Poems.* New York: Macmillan.

COOK, STANLEY. 1982. "The Fish." In John Foster (comp.), *The Fourth Poetry Book.* Oxford: Oxford University Press.

CORSARO, WILLIAM. 1984. *Friendship and Peer Culture in the Early Years.* Norwood, NJ: Ablex.

CRAVEN, MARY ANN. 1980. *A Survey of Teacher Attitudes and Practices Regarding the Teaching of Poetry in the Elementary School.* Unpublished doctoral dissertation, Lamar University.

ERICKSON, FREDERICK. 1977. Some Approaches to School-Community Ethnography. *Anthropology and Education Quarterly* 8: 58–59.

EVERTSON, CAROLYN, AND JUDITH GREEN. 1986. Observation as Inquiry and Method. In Merlin Wittrock (ed.), *Third Handbook of Research on Teaching.* New York: Macmillan.

FISHER, CAROL, AND MARGARET NATARELLA. 1982. Young Children's Preferences in Poetry: A National Survey of First, Second and Third Graders. *Research in the Teaching of English* 16: 339–55.

FOLTA, BERNAR PAUL. 1979. *Effects of Three Approaches to Teaching Poetry to Sixth Grade Students.* Unpublished doctoral dissertation, Purdue University.

FROST, ROBERT. 1969. "The Road Not Taken." In Edward Connery Latham (ed.), *The Poetry of Robert Frost.* New York: Holt, Rinehart & Winston.

GARDNER, H., AND E. WINNER. 1979. The Development of Metaphoric Competence: Implications for Humanistic Disciplines. In Sheldon Sachs (ed.), *On Metaphor.* Chicago: University of Chicago Press.

GEERTZ, CLIFFORD. 1974. *The Interpretation of Cultures.* New York: Basic Books.

GIOVANNI, NIKKI. 1985. "The Drum." In *Spin a Soft Black Song: Poems for Children.* New York: Hill and Wang.

GRAVES, DONALD. 1983. *Writing: Teachers & Children at Work.* Portsmouth, NH: Heinemann.

GREEN, JUDITH, AND DAVID BLOOME. 1983. Ethnography and Reading: Issues, Approaches, Criteria and Findings. *The Thirty-Second*

Yearbook of the National Reading Conference. Rochester, NY: National Reading Conference.

HARRISON, GREGORY. 1982. "Posting Letters." In John Foster (comp.), *The Fourth Poetry Book.* Oxford: Oxford University Press.

HEATH, SHIRLEY BRICE. 1982. Ethnography in Education: Defining the Essentials. In P. Gilmore and A. Glatthorn (eds.), *Children In and Out of School.* Washington, DC: Center for Applied Linguistics.

HECHT, SANDRA. 1978. *The Teaching of Poetry in Grades Seven and Eight: A Survey of Theory, Practice and Materials.* Unpublished doctoral dissertation, Boston University.

HEPLER, SUSAN. 1982. *Patterns of Response to Literature: A One-Year Study of a Fifth and Sixth Grade Classroom.* Unpublished doctoral dissertation, The Ohio State University.

HICKMAN, JANET. 1979. *Response to Literature in a School Environment, Grades K–5.* Unpublished doctoral dissertation, The Ohio State University.

HUCK, CHARLOTTE. 1987. *Children's Literature in the Elementary School.* New York: Holt, Rinehart & Winston.

HYMES, D. 1982. What is Ethnography? In P. Gilmore and A. Glatthorn (eds.), *Children In and Out of School.* Washington, DC: Center for Applied Linguistics.

INGHAM, ROSEMARY. 1980. *The Poetry Preferences of Fourth and Fifth Grade Students in a Suburban School Setting in 1980.* Unpublished doctoral dissertation, University of Houston.

KOCH, KENNETH. 1970. *Wishes, Lies and Dreams: Teaching Children to Write Poetry.* New York: Vintage.

———. 1973. *Rose, Where Did You Get that Red? Teaching Great Poetry to Children.* New York: Random House.

KORIYAMA, NAOSHI. 1966. "Unfolding Bud." In Stephen Dunning, Edward Leuders, and Hugh Smith (comp.), *Reflections on a Gift of Watermelon Pickle . . . and Other Modern Verse.* Glenview, IL: Scott Foresman.

LAKOFF, GEORGE, AND MARK JOHNSON. 1980. *Metaphors We Live By.* Chicago: University of Chicago Press.

LANGER, SUSANNE. 1951. *Philosophy in a New Key.* Cambridge, MA: Harvard University Press.

LINDSAY, VACHEL. 1986. "The Moon Is the North Wind's Cooky." In Jack Prelutsky (ed.), *The Random House Book of Poetry*. New York: Random House.

LIVINGSTON, MYRA. 1971. What the Heart Knows Today. In Nancy Larrick (ed.), *Somebody Turned on a Tap in These Kids*. New York: Delacorte.

———. 1972. 'Beginning." In *The Malibu and Other Poems*. New York: Atheneum.

———. 1973. *When You Are Alone/It keeps you Capone: An Approach to Creative Writing with Children*. New York: Atheneum.

———. 1974. "Street Song." In *The Way Things Are and Other Poems*. New York: Atheneum.

———. 1982. Imagination: The Forms of Things Unknown. *Horn Book Magazine* 43: 257–65.

MCCALL, CAROLYN. 1979. *A Determination of Children's Interest in Poetry Resulting from Specific Poetry Experiences*. Unpublished doctoral dissertation, University of Nebraska—Lincoln.

MCCLURE, AMY. 1985. *Children's Responses to Poetry in a Supportive Literary Context*. Unpublished doctoral dissertation, The Ohio State University.

MACKINTOSH, HELEN. 1924. A Study of Children's Choices in Poetry. *Elementary English Review* 1: 85–89.

———. 1932. "A Critical Study of Children's Choices in Poetry." *University of Iowa Studies in Education* 7.

MASTERS, MARCIA LEE. 1966. "April." In Stephen Dunning, Edward Leuders, and Hugh Smith (comp.), *Reflections on a Gift of Watermelon Pickle...and Other Modern Verse*. Glenview, IL: Scott Foresman.

MATANZO, JANE, AND JOHN MADISON. 1979. A Poem-A-Day Can Make a Difference. *Connecticut English Journal* 10: 410–30.

MERRIAM, EVE. 1962. "Where Is a Poem?" In JAMBOREE: *Rhymes for All Times*. New York: Atheneum.

———. 1964. "It Doesn't Always Have to Rhyme." In It *Doesn't Always Have to Rhyme*. New York: Atheneum.

———. 1976. "From the Japanese." In *Rainbow Writing*. New York: Atheneum.

————. 1986. "'I,' Says the Poem." In *A Sky Full of Poems*. New York: Dell.

MILES, MATTHEW, AND MICHAEL HUBERMAN. 1984. *Qualitative Data Analysis*. Beverly Hills, CA: Sage Publications.

MOFFITT, JOHN. 1966. "To Look at Anything." In Stephen Dunning, Edward Leuders, and Hugh Smith (comp.), *Reflections on a Gift of Watermelon Pickle . . . and Other Modern Verse*. Glenview, IL: Scott Foresman.

MOORE, LILIAN. 1988. *I'll Meet You at the Cucumbers*. Illustrations by Sharon Wooding. New York: Atheneum.

MOORE, ROSALIE. 1966. "Catalogue." In Stephen Dunning, Edward Leuders, and Hugh Smith (comp.), *Reflections on a Gift of Watermelon Pickle . . . and Other Modern Verse*. Glenview, IL: Scott Foresman.

NATIONAL ASSESSMENT OF EDUCATIONAL PROGRESS (NAEP). 1981. *Reading, Thinking and Writing: Results from the National Assessment of Reading and Literature*. Denver, CO: Education Commission of the States.

NORVELL, GEORGE. 1958. *What Boys and Girls Like to Read*. New York: Silver Burdett.

PAINTER, HELEN. 1970. *Poetry and Children*. Newark, DE: International Reading Association.

PIAGET, JEAN. 1952. *The Language and Thought of the Child*. London: Routledge and Kegan Paul.

PURVES, ALAN, AND RICHARD BEACH. 1972. *Literature and the Reader: Research in Response to Literature, Reading Interests, and the Teaching of Literature*. Urbana, IL: National Council of Teachers of English.

REDMOND, SISTER ANN. 1978. *Children's Response to Metaphor in Poetry*. Unpublished doctoral dissertation, University of Minnesota.

RICHARDS, I. S. 1929. *Practical Criticism*. New York: Harcourt Brace.

ROSEN, CONNIE, AND HAROLD ROSEN. 1973. *The Language of Primary School Children*. New York: Penguin.

ROSENBLATT, LOUISE. 1965. *Literature as Exploration*. New York: Barnes & Noble.

————. 1978. *The Reader, the Text, the Poem: The Transactional Theory of the Literary Work*. Carbondale, IL: Southern Illinois University Press.

———— 1982. The Literary Transaction: Evocation and Response. *Theory into Practice* 21 (Autumn): 268–77.

SANDBURG, CARL 1970. *The Complete Poems of Carl Sandburg*. New York: Harcourt, Brace, Jovanovich.

SCHULTE, EMERITA. 1967. *The Independent Reading Interests of Children in Grades Four, Five and Six*. Unpublished doctoral dissertation, The Ohio State University.

SHAPIRO, PHYLLIS, AND BERNARD SHAPIRO. 1971. *Poetry Instruction: Its Effect on Attitudes toward Literature and the Ability to Write Prose*. ERIC Document Reproduction Service No. Ed. 061–203. Washington, DC: ERIC.

SIMMONS, MARTHA. 1980. *Intermediate-Grade Children's Preferences in Poetry*. Unpublished doctoral dissertation, University of Alabama.

SKELTON, GLENN. 1963. *A Survey of Children's Responses to Selected Poems in the Fourth, Fifth and Sixth Grades*. Unpublished doctoral dissertation, University of California, Berkeley.

SMITH, JOHN. 1973. *Children's Understanding of Written Metaphor*. Unpublished doctoral dissertation, University of Alberta.

TERRY, ANN. 1972. *A National Survey of Children's Poetry Preferences in the Fourth, Fifth and Sixth Grades*. Unpublished doctoral dissertation, The Ohio State University.

THOM, CHOW LOY. 1979. *What Teachers Read to Pupils in the Middle Grades*. Unpublished doctoral dissertation, The Ohio State University.

VERBLE, DAVID. 1973. *A Road Not Taken: An Approach to Teaching*. Nashville, TN: Tennessee Arts Commission, sponsored by the National Endowment for the Arts.

WILLIAMS, WILLIAM CARLOS. 1938. "Poem." In *Collected Poems, Vol. I, 1909–1939*. New York: New Directions.